'A wonderful new biography [...] readable view of Hudson's achie[vements...]

'Robert Beaumont takes us on a [...] fall of George Hudson' *Guardia[n]*

'This gripping new biography tells a splendid tale' *Sunday Business*

'Historian Beaumont charts George Hudson's life with great sensitivity and sympathy' *Lancashire Evening Post*

'An amusing, gossipy and forthright account of George Hudson's career' *Daily Telegraph*

'This is, by any standards, a remarkable human drama' *Yorkshire Post*

'Robert Beaumont is right to go out and bat for Hudson in this lively account of his life and work' Glasgow *Sunday Herald*

'This hugely entertaining read charts Hudson's wildly fluctuating fortunes with the energy and enthusiasm of the Railway King himself' *Yorkshire Evening Press*

'*The Railway King* tells Hudson's story with gusto and great confidence' *Observer*

Robert Beaumont, a journalist and author, was educated at Marlborough College and St Catherine's College, Oxford University, where he read Modern History. He worked on the York-based *Yorkshire Evening Press* for twenty-one years, winning a succession of regional and national awards for his journalism, before embarking on a freelance career six years ago. He lives near York, with his wife, two children and cat and travels by train whenever he can. He is also a long-suffering and eternally optimistic supporter of York City Football Club.

THE RAILWAY KING

A Biography of George Hudson

Robert Beaumont

review

First published in 2002
by REVIEW
An imprint of Headline Book Publishing

First published in paperback in 2003

10 9 8 7 6 5 4 3 2 1

Robert Beaumont would be happy to hear from readers with their
comments on the book at the following e-mail address:
robert@minskiplodge.demon.co.uk

ISBN 0 7472 3236 9

Typeset in Garamond by Avon DataSet Ltd,
Bidford-on-Avon, Warwickshire

Printed and bound in Great Britain by
Mackays of Chatham plc, Chatham, Kent

HEADLINE BOOK PUBLISHING
A division of Hodder Headline
338 Euston Road
London NW1 3BH

www.reviewbooks.co.uk
www.hodderheadline.com

To my father, who awakened and stimulated
my interest in history and railways

Acknowledgements

I would like to thank the following for their invaluable help, kindness and interest during the writing of *The Railway King*: Hugh Murray, Alison Menage, Jennifer Middleton, Lindy Hymes, Darrell Buttery, Emma Farquharson, Eve Delahooke, Dr John Shannon, John Clarke, David Hudson Smith, Tony Tarpey, John Kilman, Jeremy Cassel, Chris Titley, Richard Green, David Mallender, Alan Woodcock, Celia Kent (my editor), Andrew Roberts for writing the foreword, Jeremy Phillips for taking the photographs and last, but not least, my patient and loving wife Claire, for everything.

Contents

Foreword

Of very few Britons can it be said that the country would be a recognisably different place had they never lived, but George Hudson was such a man. The great Roman city of York might easily have become a minor (if beautiful) backwater had not Hudson made it the epicentre of the Northern railway system in the mid-nineteenth century, and the hub of his vast business empire.

Railways ensured that for the first time in human history man could travel faster than on a galloping horse, and in half a generation they changed civilisation. History suddenly switched from a linear to an exponential progression. Transportation, urbanisation, business practice, property law, warfare, the development of the British Empire – everything was transformed and sped up by this Promethean invention. It was the Internet of its day, with if anything an even greater propensity to create and destroy great fortunes through speculation.

That George Hudson employed extremely dubious – not to say downright crooked – financial techniques is undeniable; the profit and loss accounts and balance sheets in a Hudson prospectus ought to have been filed under Fiction in the libraries of the day, rather than providing the genesis of a new South Sea Bubble. Yet it should be remembered that over the fifteen years of 'the Railway King's' reign Hudson also employed tens of thousands of labourers and laid hundreds of miles of virgin track.

At one point George Hudson controlled one-third of the entire national track in the United Kingdom, an astonishing achievement from a largely self-made man. To appreciate the scale of his domination of the industry one might equate him with John D Rockefeller Sr in oil or Bill Gates in information technology. He pioneered the cause of cheap, fast and relatively safe freight and personnel travel, which in its turn had incalculable effects on first the British and then the whole world's economy.

In this important and thought-provoking work – based on a good deal of painstaking primary research – the author poses the central question: was Hudson 'one of the greatest Englishmen of the nineteenth century, or a fraudster on a gigantic scale'? I believe that this book shows that it was clearly perfectly possible for him to have been both.

Few authors could be better qualified that Mr Beaumont to write this book about the most controversial Yorkshireman after Geoffrey Boycott. A son of the county himself, born in Wakefield and living in Boroughbridge, Robert Beaumont is an accomplished writer who worked for the *Yorkshire Evening Press* between 1977 and 1998, becoming assistant editor and an award-winning campaigning journalist and feature writer in the process. Thus in his quest to have the city of York finally recognise George Hudson for what he did for it, Beaumont speaks with a proud and authentic Yorkshire voice.

For it is perhaps unfair of us today to judge George Hudson by the ethical criteria of the early twenty-first century, rather than by those of his own day. It is hard to escape the conclusion that he was brought down more by his inability to guarantee everlasting 10 per cent dividends than by shock at his business ethics and habit of printing and selling shares without letting on what he was doing. Modern joint-stock capitalism had to adapt very quickly to the breakneck technological advances of the mid-nineteenth century, and Hudson was part of that process. Although Hudson massively overstretched his business empire and came to (perhaps well deserved) grief eventually, he was never actually prosecuted for any illegalities.

This is a human interest story as much as an investigation into the politics and business ethics of railway-building in its heyday. It is the Icarian tale of a man who flew too high and sensationally crashed earthwards. So powerful a cautionary account was it that Anthony Trollope adapted the Hudson experience only very slightly when he created the character Augustus Melmotte in *The Way We Live Now*. At the time of the suicide of Robert Maxwell, Hudson's name was also regularly invoked as an historical precursor for the swindling 'Captain Bob', but although there are certain superficial similarities between the two men this book seeks to acquit Hudson of the worst wrongdoing. He was certainly not as bad a man as Thomas Carlyle and Lord Macaulay painted him, let alone the modern historian who has equated him with Dr Crippen!

This book certainly does not eschew controversy, as the coverage in Chapter 18 of Hudson's historiography amply proves. When writing about so contentious a figure, and one who has already been the subject of a number of biographies, such a combative stance is no bad thing. Mr Beaumont's book is a passionate yet meticulously researched work of genuine scholarship, as well as an exciting tale of a man who, for all his lack of scruples, was essentially a creator rather than – as were so many of his detractors and critics – a destroyer.

If there is a moral to this book – other than the obvious one that dividends should be paid from revenue not capital – it is that our world was made by rogues as much as by angels, and is none the worse for it.

Andrew Roberts

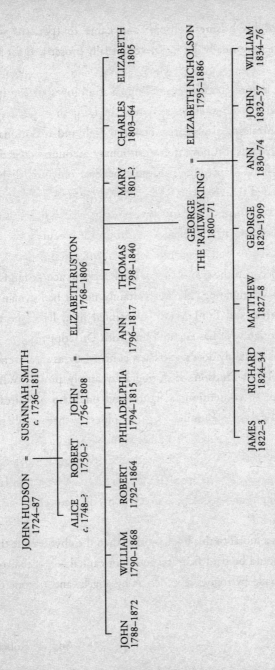

JOHN HUDSON = SUSANNAH SMITH
1724–87   c. 1736–1810

ALICE   ROBERT   JOHN
c. 1748–?   1750–?   1756–1808 = ELIZABETH RUSTON
                                        1768–1806

JOHN   WILLIAM   ROBERT   PHILADELPHIA   ANN   THOMAS   MARY   CHARLES   ELIZABETH
1788–1872   1790–1868   1792–1864   1794–1815   1796–1817   1798–1840   1801–?   1803–64   1805

GEORGE
THE 'RAILWAY KING' = ELIZABETH NICHOLSON
1800–71   1795–1886

JAMES   RICHARD   MATTHEW   GEORGE   ANN   JOHN   WILLIAM
1822–3   1824–34   1827–8   1829–1909   1830–74   1832–57   1834–76

Simplified Family Tree of the Hudsons of Howsham

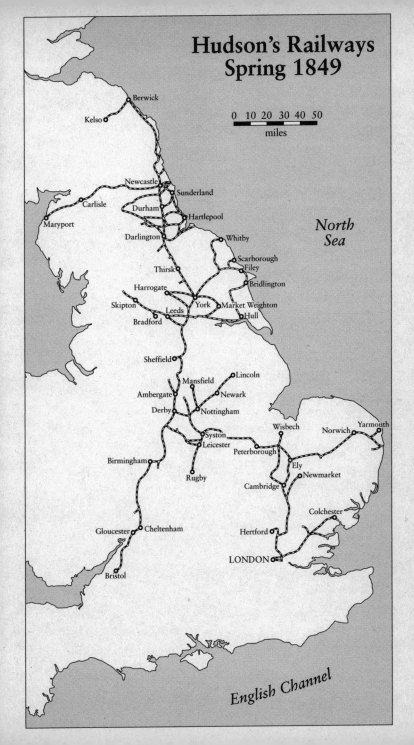

Hudson's Railways
Spring 1849

0 10 20 30 40 50
miles

*North
Sea*

Berwick
Kelso

Newcastle
Sunderland
Carlisle
Durham
Maryport
Hartlepool
Darlington
Whitby
Thirsk
Scarborough
Filey
Harrogate
Bridlington
Skipton
York
Market Weighton
Leeds
Bradford
Hull
Sheffield
Lincoln
Mansfield
Ambergate
Newark
Derby
Nottingham
Wisbech
Norwich
Yarmouth
Syston
Leicester
Peterborough
Birmingham
Ely
Newmarket
Rugby
Cambridge
Colchester
Gloucester
Cheltenham
Hertford
Bristol
LONDON

English Channel

A Life Less Ordinary

*The great end of life is not knowledge,
but action*

T. H. Huxley

George Hudson could have walked straight out of the pages of a Charles Dickens novel, although Dickens – who prided himself on his realism – might have baulked at incorporating some of the more bizarre twists and turns of Hudson's extraordinary life into one of his books.

Even by the standards of the nineteenth century, when the consequences of the industrial revolution and the rise of the middle classes turned established society upside down, George Hudson led a turbulent and mould-breaking existence. Thrown out of his North Yorkshire village when he was only fifteen, for fathering an illegitimate child, he inherited £30,000 in the most dubious of circumstances twelve years later. That enabled him to reinvent himself as the Railway King and become, at the height of his fame and fortune, one of the very richest men in England.

He made his money by forming his own railway companies and,

in 1845, he was able to buy the Londesborough estate in East Yorkshire for £500,000. That was a huge amount of money in early Victorian Britain. By 1848 he controlled nearly a third of Britain's rail network and was a leading Conservative member in the House of Commons.

His fall was as spectacular as his rise, ending in a debtors' prison and then in France, forlorn and penniless, dependent on his few remaining friends to keep him alive. He died a broken man and was buried only a couple of miles away from his birthplace. The wheel had turned full circle, but within that circle lies a journey of epic and tragic proportions.

Inevitably, these bald facts (a touch of bastardy here, a little fraud there, a spell in prison here and heartbreaking exile there) merely hint at the mercurial life that Hudson first enjoyed and then endured. It epitomised the possibilities and the pitfalls of one of the most exciting eras in British history.

George Hudson was a mass of contradictions: immensely hard-working, yet dangerously self-indulgent; tremendously generous, yet a purveyor of the sharpest financial practices; poorly educated and roughly spoken, but a quick-witted visionary; and unbearably arrogant, yet strangely humble at the end. He was a highly complex individual, whose character mixed both the grander and the baser elements of human nature in equal measure.

Most commentators have failed to understand, let alone look beyond, these contradictions, preferring to attack George Hudson for his financial sharp practice, his ostentatious display of wealth and his boorish manners. The city of York, busily rewriting history, has tried to remove all trace of the Railway King from its civic annals. York, it appears, has conveniently forgotten that it owes its position as the railway capital of the north primarily to Hudson.

Today the city's ugliest street, a nasty little road which runs from a dingy bus station to a derelict supermarket, carries his name, while a statue of his great enemy George Leeman dominates the station complex. That bears scant relation to the two men's differing legacies to their city.

It is debatable whether Hudson would have minded about all the opprobrium that has been heaped upon his head since he died. After all, he had suffered enough abuse when he was alive. Thomas Carlyle, most probably motivated by snobbery, wrote with typically extravagant rhetoric on Hudson's fall:

> This big swollen gambler . . . who, in his insatiable greed and bottomless atrocity, had led multitudes to go in the ways of gilded human baseness, seeking temporary profit where only eternal loss was possible.

Charles Dickens, meanwhile, was equally scathing:

> I find a burning disgust arising in my mind – a sort of morbid canker of the most frightful description – against Mister Hudson. His position seems to be such a monstrous one. There are some dogs who can't endure one particular note on the piano. In like manner I feel disposed to throw up my head and howl whenever I hear Mr Hudson mentioned.

And Lord Macaulay, the great Whig historian, likened Hudson to 'Mammon and Belial rolled into one' and called him 'a bloated, vulgar, insolent, purse-proud, greedy, drunken blackguard'.

Well, the Railway King was a Tory – the greatest sin in the world in Macaulay's eyes.

Clearly George Hudson was no saint. But he did not deserve

these vitriol-drenched assessments by men who did not fully understand his achievements – or his genius.

Hudson was a man of the spoken, not the written, word; so he never availed himself either of letters or diaries to put his own case.

Indeed, it was left to William Gladstone, not one of Hudson's greatest supporters, to give a much more balanced appraisal of his talents, writing, 'He was no mere speculator, but a projector of great discernment, courage and rich enterprise'.

The London *Evening Standard*, in 1846 at the height of his fame, was more forthcoming:

> Two hundred thousand well-paid labourers, representing, as heads of families, nearly one million men, women and children, all feasting through the bold enterprise of one man . . . Let us hear what man, or class of men, ever before did so much for the population of a country?

The Times, too, paid handsome tribute to the Railway King on his death in the late autumn of 1871:

> There was a time when not to know George Hudson was to argue oneself unknown; now he is only a tradition. He was a man who united largeness of view with wonderful speculative courage. He went in for bigger things than anyone else and, for two or three years, he was looked upon as having the key to untold treasures.

A drunken blackguard or a courageous speculator? A swollen gambler or an inspired visionary? Well, as the story of Hudson's amazing life unfolds, the reader must decide.

Whatever the conclusion, though, there is no doubt that George

Hudson played a crucial part in the industrial and commercial development of Britain in the first half of the nineteenth century and left an indelible imprint on the history of this country's railway network.

Today George Hudson's grave lies, neglected and overgrown, in a corner of an unkempt graveyard at Scrayingham, near Malton, in North Yorkshire. One might suppose, gazing at this sad memorial, that Hudson's reputation and legacy had likewise fallen into permanent disrepair.

But then the faint and eerie hooting of a train in the distance, on Hudson's beloved York to Scarborough line, acts as an eloquent and timely reminder of the Railway King's achievements. It is, metaphorically at least, the sound of George Hudson having the last laugh.

CHAPTER ONE

A Troubled Country Boy

The childhood shows the man,
as morning shows the day

John Milton, *Paradise Regained*

George Hudson was born in the picturesque Yorkshire village of Howsham, on the eastern bank of the River Derwent, on 10 March 1800. Today Howsham, with its quaint cottages and gently undulating main street, is a highly desirable commuter village. In 1800 it was home to a comparatively wealthy farming community, with the large Hudson family at its heart.

There could not have been a greater contrast between the peaceful, pastoral environment into which young George was born and the turbulent life he was to lead. It was to take him only fifteen years to bid farewell to Howsham – and he did so in some style and controversy. After all, not many fifteen-year-olds get drummed out of their community for fathering an illegitimate child.

There has been some debate over the exact nature of Hudson's social origins. When he was an MP in the 1840s, George Hudson was frequently lampooned for his Yorkshire accent and his loose grasp of the niceties of the English language. But he was far removed from a country bumpkin, for the Hudsons were a prominent and relatively affluent family in the social world of Howsham and beyond.

Father John held the glorious title of 'High Constable of the Wapentake of Buckrose', which meant he carried administrative duties in the district, giving him a certain social cachet among his peers. He farmed land at nearby Scrayingham and Leavening, as well as at Howsham, and it was naturally assumed that George himself, the fifth of six sons, would inherit some of his father's lands when he came of age. Fate, however, intervened.

By the time he was eight, both his parents were dead. Mother Elizabeth, perhaps worn out by bearing ten children in seventeen years, died in 1806 when she was just thirty-eight, while father John passed away two years later. Luckily George's elder brothers John and William were old enough – and William sensible enough – to look after the Hudson brood.

Yet the lack of parental supervision, combined with the absence of a formal education, were to have a strong influence on the adolescent George. He grew up quickly, learning to trust his own instincts and to be dependent upon nobody but himself. He despised learning for learning's sake and was contemptuous of anyone who could not, or did not, turn their education into money.

The details of George's own education are sketchy. There was no record of a village school at Howsham in the early nineteenth century and it is unlikely that the Hudson family set much store by formal tuition. They would have been more concerned that George grew up knowing how to farm. But a contemporary report suggests that the young boy had a good mathematical brain. He certainly used that brain to great effect in later life.

Hudson's first and most accomplished biographer, Richard S.

Lambert, in his *The Railway King: A Study of George Hudson and the Business Morals of His Time*, shrewdly points out that George always retained a yeoman farmer's outlook on life:

> All through the ups and downs of his giddy career, in politics and in transport, George Hudson remained at heart the farmer's boy, racy, of the soil, coarse-grained and with a constitution as tough as the roots of an old tree. And his outlook – even when the view was railways – was that of a shrewd peasant.

He quickly realised that farming in the early nineteenth century, as it is today, was a precarious business and was subject to a whole series of unpredictable outside forces. A period of severe agricultural depression, in which the price of wheat fell through the floor, ruined many farmers at the end of the debilitating Napoleonic wars in 1815 and it became apparent to George that the town might offer more to him than the country.

In any case, the sudden death of John Hudson had thrown the family finances into chaos. There is some dispute as to how much money, if any, Hudson senior left, but it was probably not enough to keep George, together with all his brothers, gainfully employed on the farm. The historic, bustling city of York, just ten miles down the road, must have looked an attractive proposition to a young man of ambition and vision.

At this juncture fate took another hand, as it was to do quite regularly in his topsy-turvy life. An entry in the *Howsham Poor Book* for 1815–16 reads: 'Received of George Hudson for Bastardy, 12s 6d'.

Unfortunately, the *Howsham Poor Book* gives nothing else away. Who was the mother of this child? How old was she? Did the child survive childbirth? Did mother and child continue to live in Howsham? And, crucially, is there a whole illegitimate branch of the Hudson dynasty living in Yorkshire – or further afield – today? It is unlikely we shall ever know.

Hudson himself never alluded to this 'bastardy episode' in later life. Indeed he liked to maintain that he left Howsham for York when he was only thirteen, discreetly drawing a veil over the unsavoury incident. In the House of Commons, for example, in 1845, he claimed he had lived in York for thirty-two years – and no one had either the information, or the inclination, to dispute this.

There were other reasons, too, why young George might have wanted to leave Howsham. His eldest sister Philadelphia died in 1815, aged only twenty-one, and there are strong suggestions that his eldest brother John buckled under the pressure of being head of such a large family at such a young age. Indeed, John did not last long in the office of the Chief Constable of the Division of Buckrose, as he was often 'unsteady on his feet'. Brother William succeeded him and held the post, without incident, for more than fifty years.

The death of George's father, mother and eldest sister in quick succession, coupled with his eldest brother's excessive drinking and the family's flagging financial fortunes, all combined to create a pressurised household. No wonder his eyes strayed to York, especially after fathering an illegitimate child.

The pretty village of Howsham, which had promised so much when George was born in 1800, had nothing more to offer him. He needed a bigger stage, a happy family of his own making and a career to test his undoubted talents. York would provide all three – and much more besides.

The succession of disasters which struck the Hudsons made George's formative years a difficult and testing time. In retrospect, though, they equipped him to cope with all the challenges that life presents – and it is extremely significant that he bore his later misfortunes with humility and stoicism. He had been there before.

It was highly appropriate, and symbolic, that George Hudson was born in the opening year of the nineteenth century. For this was a century destined to be full of innovation and revolution, and George's winning combination of talent, hard work and vision, plus a little luck, would enable him to take advantage of the unique opportunities provided by the Victorian era. It was only when his vision became clouded by extraordinary wealth, and his luck ran out, that the Hudson train careered off the rails.

In 1815, however, the train was just pulling out of the station.

CHAPTER TWO

Those were the Days of his Life

You don't know what you've got till it's gone

Joni Mitchell

It is highly likely that fifteen-year-old George set off to York with a light and happy heart. His early years in Howsham had been traumatic and he would doubtless have been glad to leave them, and the village, behind. In contrast, the city of York offered independence, self-determination and advancement. George might even have seen himself as a latter-day Dick Whittington, which was appropriate enough, since he was to find that the streets of York were paved with gold.

In 1815 the city of York was a sleeping giant. The industrial revolution, which had transformed the landscape and the economy of neighbouring West Yorkshire, had all but passed by this proud, historic city. It was still dependent on the patronage of farmers, clergy and the leading county families for its prosperity and looked on jealously as towns such as Leeds and Bradford tapped into the riches generated by huge changes in production and manufacturing. There was a real danger that York, resting on its illustrious laurels, would be consigned to the backwaters of nineteenth-century British history.

This would not have worried young George in 1815 – though it certainly did twenty years later. He was simply concerned with finding a job, which was not too much of a problem for a willing, able-bodied and hard-working young man. Before long he became an apprentice at Nicholson and Bell's drapers' shop on the edge of Goodramgate and College Street, under the benign shadow of York Minster. Today these premises are owned by the National Trust, but a little plaque draws attention to where George Hudson learned his first trade.

William Bell had actually died two years before young George arrived in York, but his widow Rebecca (née Nicholson) carried on the business and it was she who first employed the lad. This was a move that was ultimately to have tragic consequences for the Nicholson family but, in 1815, a pushy and self-confident young man was just what the business needed.

In his old age, when he gazed back over the wreckage of his life, George Hudson was fond of saying that the years he spent in the quaint little drapers' shop in College Street were the happiest of his life. Nostalgia can be a deceptive emotion, but there is no doubt that George was good at his job, lived an ordered existence and had no enemies baying for his blood. It was a time of contentment – and of hope. It was also a time of love.

There were three members of the Nicholson family who were involved in the running of the shop: Rebecca and her younger brother and sister, Richard and Elizabeth, who were both to play a much more crucial, and traumatic, part in George Hudson's life. Rebecca handed over the running of Nicholson and Bell to Richard in 1817 and everything progressed smoothly, with George learning the drapers' and silk mercers' trade, together with the art of salesmanship, behind the counter at College Street. He also found time to befriend and court Elizabeth, who was five years his senior.

By all accounts, Elizabeth Nicholson was both a very plain and a very stupid young woman. Brains and beauty, however, were of little consequence to her suitor. He was more interested in her money and her connections. They, after all, could unlock doors – and usher him into a wealthy world within.

Yet George, in his own, emotionally buttoned-up Yorkshireman's way, did love his Elizabeth. They were to remain married throughout his extraordinary life and she would share his triumphs and his tribulations, often without understanding exactly what was going on.

In 1821 George Hudson came of age – and celebrated in style. He became Richard Nicholson's partner and he married Elizabeth. These events, not entirely unconnected, occurred within exactly five months of each other.

The deed of partnership between George Hudson and Richard Nicholson, which is dated 17 February, still survives in the city of York archives. It reveals that George and Elizabeth were to live on the premises at College Street, paying a rent of £35 a year. Intriguingly, it also reveals that £6,000 worth of equity was sunk into this partnership. Most of that, surely, must have come from the Nicholsons.

On 17 July George Hudson and Elizabeth Nicholson were married in Holy Trinity Church, Goodramgate, arguably the city of York's most beautiful church. Richard, together with George's older brother William and his younger sister Mary, were the witnesses. The newly-weds seemed set fair for a happy, productive and untroubled existence, though George's impatient character – always straining at the leash – suggested their life would never be dull.

They settled down together in the pretty bay-windowed shop

and started a family. Their first three children, James, Richard and Matthew, all died young, which cast a shadow of sadness over their early life in College Street. But Elizabeth was as proficient at childbearing as she was deficient in brains, and there was never any doubt that the Hudsons would soon have a young family of which they could justifiably be proud.

As he approached his death in 1871, a reflective George Hudson looked back on his carefree days as a young York draper.

> The happiest part of my life was when I stood behind the counter and used the yard measure in my own shop. I had one of the snuggest businesses in York, and turned over my thirty thousand a year, five-and-twenty per cent of it being profit. My ruin was having a fortune left to me.

It is highly unlikely that a comparatively small drapery business would have had a turnover of £30,000 a year in the 1820s, but the old man's point remains valid. These were happy times, when his ambition was curtailed by his circumstances, and the lure of the railways with their promises of instant riches were just a distant mirage at the end of a very dark tunnel.

The seeds of George Hudson's destruction, however, were already being sown.

CHAPTER THREE

'My Ruin was having a Fortune left to Me'

All the riches in the world may be
gifts from the devil

William Blake

One of George and Elizabeth Hudson's closer friends in the early years of their marriage was George's great-uncle Matthew Bottrill. Uncle Matthew was an extremely rich man, who lived in a grand seventeenth-century house in Monkgate, just a couple of hundred yards down the road from the Hudsons' College Street shop-cum-home.

In the early months of 1827 Uncle Matthew, who was seventy, fell ill. George, who was not normally the most sympathetic of souls, suddenly began to spend a great deal of time at his great-uncle's bedside. He might have been genuinely concerned about Uncle Matthew's health, but he would also have been acutely aware of his wealth.

Matthew Bottrill was one of the richest men in York. Apart from his house in Monkgate, he had property in the suburbs of Osbaldwick and Huntington as well as in Westow (near Malton),

Whitby and in the East Yorkshire villages of Hutton Cranswick and Newton-on-Derwent. He was cash rich, too. No doubt George and his uncle talked about this extensive portfolio of property as the latter lay dying. No doubt George, employing more subtlety than usual, was attentive and understanding.

Uncle Matthew died on 25 May 1827, leaving George Hudson an estate worth about £30,000. That was a fortune in those days and, at a stroke, transformed the College Street draper from a run-of-the-mill, lower middle-class businessman into one of York's wealthiest men. This was a transformation which did not go unnoticed, and Hudson had to suffer malicious rumours and snide innuendo for the rest of his life. He did not mind too much at the time, because £30,000 goes a long way to soothing all forms of criticism, no matter how vitriolic. Only later, as he looked back on this pivotal moment of his life, did he voice regret at the £30,000 legacy, the bitterness it caused and the havoc it wreaked.

It might all have been so different. For Matthew Bottrill had changed his will only weeks before his death – and it is highly likely that the original will did not leave his vast fortune to his great-nephew. Why was the will changed? And why wasn't the bulk of Bottrill's wealth left to his nephews and nieces, who were more closely related to him than George?

Dr Alf Peacock, one of York's more prominent historians and an implacable opponent of George Hudson, is in no doubt that Hudson had behaved deviously, if not immorally, by Bottrill's bedside.

In his hard-hitting biography of the Railway King, *George Hudson*, Dr Peacock writes:

> If George acted shabbily in 1827 – long before railways were considered – then his behaviour later on can be presented as being in character. Certainly, by the time he became a railway

promoter, he had enjoyed considerable experience in influencing men by dubious methods. Matthew Bottrill might have been the first in a long line.

Dr Peacock was being too harsh. It is quite possible that Bottrill introduced young George to the Nicholsons (his house was less than half a mile from their shop) and that he subsequently regarded George as his surrogate son. It is equally possible that Bottrill, seeing that the young man was making a success of the drapers' shop, provided some of the £6,000 needed for the partnership in 1821.

Either way, Matthew Bottrill's astonishing legacy was the defining moment of George Hudson's life. The poorly educated farmer's boy from Howsham, expelled from the village for bastardy, had become one of the richest and most influential citizens in York's social and political firmament.

'It was the very worst thing that could have happened to me. It let me into the railways, and to all my misfortunes since,' said a wiser, older Hudson as he contemplated his turbulent life from miserable exile in France.

At the time, however, George could see no further than the dazzling opportunities with which his newly inherited wealth presented him. His first decision was to move house. It was clearly inappropriate for one of York's richest businessmen to 'live above the shop', so the Hudsons made the short journey from College Street, in the shadow of Monk Bar, to Monkgate and Matthew Bottrill's elegant Charles II home at Number 44. Today, incidentally, 44 Monkgate is occupied by a firm of chartered accountants – which is ironic, given Hudson's own dubious accounting practices!

While Elizabeth busied herself with bearing and raising a family (George was born in 1829, quickly followed by Ann, John and

William), her husband surveyed York's political scene with his sharp and canny eye. Then, as now, local politics was an incestuous, back-stabbing and parochial affair, dominated by 'worthies' whose vanity far outstripped their intellect. The field was wide open for a young man with brains, vision and money.

There has been some controversy over George Hudson's early political and religious beliefs. Richard S. Lambert, in his engaging biography, suggests that Hudson was a Methodist in the 1820s but the evidence for this is flimsy. Hudson denied it vehemently towards the end of his life, when there would have been no harm in admitting it, and it is much more likely that he was always a traditional member of the Church of England. Significantly, his four children were all baptised into the established Church.

His politics, however, were never in any doubt. He grew up, politically and intellectually, during Lord Liverpool's great Conservative administration of 1812 to 1827. Liverpool, with a judicious mixture of consolidation and reform, helped to create a relatively peaceful Britain as the fires of revolution burned abroad. Hudson would have been impressed by the considerable achieve-ments of the Tories in the 1820s and his own plain-speaking, pragmatic approach to life was more in tune with Liverpool's party than with the patronising élitism of the Whigs.

There was one problem, though. York was a Whig city. It was dominated by a closed Whig corporation and it would have been much easier for a young politician, eager for advancement, to espouse the Whig cause. It says much, therefore, about George Hudson the man that he did not tailor his beliefs to the prevailing political climate of the time. By 1830 he was a staunch Church of England Tory – and he never once deviated from this quintessential establishment position to his dying day.

The opening that Hudson needed came in 1832, when the

dreaded cholera visited York and caused widespread misery and distress. Altogether 185 people died, while another 265 recovered, as the disease swept through the city's fetid slums. The situation would have been far worse, however, but for the efforts of the York Board of Health, of which Hudson was a prominent member. This task force, which had been set up specifically to deal with the cholera crisis, performed a number of brave and commendable tasks and Hudson himself distinguished himself as a spirited public servant by visiting the sick and reporting on their welfare.

Once the cholera crisis was over, a nasty row erupted between the board and the corporation over the exact site of the burial ground for the victims of the epidemic. George Hudson, rapidly establishing a name for himself in the city, was at the centre of this row – demonstrating for the first time, in public at least, his intemperate and aggressive nature. He obviously felt deeply about the issue of the burial ground, but his rude tone and the personal nature of his attacks on his opponents made him deeply unpopular. As a result, even at the height of his fame and fortune in the 1840s, a significant section of the York establishment hated him with a vengeance.

In the same year the Whigs introduced the Great Reform Bill, which changed the political landscape of the country by giving the middle classes the vote. It was a canny move by the Whigs, who needed to extend their narrow political power base if they were to survive the economic and social revolution that was sweeping nineteenth-century Britain. Hudson himself was not impressed. Speaking at a Tory meeting in the George Inn, Coney Street (to which the poet Shelley had eloped twenty-one years earlier), he castigated William IV and Lord Grey, the Prime Minister, for threatening to flood the House of Lords with new peers to get the Reform Bill through.

His comment that he had 'no objection to reform, but wished it to be carried and obtained in a constitutional way, and not by inundating the House of Lords with mere delegates' has a special resonance today.

Inevitably, with electoral reform in the air, the political temperature in York was high. Hudson was howled down on a couple of occasions by an unruly mob, but he had acquired a taste for the cut-and-thrust of political debate (and abuse) and he furthered his ambitions by becoming the treasurer of the York Tory party in the summer of 1832. His money had opened a crucial door, the first of many that were to swing wide open when faced by the Hudson fortune.

The York Tories were a pretty dispirited bunch in 1832. Apart from the fact that the city was traditionally Whig, the party's damaging split over Catholic emancipation in 1829 and the consequences of the Reform Act meant that their chances of winning even one of the two York seats in the autumn election that year were remote. And so it proved.

That election, however, enabled George Hudson to make an indelible mark on the York political scene. He supported the candidature of John Henry Lowther, son of the wealthy baronet Sir John Lowther of Swillington Park, near Wakefield, and impressed both father and son with his enthusiasm and – almost needless to say – with his money. John Lowther may not have secured a seat in York in 1832, but George Hudson had won his first battle in what was to be a tumultuous and bloody war.

It was inevitable, given Hudson's political ambitions, that his drapery business would take a back seat. There was simply no way in which the College Street shop could generate the kind of money he aspired to. Brother-in-law Richard and wife Elizabeth, when she could spare the time from her young family, kept the business ticking over. Meanwhile George concentrated on looking for ways to make the Bottrill fortune work for him – and in the spring of 1833 he saw his chance.

He became closely involved in the formation of the York Union Bank, buying a number of shares and being appointed a director. On 1 May 1833 the York Union Banking Company opened its doors for the first time, with capital of £500,000 and deposits from Sir John Lowther and other wealthy local men. Significantly the York Union Bank had close ties with Glyn's, one of the best-known banks in London. The chairman of Glyn's, George Glyn, just happened to be the chairman and chief promoter of the London and Birmingham Railway and other lines. Once George Hudson's eyes alighted on the untold benefits of railway speculation, this was to be an alliance made in heaven.

It was to prove a busy year for Hudson. The sudden death of Samuel Baynton, one of York's two sitting MPs, forced a by-election and John Lowther junior – somewhat reluctantly – stood again. Again he was defeated, but his vigorous, high-profile campaign had been expertly managed by Hudson. The city of York was beginning to sit up and take notice of this rich, confident and pushy young man, who seemed to have a habit of getting things done – by every means at his disposal.

It was no surprise, therefore, to discover George Hudson being nominated for, and accepting, the post of treasurer of the York Railway Committee in December 1833. This committee had been set up to examine the possibility of bringing a railway line to York, and Hudson was quick to invest in the enterprise. He could see further, much further, than the other members of the committee who simply wanted a line which would bring coal to the city. He could see, dimly at first but then ever so clearly, a vision in which he presided over the finest railway network in the world.

The committee, blissfully unaware of the fact that they were in the process of making history, first met in Mrs Tomlinson's Hotel in Low Petergate, York, on 30 December 1833. Composed of York's leading lawyers and businessmen, the committee discussed the importance of transporting cheap coal into York by rail. Everyone agreed that the city was missing out on the benefits of the industrial revolution, which were being so clearly enjoyed in the neighbouring West Riding, and it was hoped that cheap coal might drag York into the nineteenth century.

As the meeting broke up, with officers elected and a plan of action formulated, George Hudson's head must have been swimming with ideas. The railways might have been in their infancy, but their rapid growth was creating a brand-new world full of exciting opportunities. Their time had come – and so had George Hudson's. At Mrs Tomlinson's that night, the Railway King had taken the first step towards his throne. His life would never be the same again.

CHAPTER FOUR

On the Right Tracks

I have been ever of the opinion that revolutions are not to be evaded

Benjamin Disraeli

As the year 1833 drew to a close, the age of the railways was about to begin in earnest. The nature and extent of this railway revolution was as yet but dimly understood, but the more perspicacious of men realised that life would be transformed once the rail network began to spread its tentacles across the country.

It is always dangerous to place precise dates on the beginning of a movement or an age, but the opening of the Stockton and Darlington Railway on 27 September 1825 is generally regarded as the symbolic start of the great railway era. This was the first public railway worked by steam and it set the pattern for the development of railway systems across the world.

Enthusiasts will point out that the Loughborough and Nanpantan line, opened in 1788, was the world's first public railway. They might also claim that the Swansea and Mumbles line became the first passenger railway in 1806. But it is generally agreed that the Stockton and Darlington line was the first railway to be worked by steam, although for several years after its gala opening that September day, its steam traction was reserved for freight.

The prime mover in the development of the railways was George Stephenson, a brilliant engineer who was to play a significant part in George Hudson's own meteoric rise to fame and fortune. Stephenson, born in 1781 in a mining village not far from Newcastle, had developed the *Locomotion*, a pioneering mobile steam engine, and it was the *Locomotion No 1* which pulled the freight train from Darlington to Stockton Quay on that historic occasion in 1825. Hudson was still in his drapers' shop when Stephenson was being hailed as a national hero, but their paths were to cross presently – with far-reaching consequences.

Once the Stockton and Darlington line had proved to be a viable money-making exercise, it was followed by the Liverpool to Manchester railway, which was opened in September 1830 to carry passengers as well as freight, and then a succession of other smaller lines up and down the country. Circumstance and need, rather than any grand design, shaped the geographical position and routes of these tracks. It was a lottery, but it was a very lucrative lottery. That is why railway committees, such as the one formed at Mrs Tomlinson's Hotel at the end of 1833, sprang up in every large English town.

It must be said that George Hudson took his role on the York Railway Committee much more seriously than most of his colleagues. That is why he was appointed the committee's treasurer; that is why he bought most of the shares which were on offer at the committee's inaugural meeting; and that is why he accompanied the surveyor, George Rennie, on most of his site visits on the proposed York to Leeds line. No other committee member showed remotely the same level of interest. It was to be their loss, and George Hudson's gain.

The chairman of the York Railway Committee was James Meek. Meek, a leading city businessman, was a Liberal and a Methodist, neither of which endeared him to Hudson, and the two men detested each other. Meek managed to keep his hatred under control while Hudson was making fortunes for himself and others, but he was the first to dance on the Railway King's grave once Hudson fell from grace. Indeed, the hypocrisy of Meek and his acolytes would prove truly staggering – and morally reprehensible.

In 1834, however, James Meek was willing to allow the dynamic Hudson to force the pace, because it was in the general interest to build a railway line between York and Leeds and bring cheap coal into the ailing cathedral city.

As Meek himself explained:

> The great advantage attendant on this project would be the reduction in the price of that necessary article of consumption, coal, and I have no doubt that York will one day become a manufacturing town as there could be little obstacle when coal could be delivered here at the same expense as Leeds.

In 1834 George Rennie presented his report to the committee and suggested that horses, rather than locomotives, should 'power' the trains on the York–Leeds line on the grounds of cost. This was not at all what the committee had expected, but Hudson's interest in the potential of a railway linking York and Leeds had been awakened. It was quickened when he met the legendary George Stephenson, quite by chance, in Whitby that summer.

Hudson was visiting Whitby to inspect some of the property on West Cliff which had been left to him by great-uncle Matthew

Bottrill. By an extraordinary coincidence, Stephenson was also in town. The two men were introduced and struck up a firm friendship, which was only threatened when Hudson became very grand at the height of his fame in the 1840s. In the 1830s and early 1840s, they complemented each other perfectly. It was Stephenson's genius to design and build engines and lines; it was Hudson's to promote and finance his friend's schemes and turn his dreams into reality.

It would be stretching the truth, however, to say that this partnership bore immediate fruit. In 1834 George Hudson was not yet a railway entrepreneur and George Stephenson was more interested in a series of projects in the Midlands. Legend has it that Hudson told Stephenson to 'mak all t'railways cum t'York', but there is no evidence for this. Nevertheless, when the two Georges did team up, York's position as one of the country's most important railway centres was assured.

It was clear that Rennie's idea of horse-drawn trains was a retrograde step – even if it might save money in the short term. In 1835 Stephenson was able to persuade the members of the York committee that they must use locomotive engines, rather than horses, on any line to be built between York and Leeds. More importantly, he also drew the attention of Hudson and his committee colleagues to his 'Midland projects', one of which was a line between Derby and Leeds. This line, as Hudson understood at once, had immense possibilities. It would open up links between Leeds and London – and revolutionise Britain's rail network.

But how could the city of York become involved? Wasn't it in danger of losing out again to Leeds, as it had during the industrial revolution? George Hudson, with his razor-sharp mind and uncluttered vision, seized the moment. Why didn't the railway committee's proposed line from York to Leeds connect with George Stephenson's Leeds–Derby project at a West Yorkshire town such as Normanton or Methley? This was a stroke of genius, and the railway committee, meeting at the York Guildhall in the summer of 1835, needed no persuading to accept Hudson's bold plan. Thus the historic York and North Midland Railway was born.

Hudson was convinced, with George Stephenson and his talented son Robert on board, that the York and North Midland Railway could not fail. He was right. York would now become the pivot of any future lines George Stephenson might plan to his native north-east, while the Stephenson name would inspire confidence among potential financial backers of the York and North Midland. No wonder Hudson threw himself wholeheartedly into the running of this new railway company. It would, he believed, be his passport to untold riches.

The York Railway Committee, which all of a sudden sounded terribly parochial, was transformed into the North Midland Railway Company, with Hudson as treasurer, his loyal friend James Richardson as solicitor and Robert Stephenson as its engineer. A survey was commissioned, a capital sum of £300,000 raised and a Bill drafted for Parliament. By the spring of 1836, railway fever was beginning to grip the city of York for the very first time.

In the meantime, George Hudson's personal and political lives were proceeding at an impressive pace. By 1835 the Hudsons were the proud parents of four children, George, Ann, John and William, and living in some splendour in their seventeenth-century Monkgate town house. They were also spreading their social wings. In his 1995 biography, *George Hudson*, Brian Bailey quotes from the unintentionally hilarious diary of the nineteenth-century 'It girl' Lady Charlotte Guest, who had met the Hudsons at a London dinner party in May 1834.

Lady Charlotte, daughter of the Earl of Lindsey, wrote with shrill indignation:

It was such a dinner, so stupid, so hot, that I nearly fainted. Conceive the horror of seeing a fat woman sit opposite to one in a yellow gown, and an amber hat with red flowers, and the still greater horror of that fat lady claiming to be an acquaintance. She proved to be Mrs Hudson . . . I had taken great pains to avoid the Hudsons in London, so it was supremely unlucky to have met them here.

This was Elizabeth Hudson's first foray into London society. It was not to be her last. In the 1840s, when the Hudsons were the proud owners of Albert Gate in Kensington, Mrs Hudson's wholly unintentional yet immaculate portrayal of Sheridan's Mrs Malaprop caused mirth and indignation in equal measure throughout polite society in the capital. She, like Richard Brinsley Sheridan's stage original, was blissfully ignorant of the effect of her social gaffes. On one occasion, for example, when asked whether she wanted sherry or port, she replied, 'A little of both please.' And once, when she ordered two globes, one terrestrial and one celestial, she sent them back because they did not match. Her loyal and loving husband never complained about her dreadful dress sense or her massacre of the English language.

It is instructive to note the date of this encounter with Lady Charlotte. It was May 1834, before George Hudson's grand railway projects or far-reaching political ambitions had taken off. The host of the dinner was William Thompson, the Conservative MP for Sunderland, a London Alderman and a former Lord Mayor of the City of London. Clearly the young man from the small draper's shop in York was aiming high, even before the railways shunted him into the limelight.

Meanwhile it was crucial that George Hudson established a firm political base in York if he was to fulfil the dreams he had for the

York and North Midland Railway Company. He could not possibly promote the company, either financially or in the House of Commons, unless he had solid and effective political support. Hudson, like the pragmatic political animal that he was, had been working on this assiduously since he had first become treasurer of the York Tories in 1832. Significantly, he had been helped by a change in the national political climate.

The euphoria which had greeted the Great Reform Act of 1832 and which had swept the Whigs to electoral triumph later that year was evaporating fast. It had become painfully apparent that the Whigs were little more than a self-seeking oligarchy and had lost much of the radical zeal which characterised the party under Charles James Fox. The ill-conceived and patronising Poor Law of 1834, combined with the attempt by Lord John Russell to appropriate Church of England land for secular purposes, caused widespread outrage, while Sir Robert Peel's seminal Tamworth Manifesto of 1834 reinvented the Conservative Party and proved there was life left in the Tories in the post-Reform Act era.

All this was of immense benefit to George Hudson and his fellow Conservatives in York. In January 1835 Sir John Lowther, standing in York for the third time, was finally elected and Hudson had an ally in the House of Commons. Basking in the afterglow of Lowther's victory, Hudson allowed the cheering Tory crowd a tantalising glimpse of his politics, as the *Yorkshire Gazette* reported:

> Mr Hudson returned thanks and declared that his highest gratification he could receive was to promote so glorious a cause as that in which they (i.e. the Tories) had been engaged. His politics were in a little room, they consisted in a sincere love of the king and constitution, and a desire to hand it down unsullied to their children.

It had been, however, a bitterly contested election in York, and allegations of bribery and corruption circulated long after Sir John had taken his seat in Parliament. Unfortunately for George Hudson, he was at the centre of these allegations.

There is no doubt that bribery was an integral part of the political process in the 1830s, just as sleaze appears to be today. But Hudson had broken the eleventh commandment, 'Do not get found out', and he had to face the consequences. As Lowther's political opponents tried to prove that he had been elected on a tide of alcohol and gold, Hudson gave them a helping hand. In an uncharacteristically – and unbelievably – stupid move, he sent gold sovereigns through the post to those poor people who had voted for Lowther. He played straight into the hands of the Whigs, and it was his fault, and his fault alone, that he was summoned to a House of Commons Select Committee to explain himself.

The Yorkshireman, a new radical newspaper which was soon to prove an implacable and vitriolic opponent of the Railway King, sent Hudson to London with these comments ringing in his ears:

The 1835 elections had been a struggle between the purity of election on the one hand and Tory corruption on the other. Never, in the annals of electioneering, did the votaries of drunkenness, bribery and treating hold their hands up and stalk through our streets with more effrontery and less shame, than during our late city contest.

Hudson, who was accompanied by his solicitor friend James Richardson, gave evidence to the House of Commons for three days in the summer of 1835. It has to be said that he proved to be the master of obfuscation and evasion. At one stage he denied paying out any money on Lowther's behalf, prompting the tart and pertinent question: 'Were you treasurer without a treasury?'

Hudson's reply was a wonderful concoction of meaningless waffle. He said: 'Well, perhaps that admits of some explanation. The fact is, that I believe in 1832, I was what they call treasurer, but I received no monies; but I was told by the chairman that cheques on the city and county bank would be answered, if I drew them on account of the expenses of the election; that is the explanation.'

It transpired that the total amount drawn from the bank had been £3,240 and Hudson was asked, by one of the more dogged Select Committee members, whether this was 'polling money'. Polling money, to the uninitiated, was money used to bribe the electorate.

Hudson retorted: 'I don't know what you mean by polling money. I don't like to be entrapped into an answer by a question of that sort; let him put his question in a straightforward way.'

The dogged member responded: 'I ask you, do you know whether any polling money was paid on behalf of Mr Lowther?'

'That question,' Hudson replied, with remarkable sang froid, 'I respectfully decline to answer.'

The York historian, Dr Alf Peacock, has seized upon this reply as damning evidence of Hudson's fundamental dishonesty. What Dr Peacock fails either to appreciate or accept is that Hudson was simply playing by the political rules of the day. Bribery was an integral part of the electoral process. Had the York Whigs eschewed corruption, then Hudson would have been in deepest trouble. They hadn't, and he wasn't.

It was precisely because the Select Committee uncovered corruption in the Whig camp during the elections between 1832 and 1835 that the inquiry into Hudson's own questionable behaviour was dropped. Interestingly enough, the chief perpetrator of the Whig misdemeanours was James Meek, that holier-than-thou

Methodist and implacable Hudson foe. No doubt George Hudson allowed himself a wry smile at Meek's double standards, but he wouldn't have been too concerned by the stench of his enemy's hypocrisy. He had more important things on his mind.

In December 1835, Hudson was elected to the York Corporation for the first time and became one of the twelve aldermen of the city. This was a real triumph for the farmer's boy from Howsham, now known as the magnate from Monkgate, and it provided him with the political platform he needed to further his burgeoning railway ambitions. The momentum was with him now, and the city of York was never going to be the same again.

The York and North Midland Railway Bill passed through Parliament in 1836, with relatively little trouble, and by August the new York and North Midland Railway Company held its first formal meeting. It came as no surprise to anyone when Hudson was elected chairman. After all, it was his vision and his drive that had led to the formation of the company in the first place. The other directors of the company, incidentally, included James Richardson, Richard Nicholson (Hudson's brother-in-law) and James Meek.

Work began on the historic new line in April 1837. It was to run from Tanner Row, from within the city walls, crossing the Leeds–Selby line at South Milford and joining the North Midland at Altofts, near Wakefield. George Hudson was taking the first steps towards fulfilling his dream and, as the new line neared completion, his stock continued to rise within the York Corporation.

Richard S. Lambert, Hudson's faithful biographer, explains how:

> For some time past, Hudson had been steadily consolidating
> his influence on the York Council, where he showed himself
> an unsparing advocate for public parsimony – in strong
> contrast with the lavish provision he made for private

hospitality and charity. One day he would demonstrate the former by the cutting down of some petty official's salary; the next he would ostentatiously display the latter by heading a subscription list opened on behalf of the suffering poor. Thus he gained a reputation for efficiency and benevolence combined.

Yes, Hudson was certainly getting up a head of steam. By the end of 1837 the York Tories had made sufficient progress at the local elections to hold the balance of power within the Corporation and to appoint the new Lord Mayor. There was but one choice: George Hudson. What an amazing reworking of the legend of Dick Whittington this was, as the ill-educated farmer's boy from Howsham rose to be the Lord Mayor of the second most important city in the land.

A more introspective man might have stopped and wondered about his extraordinary good fortune at this stage in his roller-coaster life. But not George Hudson. He was already plotting and planning ahead, convinced that even if the streets of London weren't paved with gold, the brand-new rail tracks of Yorkshire were.

CHAPTER FIVE

Action Stations

Blessed is he who has found his work;
let him ask no other blessedness

Thomas Carlyle

The city of York must have been an enjoyable place in which to live in 1837, unless you happened to be very poor, because the new Lord Mayor decided that the three themes of his term of office should be hospitality, more hospitality and even more hospitality. George Hudson might not have been a keen student of human nature, but he was acute enough to realise that a series of lavish Mansion House feasts, washed down by gallons of champagne, beer, sherry and wine, would win the hearts – as well as the stomachs – of his fellow citizens. It was a recipe for success, especially since his predecessor as Lord Mayor was the ascetic and penny-pinching glass manufacturer James Meek.

However, *The Yorkshireman*, which was emerging as an implacable enemy of Hudson, regarded his election as Lord Mayor as an unmitigated disaster:

With Mr Hudson as an individual, we have not fault to find. We have no objection that he should possess the civic honours of York; but that the corporation and representation of this important city should be held in his hand is a thing most monstrous.

The vehemence of these comments is significant. *The Yorkshireman* was a Whig newspaper and was inevitably going to oppose the appointment of an archetypal Tory like George Hudson. But the use of such strong language, notably the word 'monstrous', went far beyond mere opposition. It suggested an ingrained dislike of Hudson, which was soon to blossom into full-scale loathing. It was a measure of Hudson's success thus far that he had aroused such passions among his enemies before he had served a single day as Lord Mayor. And it was a measure of his insouciance that he would not have given *The Yorkshireman*'s tirade a second thought. There was, after all, some entertaining to be done.

The inaugural civic banquet, which was held at the beginning of 1838, was lavish enough, but it was followed by a ball for eight hundred guests at the Mansion House in March and two royal celebrations, one for Queen Victoria's nineteenth birthday in May and one for her Coronation in June. There were also banquets for the Assizes in July, the Archbishop of York and his clergy in September and the York Hussars in October. York was afloat on a tide of lavish hospitality and the *York Herald* was suitably impressed, describing the March banquet thus:

The Guildhall, venerable, grave and picturesque in its gothic taste, was illuminated by innumerable gaslights arranged in various devices, the whole fitted up for the occasion at great expense and with excellent taste and judgement. The first object which struck the eye was a brilliant design in gaslight beneath the roof displaying a large imperial crown in the centre, and with the letters V.R. (Victoria Regina) in characters of about three foot high. There were seven tables, all laden with the most sumptuous delicacies. We have never witnessed so splendid an entertainment in this city on any previous occasion whatever.

The Lord Mayor was clever enough to dispense his largesse to all sections of York society. On Queen Victoria's Coronation Day, for example, he organised a free feast for 14,000 adults and children, while his magnificent balls and dances had the most beneficial consequences for York's tradesmen and shopkeepers. Thus the York Union Gas Light Company masterminded the illuminations at the March banquet and made Hudson a company director as a result. The York Whigs, so used to getting their own way, could only watch with impotent rage as Hudson's junketing kept them in the political wilderness.

It came as no surprise, therefore, when the Tories swept the board at the municipal elections in November 1838. They tightened their grip on the corporation, enabling them to nominate their hero Hudson as the Lord Mayor for a second time. The Whigs were aghast, because this was against all the unwritten (and some of the written) rules of the corporation's constitution. It had long been the case that only an alderman could become Lord Mayor, and Hudson's period as alderman had expired at the same time as his mayoralty. No matter. The Tories re-elected Hudson as an alderman, and then Lord Mayor. The Whigs, backed by the vociferous *Yorkshireman*, took legal action, but it was nearly two years before the case was decided and, by then, Hudson's second period as Lord Mayor had long since been and gone.

George Hudson himself was reported as saying that he was most anxious to retire from office, and that only a sense of duty prompted him to stand again. If he was serious about this, he was being most economical with the truth. For it was absolutely crucial that he held the most influential position in the city as his grand railway plans inched nearer towards reality.

The highlight of 1839, for both Hudson and the city of York, was the official opening of the York and North Midland Railway. The initial enthusiasm which had greeted the project in 1836 had waned, as delays hampered its construction and the value of its shares sagged, but by 1839 a tunnel had been built under York's historic walls and land had been bought at Tanner Row and Toft Green, off Micklegate, for a station. In April of that year the first engine arrived from George Stephenson's factory at Newcastle and it was christened the *Lowther*, in honour of York's Conservative MP. By May, everything was in place for the grand opening on the 29th.

And what an opening it was. J. L. Foster, an eager young reporter on the *Yorkshire Gazette* who was to become one of Hudson's firmest supporters, recorded it for posterity with twelve-and-a-half columns of tiny print. Here is an excerpt:

A cloudless sky of an azure more deep than is often seen above our misty atmosphere and a sign of intense brightness and warmth might have belonged to a southern clime, but a gentle breeze from the north-east of refreshing coolness preserved the temperature at such a point to present the lassitude and enervation which are felt under a too sultry day. The cathedral bells were rung, flags were hoisted and every sight, every sound, every movement seemed to bespeak a holiday; even the sulky booming of the cannon on the river had a gladsome interpretation.

After breakfast, which was a massive feast, the four hundred carefully selected guests moved en masse in a series of carriages from the Mansion House to the railway terminus at Thief Lane, where a train was ready and waiting. It consisted of five first-, ten second- and three third-class coaches, with the Stephenson locomotives *Lowther* and *York and Leeds* at the front and back respectively. It took just thirty-six minutes to reach South Milford, to the south-west of Selby, at the average speed of just under 24 mph. The guests then spent half an hour at South Milford, reflecting on their historic journey and inspecting the brand-new line, before returning to York.

The day was not yet over. Two immense dinners had been laid on (as if the huge breakfast had not been enough), one for the clerks and the engineers and one for George Hudson and his illustrious guests at the Guildhall. Hudson and his good friend and fellow pioneer George Stephenson sat down at 4.30 p.m. and did not rise until after 10.00 p.m. No doubt some, including Hudson himself who had a voracious appetite for both food and drink, had a little difficulty rising when the time came to leave!

During the dinner Hudson paid a lavish tribute to Stephenson, whose name had given this project the gravitas and respectability it needed. He said: 'If ever there is a man who deserved to be held up to the public approbation of the whole world, that man is Mr Stephenson . . . He has brought us through our difficulties, and when doubts were entertained as to this railway being a profitable investment, he has said: "I know the York and North Midland Railway will be a good concern – buy me some shares." The effect of this we all know.'

Meanwhile James Meek, for once jettisoning his dour Methodist demeanour, enthused: 'London will be the head of our railway, Edinburgh the feet and York the heart. I hope that the head will never be affected with apoplexy, nor the feet with gout, and that York will continue sound at the heart.' Was this a thinly veiled jibe at the expense of his arch enemy George Hudson, who suffered badly from gout? We shall never know. But we do know that York's heart remained sound until Hudson himself came tumbling down – pushed by, among others, Meek.

Once the celebrations were over, Hudson could sit back and savour his considerable achievement. The opening (albeit partial) of the York and North Midland Railway paved the way for a crucial link with London. Within twelve months the capital could be reached from York, via Normanton, Derby and Rugby, in no more than ten hours at an average speed of just over 20 mph. It was remarkable – and it opened up a whole new world of opportunities for the city of York.

If George Hudson thought this achievement would endear him either to his colleagues on the corporation or within the York and North Midland Company, he was sadly mistaken. Although he had an aptitude for making money, he had a real talent for making enemies. By November 1839, at the end of his second stint as Lord Mayor, those enemies were circling, like vultures, around him.

It is fair to say that Hudson brought most of his unpopularity upon himself. He had a vicious tongue and an ability to tease and taunt less quick-witted opponents which caused deep and lasting offence. The Whigs on the corporation were still smarting from the effective manner in which Hudson had removed them from power, and they were incensed by the partisan way in which he had behaved as Lord Mayor. The more scrupulous committee members on the York and North Midland, meanwhile, were becoming worried about his apparently cavalier approach to the company's finances and to his plans for running trains on Sundays.

So it was not too surprising that George Hudson stepped down as Lord Mayor that November in a blaze of controversy and abuse. The vultures were led by a young solicitor called George Leeman, who, instead of praising Hudson's two years as Lord Mayor, said that he was delighted that Hudson was going. His was a nasty piece of invective, accusing the Tories of 'bowing down before the golden calf of Hudson's wealth and worshipping it'. He was presupposing that all Whig councillors were morally beyond reproach, which was simply not true.

A vote of thanks to Hudson was carried, nonetheless, by a substantial majority and then the outgoing Lord Mayor rose, like a wounded stag, to reply to Leeman and his acolytes. He denounced his critics as 'actuated by a littleness of feeling which, when exhibited in its deformed state, as it has been this day, is disgraceful'. He then described them as toadies who touted for meals and invitations, resorted to backbiting and invented conversations which never occurred. Hudson's anger and frustration at the behaviour of his opponents was understandable, for he was forging ahead while the rest of York followed. He could not work out why he should attract such hatred – and that was to be one of the reasons for his eventual downfall. He believed his achievements would destroy his opponents. He was wrong.

The political life of York was becoming ever more feverish. As the Whigs continued to brood over Hudson's contemptuous attitude towards them, a terrible row broke out between Hudson and the Recorder of York, the Whig Charles H. Elsey, during a prestigious civic dinner. Both men were exceptionally drunk and got themselves into a ridiculous argument (as only drunks can) over who should reply to the toast 'The Aldermen of York'. Both considered themselves the senior alderman present, and exchanged insult after insult until the band struck up and drowned them out. Hudson, struggling to get his words out through a haze of alcohol and anger, stormed:

'I beg to stress my abhorrence of that individual who, with an audacity which belonged to his ignorance, had thus insulted me . . . Because I dared to differ from a certain individual, was that person to forget all the kindly feelings of human nature, and wantonly attack me on all occasions. Was a gentleman to be insulted to his face, as I had been?'

The dinner broke up with food and missiles being thrown across the room and there were fears that Hudson and Elsey would come to blows in St Helen's Square, outside the Mansion House. Luckily both were too drunk actually to fight, and a most embarrassing and unbecoming scene was averted. But this was a graphic reminder of George Hudson's hot temper and the hatred that he was capable of inspiring. This did not matter when his star was in the ascendant, as it was in 1839 and 1840, but his unpopularity was a crucial factor when the Hudson edifice began to crumble in 1848.

It was generally believed that the 'battle of the alderman's toast' had been won by George Hudson. The *Yorkshire Gazette* blamed Elsey for the disgraceful scenes and the Tories put forward a motion to cut his salary. It is doubtful that Hudson himself gave this embarrassing incident any further thought, because his involvement in the railways was moving on apace. Like most great men, he did not spend too much time worrying about what might have been.

By 1840 George Hudson was the undisputed king of the York and North Midland Railway Company, even if he had not yet been crowned the Railway King. In the summer of 1839, two company members, James Meek and Samuel Tuke, had suggested that York and North Midland trains should not run on a Sunday for religious reasons. Hudson was astounded, as well he might have been because both Meek's glassworks and Tuke's gasworks operated on a Sunday, and their motion was roundly defeated. Meek, in a fit of hypocritical pique, resigned immediately. With his enemy gone, Hudson could run the York and North Midland in exactly the way he wanted. And so he did.

In the spring of 1840, the shareholders of the York and North Midland received their first dividend, one guinea. This was a princely sum, especially since the railway had only been opened as far as South Milford on the Leeds–Selby line. Hudson boasted about this, saying that he was not aware of any other railway company that had paid a dividend before it was fully operational. He also admitted, presumably because he had to, that this dividend had been paid out of capital. No shareholder complained then, but they certainly screamed eight years later.

The year 1840, though, was a golden one for George Hudson. His admirers, headed by the new Lord Mayor, William Stephenson Clark, voted to raise a public subscription for him and £700 was collected within two months. He was subsequently presented with a beautiful piece of silverware. Even though the Whigs, victims of both his Machiavellian political machinations and his vicious tongue, hated Hudson, the rest of York loved him. It was no wonder that Whig resentment festered, until it erupted when the crown began to slip from the Railway King's head.

During the summer of 1840, Hudson's stock (if that isn't too ironic a word) rose even higher with the completion of the York and North Midland Railway. On 11 May the South Milford to Burton Salmon section of the line was opened and, six weeks later, the last seven miles from Burton Salmon to the junction with the North Midland at Altofts, near Normanton, was finished. It was time for another grand opening!

This was held on 30 June. The occasion celebrated the completion not only of the York and North Midland line, but also the completion of the third and final portion of the Midland Counties Railway between Leicester and Rugby. This meant that there was an uninterrupted line, 217 miles long, from York to London, via Normanton, Derby and Rugby. The journey would take no more than ten hours and four trains would run daily, each way. A similar journey by coach and horses would have taken twice as long.

The two Georges, Hudson and Stephenson, travelled together in triumph on the special train which steamed from York to Derby on that historic June day. United in friendship, talent and ambition, there seemed no limit to what they could achieve together. With Hudson's entrepreneurial flair and Stephenson's technical brilliance, they were a formidable combination. It was clear, as railway mania gripped the country, that the York and North Midland project would be the first of many.

Significantly, the celebrations of 30 June were less sustained and lavish than those of the previous year when the first section of York and North Midland line was opened. That was because Hudson, who was looking to cast his net much wider than a single line between York and the West Riding, had work to do the very next day.

He decided to attend another opening ceremony, that of the little Selby to Hull railway. Although George Hudson always looked at the broader picture, he never neglected the detail (unless he was dealing with the accounts!). So he believed that a rail link with Hull, the principal English port for trade with the Baltic, could be of great strategic importance for York. Hudson's appearance at the opening ceremony would have been noted and must have filled the directors of the new railway with an uneasy mixture of fear and anticipation.

However, Hudson was not in the habit of sitting back and watching what other people were doing. George Stephenson returned to York in July, armed with an ambitious plan which he and Hudson believed would underline the city's growing reputation as a major strategic railway centre. They wanted to build a railway from York to Scarborough and Whitby, thereby linking Yorkshire's most beautiful city with its attractive and under-used coastline. Hudson had an especial fondness for the atmospheric port of Whitby, and he believed that Scarborough could become the 'Brighton of the north'. He was also aware that any railway link between York and Scarborough would pass through the stunning Derwent Valley and his birthplace of Howsham. This would have appealed to someone with a strong sense of his past, and of his destiny.

The plan was to build a railway from York to Scarborough with a branch line to Pickering, thus making a connection from York to Whitby as there was already a Pickering–Whitby line. The project was announced, with impeccable timing, at the annual meeting of the York and North Midland, whose shareholders, delighted with a dividend of six per cent, were only too delighted to grant £500 for a survey of the proposed line. Only the Quaker Joseph Rowntree sounded a note of caution, questioning the vagueness of the company accounts. The other shareholders did not appear to mind, so long as healthy dividends were paid. The appointment of George Stephenson to the board of the York and North Midland, meanwhile, reassured any other doubting Thomases.

Incidentally, Hudson himself could not believe that anyone should be concerned about his accounting practices and poured scorn on the suggestion that independent auditors be appointed:

> This is the first time that I have ever heard such a suggestion
> in a meeting of railway projectors. The accounts are always
> audited by the directors themselves. Does anyone doubt these
> worthy gentlemen? Are not the books always open for every
> shareholder to inspect for himself?

These words would return to haunt him.

Meanwhile, now that the York to Scarborough line had been approved, at least in theory, George Hudson turned his attention once more to the little Leeds–Selby railway. He was frightened that it could become a serious rival to the York and North Midland by becoming the crucial link in the Liverpool, Manchester, Leeds and Hull chain and thus cornering all the east-to-west traffic. So he approached the directors of the Leeds and Selby and suggested they lease their line to the York and North Midland. They agreed and, in November 1840, a thirty-one-year lease was negotiated at an annual rental of £17,000 with an option to purchase at a later date. Another brick had been laid in the foundations of George Hudson's burgeoning empire.

If Hudson thought, however, that he could deal as easily with the directors of his next target, the Selby–Hull railway, he was mistaken. These directors had distanced themselves from Hudson's successful negotiations with their neighbouring Leeds–Selby line and were in no mood to be bought out. Neither were they prepared to share the line with the York and North Midland. So the Selby and Hull retained its independence – for a few years. But it was a minnow swimming in a shark-infested sea, and its days were inevitably numbered.

George Hudson's enemies had been having a barren time in 1840, as he went from strength to strength with a growing band of disciples, hangers-on and satisfied shareholders in his wake. Then, on the night of 11 November, just two days after the lease had been signed for the Leeds–Selby line, a goods train crashed into the rear of a passenger train standing at the junction between the York and the Leeds–Selby lines. Two passengers were killed. It transpired that the driver of the goods train had poor eyesight, prompting the *Halifax Guardian* to denounce 'those whose grasping cupidity allows their own aggrandisement to supersede the necessity of carefully watching and directing their servants, or of studying the comfort and protection of the public'.

This thinly veiled attack on George Hudson, which has an unfortunate resonance today, echoed right across Yorkshire. But it was in York, where his frustrated foes had been biding their time, that anti-Hudson feeling found its fullest expression. The success that he was enjoying with the York and North Midland, and his popularity in the city itself, was becoming intolerable to enemies such as James Meek, Charles Elsey and George Leeman. They sought every opportunity to denigrate Hudson, but in the early 1840s, those opportunities were limited and so they had to make the best of them.

The feud with Recorder Elsey was still simmering and Elsey, smarting from the fall-out from that embarrassing dinner, rounded on Hudson at the York Sessions in January 1841. He fumed that Hudson 'held an undivided sovereignty and dominion over all ranks and denominations in the city of York'. Elsey was probably right, but that did nothing to assuage his anger.

If Elsey hated George Hudson, George Leeman positively loathed him. It is impossible to say exactly why this radical young solicitor was so implacably opposed to everything Hudson did, but jealousy must enter into the equation. Certainly a difference of political views, and temperament, cannot explain the depth of Leeman's dislike of the 'magnate of Monkgate'. This dislike erupted again in the summer of 1841 when Hudson – on behalf of the York and North Midland Company – put forward an imaginative scheme to build a new bridge across the Ouse into Lendal and St Leonard's Place in the heart of York. This would improve the access to York Station in Tanner Row.

It was an admirable scheme, in the best interests of both the

York and North Midland and the city of York. There was some opposition, notably from the shopkeepers by Ouse Bridge in Micklegate and Ousegate and from the owners of the ferry which crossed the Ouse at Lendal, but that did not amount to much until Leeman intervened. He persuaded Parliament to compel the York and North Midland to build a new road from the station to Micklegate, as a condition for the bridge being given the go-ahead. Hudson was having none of this, and the city had to wait another twenty years for a new bridge at Lendal.

Interestingly enough, the family that owned the ferry at Lendal were called Leeman. Might this explain George Leeman's violent opposition to this new bridge? It is ironic that George Hudson's detractors have always painted Hudson as a self-interested hypocrite and George Leeman as a dedicated upholder of the city of York's good name. That is one reason why a statue of Leeman stands proudly next to York Station, while Hudson must make do with an ugly little thoroughfare between Rougier Street and Micklegate. The episode of the new bridge at Lendal underlines that Leeman might not only have been an opportunist, but also a rogue, and suggests that York's opinion of two of its most famous sons needs to be radically revised.

Hudson's most recent biographer, Brian Bailey, points out that he had a genuine interest in York's advancement and prosperity:

Hudson's motives in promoting improvements in York were not so sordidly mercenary as his political opponents liked to make out. It was he, for instance, who helped to promote the building which was to serve as an officers' mess for the Yorkshire Hussars and as a venue for other events. Designed by his friend George Townsend Andrews, it was financed by public subscription. What are now known as the De Grey

Rooms, built in St Leonard's Place in 1842, subsequently became the scene of many of Hudson's railway meetings.

George Hudson, though, did not let the episode of the new bridge at Lendal worry him unduly. He had other, larger projects in mind. He was about to try out the throne of the Railway King for size.

CHAPTER SIX

The Golden Touch
of a Railway Visionary

Where there is no vision, the people perish

Proverbs

While George Hudson was probably not a subscriber to the theory that life begins at forty, since his began in earnest at twenty-seven when he inherited £30,000, he had every reason to be extremely positive and confident about the future as he entered his forty-first year.

On a personal level, Hudson's life was on an even keel. Although his father-in-law James and his brother Thomas had recently died, his wife Elizabeth and their four children were in good health. George, the eldest, was now eleven, with Ann nine, John eight and William six. George Hudson was immensely proud of his children and was determined to give them the secure upbringing and first-class education that he had so conspicuously lacked. Young George would soon be off to Harrow, one of the finest independent schools in the country, where he would lose those rough edges in his character that his father was to carry to the grave.

The Hudsons lived in domestic bliss at 44 Monkgate, their

most elegant Restoration town house, which proved a reassuring refuge from the vicious politics of the York council and the rigours of running the York and North Midland Railway. The garden was spacious by town house standards and overlooked the River Foss, providing an element of much-needed tranquillity. Elizabeth Hudson was a good wife and mother, and her husband loved her dearly. He did not mind if she was an object of ridicule among the chattering classes, because those classes were – in Hudson's opinion – ridiculous anyway. He and his wife had been through a great deal together during their twenty-year marriage; Elizabeth was a kindly and loyal soul and was a tremendous support in the bad times as well as an enthusiastic companion in the good.

Hudson's own character was by now set in stone. He was hard-working, unscrupulous, quick-witted, rude, confident, self-indulgent and obstinate. He did not suffer fools gladly and never forgave anyone who crossed him. His life thus far had been remarkably successful, by any personal, political or financial criteria, and he had no reason to doubt himself or his *modus operandi*. He had risen from the obscurity of a North Yorkshire farming village to become the leading political figure in York and he was in the process of creating a national network of railways out of anarchy and chaos. Why should he be beset by uncertainty or doubt, when everything he had touched had turned, sometimes literally, to gold?

It is said that everyone has the face they deserve at forty, so it is worth quoting D. Morier Evans' description of Hudson's physical appearance at the time:

He is about five feet eight inches in height, of a stout burly frame, with a short bull-neck, surmounted by a head not conspicuous for intellectuality. His face attracts attention, and the expression in his eye is not peculiar. At first sight one dislikes him . . . Notwithstanding the sinister leer of his eyes, the ungainly frame, and the unharmonious voice, his person, however rude exteriorly, is the cover of a fairer mind than was first imagined.

In his fascinating essay *Facts, Failures and Frauds*, published in 1859, D. Morier Evans describes Hudson thus:

Mr Hudson's personal appearance is calculated to strike if not absolutely command attention. There is a massiveness in the proportions of his bodily frame, evidently hereditary in his stock, and inclining to symmetric development. His head is large; his forehead broad, and somewhat elevated. The features of his face, lighted up with small and somewhat penetrating grey eyes might, from their severity of outline, convey to a casual observer, the impression of harshness of disposition. This severity, however, is of a purely mental character – the indication of a powerful will acting on thoughts arranged and re-arranged with incessant activity, or upon schemes either altogether ideal or rigidly practical, and long and closely nurtured and stimulated by a vast range of feeling, which covers the whole ground of his sympathies and passions. When animated by conversation, his countenance – usually hard and rugged – relaxes into a pleasing smile.

A famous European graphologist, one Dr Robert Saudek, was given a specimen of Hudson's handwriting – without knowing anything of his subject's career or personality. He concluded:

Here is a man of tremendous temperament. Nervous, irritable, neurotic and impatient – with himself as well as others – gifted in far-sightedness, grasping things at a moment's notice, ever ready for combinations, and regrouping facts with creative originality. His temperament is so strong and his convictions so powerful that, as a personality, he exercises a great influence on others, who are often prepared to follow his leadership without taking the trouble to examine his arguments. He is half genius and half madman, a typical example of how a neurotic constitution can produce quite exceptional brilliancy.

There is much truth in Dr Saudek's analysis. The problem was, as Dr Saudek also pointed out, that there was no one to temper Hudson's wilder flights of fancy with reason and no one to point out that his idea of efficient accounting could, in fact, be interpreted as fraud. He needed a friend whose intelligence, as well as loyalty, he could trust. George Stephenson performed that role in the early days, but by 1845 Stephenson was complaining that Hudson had become 'too grand' for him. Hudson was to find it was lonely – and dangerous – at the top.

In 1841, nevertheless, the Hudson–Stephenson bandwagon was well and truly on the rails. The York and North Midland was prospering in 1841, as the benefits of the railway revolution began to filter through to all sections of Yorkshire society. But its neighbouring line, the Great North of England, was in terrible difficulties. It had been assumed that this railway, which was to link York with Newcastle, would be a natural money-spinner, but it had run into a succession of problems. By the end of March 1841, all its capital had been used up and the line only stretched as far north as Darlington.

On 30 March 1841, the directors of the Great North of England railway decided to make the best of a bad job and opened the forty-five miles from York to Darlington to passenger traffic. Hudson's presence at the opening ceremony must have unnerved the Great North of England directors, because he was clearly not just there for the gallons of free champagne on offer. He allowed himself a few words during the speeches, saying: 'All railways are as yet in their infancy and day after day, week after week, and month after month, they will go increasing their resources.' A director of the railway, called Oxley, replied enthusiastically in agreement: 'Yes, truly. Nothing, next to religion, is of so much importance as a ready communication.' Clearly, he couldn't see Hudson coming through the ocean of champagne!

The Great North of England directors had, in truth, made a dreadful mess of building (or trying to build) a railway between York and Newcastle. The York to Darlington link, which is one of the prettiest and fastest stretches of line in the whole country, presented few technical or economic challenges. Cutting through the heart of the picturesque Vale of York, where the terrain is primarily flat, was an engineer's dream. Moreover, there were not any competing lines, with all the vested interests that those contained, in the vicinity.

The stretch between Darlington and Newcastle, however, was fraught with difficulty. The countryside was much more hilly, while there were a number of small companies, such as the pioneering Stockton and Darlington, the Durham and Sunderland, the Brandling Junction and the Stanhope and Tyne, whose lines crossed the proposed Darlington–Newcastle link from east to west. The Great North of England company simply did not have the resources, the expertise or the vision to overcome these problems.

In the meantime, a Board of Trade report of 1841 had looked at the possibility of a rail link between London and Scotland and had recommended a western route from Carlisle to Edinburgh, connecting with the line that already stretched as far north as Lancaster. This was potentially disastrous news for Hudson, and for the city of York, whose future prosperity depended heavily on an east coast link with Scotland. But the Government report did leave the door partially open for the 'East Coast party', by stipulating: 'Should the line between Lancaster and Carlisle not be built and should parties be found to construct the line from Darlington to Edinburgh, then the western route ought to be abandoned for the present.'

George Hudson assimilated all this information, and assessed its implications, in a flash. The Board of Trade's report had concentrated everyone's minds by introducing an element of competition into the London–Edinburgh link and the petty jealousies which had beset progress in the north-east were forgotten. It was essential that the York–Darlington–Newcastle line should be completed as quickly as possible to give the East Coast lobby a fighting chance of defeating their West Coast rivals. The Great North of England company admitted that it could not help, because it had run out of money, so all eyes turned, in both hope and expectation, to George Hudson and George Stephenson.

Hudson, needless to say, had a master plan. This plan, which he unveiled in two stages, was an excellent illustration of his vision, his bravery, his quick-wittedness and his grasp of detail. Those detractors of the Railway King, of whom they are many, should study this plan carefully and then review their assessment of him as a fraudulent and self-obsessed opportunist.

The first part of Hudson's strategy was explained at a York meeting of all the companies who were interested in the east coast link to Edinburgh. He told the meeting, held in April 1841, that he proposed to build a new line from Darlington to the south of Durham, before linking up with the existing lines to complete the route to Gateshead and then Newcastle. This made perfect sense, promoting the Edinburgh link and placating the smaller rail companies at the same time.

But how was this bold project to be financed? Four months later, representatives of the eight smaller lines met in York again to hear George Hudson unveil the second part of his grand plan. It was then that he gave one of the finest speeches of his career. As John Clayton, the town clerk of Newcastle, recalled:

> We all came to York with gloomy countenances We went into the room without seeing our way through the night which beset us. This was the first occasion on which I saw my friend Mr Hudson. The room was full. All eyes were turned upon my friend, as a quarter from which light would spring upon us. He rose, and did not disappoint us. He spoke for less than half an hour, but he explained the thing in a most clear and intelligible manner.

George Hudson's plan was simple, but brave. The entire project was expected to cost £500,000, which was unlikely to be raised on the open market. So he proposed that the eight companies involved in the construction of the line from Darlington to Newcastle should offer shares in the new railway to their own shareholders – with a guaranteed dividend of six per cent. The shareholders would jointly own and administer the new railway, when it was built, and recoup their investment once the line was up and running. Clayton went on:

> When he [Hudson] had finished speaking, no man added one word – no man attempted to controvert a proposition he

had made. The light seemed to have suddenly broken upon us. We all saw our way. We saw that the thing would be achieved and achieved soon; we returned to our homes comfortable and happy.

Even Dr Alf Peacock is forced to give him some credit for this stroke of genius:

Hudson then, as he did frequently during his career, simply took up ideas that were going the rounds – and got credit for inventing them. But it was his skill, drive and enthusiasm which so often brought them to fruition.

Given Dr Peacock's distaste for Hudson, this is praise indeed.

Hudson had to move fast, because of the west coast threat, and he did. By December 1841, all the railway companies involved had ratified his plans and the Newcastle and Darlington Junction Railway was formed. The chairman, of course, was one George Hudson.

Whereas the new Newcastle and Darlington Junction Railway met with most people's approval, there were one or two dissenting voices. The most powerful and articulate of these was Captain Watts of Darlington, who wrote a succession of letters to the *Railway Times* during 1841–2. These letters are object lessons in the art of invective.

Captain Watts wrote:

I came across him at York Station crowing like a cock upon his own dunghill in the full plenitude of his tumultuary and noisy powers. Here is Mr Hudson, voluntarily addressing me at a public station in the voice of a Stentor, and with the publicity of a common crier, in terms of exaltation at carrying his point against me at the North Midland meeting. And when I state that my main objection to the measure arises from it being a violation of principle, his rejoinder is: 'Pooh, pooh, we don't mind principle in matters of business'.

There was no stopping Watts, who described the Newcastle and Darlington Junction scheme as 'an abortion, with a crooked back and a crooked snout, conceived in cupidity and begotten in fraud'. Hudson was aware that Watts was being primed by the directors of the Darlington and Stockton Railway, who were furious at their lack of influence over the new Darlington–Newcastle railway, and he simply ignored the good captain. It was the wisest course of action. Hudson had perhaps learned from his undignified spat with the Recorder of York that there was little to be gained from trading insults in public.

The success of the York and North Midland, meanwhile, had made George Hudson's power base in York even more secure. Dividends of almost ten per cent, when trading conditions were depressed and other railway companies were doing badly, kept the shareholders loyal and happy. No one was interested in asking any searching questions about Hudson's business practices when the rate of return from the York and North Midland was so good. Captain Watts could rant and rail against Hudson as much as he wished, but nobody of importance was listening.

As line after line, and company after company, sprang up all over England during the first two decades of the railway revolution, Parliament struggled to keep on top of events. New companies had to pass a private Bill through Parliament in order to start work, and this gave opponents a chance to argue a case against each line, for there was no guarantee that the railways that served the national interest best were the ones that were built. By 1840 the railways were a much sought-after haven for private savings and for speculative funds and Parliament found itself overwhelmed by applications to build new lines. It was only in 1844 that William Gladstone, anxious about the anarchy which was engulfing Britain's evolving rail network, introduced his Railway Act in an attempt to create order out of chaos.

So it was that in 1842 George Hudson, accompanied by Robert Stephenson, found himself in London watching over the progress of the Newcastle and Darlington Junction Railway Bill. It became law in June, despite vociferous opposition from the Stockton and Darlington directors, and the first meeting of the company's shareholders was held in October. Hudson promised to have the line open within two years and forecast that it would be as successful as the York and North Midland. He then appointed John Close, his former assistant at the draper's shop in College Street, as company secretary and his brother-in-law Richard Nicholson as treasurer. His control over the company was complete.

These were heady days for Hudson. Work soon began on the Darlington to Newcastle railway and progressed smoothly during the winter of 1842–3 – putting pressure on the supporters of the west coast link from London to Edinburgh. The York and North Midland, meanwhile, paid a regular ten per cent dividend and Hudson could not refrain from congratulating both himself, and the shareholders, in the spring of 1843 on the company's perform-ance during the past six months. He pointed out that 'all other railways, not even excepting the greatest of all railways, the London and Birmingham, had experienced a large diminution of income'.

It was not surprising, therefore, that the *Yorkshire Gazette* described George Hudson as 'probably the most perfect pattern of what a railway director should be', and called the York and North

Midland railway 'now, beyond any doubt, the best conducted of any line in the kingdom'. Nor was it a surprise that the North Midland railway, struggling badly in the depression, turned to Hudson for help. It cannot have escaped the attention of the directors of the North Midland line, which ran from Derby to Leeds, that the York and North Midland, which ran from Leeds to York, was doing extremely well. Why? The answer seemed simple: George Hudson.

In the spring of 1841 Hudson had refused to become a director of the North Midland, primarily because he wanted to focus on the embryonic Great North of England Railway. But he was on friendly terms with the North Midland's chairman, the banker George Carr Glyn, who was closely connected with Hudson's York Union Bank, and he accepted a request to become a member of a committee of inquiry into the North Midland's problems in August 1842. It was inevitable, given Hudson's temperament and his knowledge of the railways, that he would not only lead this committee of inquiry, but would also ensure that its recommendations were carried out.

These recommendations, which were formulated within a week, were radical. They included cutting the working expenses of the line from £44,000 to £27,000 a year by axing jobs, reducing wages and using cheaper materials. The *Yorkshire Gazette*, rapidly becoming Hudson's very own obedient poodle, applauded the 'reduction of extravagant salaries and the discharge of unnecessary officers whom the love of patronage or an ignorance of their duties has induced the directors to appoint'. The shareholders, too, liked what Hudson was proposing. It was only the 'unnecessary officers' and the workers, fearful of losing their jobs, who were appalled by these plans. But they did not have much hope of carrying the day in the face of the Hudson hurricane.

At a stormy meeting in Leeds in November 1842, the powerful alliance of George Hudson and the disgruntled shareholders of the North Midland proved far too powerful for their frightened opponents. Hudson, in fiery form, compared the different rates of pay between the two companies, pointing out:

> The servants of the York and North Midland Railway have less wages than are paid to the servants under this company, but they are as efficient and active as the servants on any other line . . . The servants of the York and North Midland are as happy and contented as any class of workmen can be.

That may, or may not, have been true, but the shareholders – sick and tired of failure – loved it. George Hudson, welcomed as a saviour, took charge of the North Midland's finances and immediately introduced a number of swingeing cuts. The company groaned under the strain and, on 12 January 1843, two trains collided at Cudworth, near Barnsley, and a passenger was killed. It was revealed at the inquest that the driver of one of the trains was in fact a fireman and had only three weeks' experience as an engine driver. There was an outcry – and the North Midland was suddenly saddled with the unfortunate, but justified, reputation of being the most dangerous railway in the land.

Hudson, of course, was not oblivious to the commercial consequences of such a reputation – especially when Queen Victoria's cousin, Prince George of Cambridge, was involved in an accident on the North Midland. Thankfully, Prince George and his fellow passenger, the Chartist leader Feargus O'Connor, were uninjured, but the damage was done. Hudson's immediate response was to blame a conspiracy among the North Midland's employees, but he needed something more substantial to placate his critics and, more importantly, the company's shareholders. In true Hudsonian fashion, he found it at once.

The North Midland was not the only railway which was struggling in the depressed times of the early 1840s. The Birmingham and Derby Junction and the Midland Counties, which had been built in the railway boom of 1836–7, were now in difficulties and George Hudson envisaged an amalgamation of all three companies. The shareholders concerned saw Hudson as their potential saviour, once he had dangled the prospect of healthy dividends before their impressionable eyes.

Addressing an unruly meeting at Derby Station in August 1843, Hudson outlined his plan to end the bitter and divisive rivalry between the Birmingham and Derby Junction and the Midland Counties, referring disparagingly to the 'struggle which was going on between the clerks at Derby Station to get one person to go by one route, and another by another'. He calculated that the amalgamation of the two companies would save £25,000 and that the Midland would soon be declaring a dividend of five per cent. It mattered not that the half-yearly dividend for the North Midland, announced that same month, had been a disappointingly low three per cent. The North Midland shareholders were mesmerised by the prospect of greater profits, once the three companies had been merged.

They did not have long to wait. Although there was some spirited opposition to Hudson, mainly from the directors of the Midland Counties, his dream of a unified rail network in the Midlands became a reality in September 1843 when the Midland Railway was formed. Hudson himself, naturally, was appointed chairman. He had, as one observer eloquently put it, 'walked straight into the thick of a quarrel between the two companies and, with courteous and plausible words, a long array of figures and a face of Corinthian brass', solved it.

This notable coup in the Midlands was George Hudson's greatest triumph thus far. He was now a major player on the railway stage, with control over lines stretching from Rugby and Birmingham to York and Newcastle, and his fame had spread way beyond the parochial confines of York. He was no longer 'the magnate of Monkgate', but the 'Railway Napoleon'. It would be only a few months before he was the 'Railway King'.

CHAPTER SEVEN

The Railway King Ascends his Throne

I think that the public would rather the railways were in the hands of companies, rather than the government

George Hudson

It was the Reverend Sydney Smith, one of the great wits of the nineteenth century, who dreamed up the soubriquet 'the Railway King' for George Hudson. Smith, who was the vicar of Foston and Thornton-le-Clay, near York, was famous for his cutting comments and his acerbic humour and once stopped the verbose Lord Macaulay (no friend of Hudson's) in full flow by saying: 'Your occasional flashes of silence make your conversation perfectly delightful.' He also endeared himself to the Swiss, by describing their country as 'an inferior sort of Scotland'. Incidentally, Smith also once referred to Hudson, rather disparagingly, as 'the retired linen draper'!

Hudson himself was delighted with his nickname and would have been touched that he is still known by it today, some 140 years after his death. The pride in his voice is almost audible as he recalled, towards the end of his life:

Sydney Smith, Sir, the Reverend Sydney Smith, the great wit, first called me The Railway King. I remember very well that he made a very pretty speech about it, saying that some monarchs had won their title to fame by bloodshed and by the misery they inflicted on their fellow creatures, I had come to my throne by my own peaceful exertions, and by a course of probity and enterprise.

Probity? That is debatable. Enterprise? Well, no one could deny that. Hudson's capacity for hard work, fuelled by a desire to make money and a few stiff drinks at the end of the day, was legendary. He combined this work ethic with an ability to focus on a number of projects simultaneously and the vision to see these projects through to their conclusion. It was a heady, potent mix, which was soon to make Hudson one of the richest and most influential men in England. By the beginning of 1844, just as the phrase 'the Railway King' was becoming common currency, a disgruntled correspondent of the *Railway Times* was complaining:

I consider Mr Hudson to be a shrewd man, but for pity's sake, Sir, call the attention of shareholders to the sway this person is obtaining . . . Shareholders should be cautious ere they raise a railway autocrat, with power greater than the Prime Minister.

Why, though, should shareholders be cautious when they were reaping the benefits of George Hudson's genius? As one grateful shareholder called Oldfield commented: 'Providence not only blessed him with intellect of which the cleverest people might be proud, but also with a constitution which enabled him to go through as much work as would have killed half a score of men.'

This was why, within days of having pulled off his audacious coup in the Midlands, Hudson was back in the north of England with ambitious plans to build a railway line to Scarborough and to buy the ailing Durham Junction and the Leeds–Selby companies. Once again he was demonstrating an uncanny ability to focus on three very different projects at the same time.

By November 1843, Hudson was ready to unfold his Scarborough plans to the shareholders of the booming York and North Midland, who were more than happy for their chairman, clearly blessed with the Midas touch, to proceed.

Hudson's biographer Richard S. Lambert calls mid-nineteenth-century Scarborough 'a small fishing village' and argues that Hudson was motivated mainly by romantic reasons. Hudson himself had encouraged this semi-altruistic interpretation of why he should wish to build a railway by declaring:

> A man who commences railway undertakings incurs a serious responsibility, and he ought to be very careful, and to weigh well and anxiously the details of his measure, before he projects such schemes and induces others to embark in them. There are many poor people who embark their property in railways, and if they prove unsuccessful, the consequences can hardly be calculated.

We shall never know whether George Hudson actually believed this sanctimonious sermon, but he was well aware that Scarborough, with its 10,000 population at the time, was much more than 'a small fishing village' and that a railway journey to Yorkshire's lovely east coast, through some of the county's most picturesque country-side, would prove exceptionally popular.

The prospering shareholders of the York and North Midland,

one of the only three companies which was making a healthy profit in 1843, needed no second bidding. Hudson told them: 'If you are not disposed to take up this project, and to embark your capital in it, I have parties who are ready to complete it, independent of this company.' But he knew he was preaching to the converted. By the end of November 1843, he had been given permission to proceed with the York to Scarborough line, to buy the Leeds–Selby line, which had been leased for the past five years, and to implement a complex personal shares arrangement, which would make him a very rich man indeed.

One or two voices were raised against this 'arrangement', notably that of the austere Quaker Joseph Rowntree, but Hudson's supporters dismissed this opposition contemptuously. They minded not that their friend George would pocket £10,000 from the Scarborough project, pointing out that he had done all the work on which the scheme was founded. They had a point.

By 1844 the Conservative Government, led by Sir Robert Peel, was becoming increasingly concerned about the haphazard and, at times, anarchic growth of the railways across the country. In effect, the railway age came to Britain (and America) before there was a railway policy. Although new railway companies had got their private Bill through Parliament in order to commence work, unfettered railway mania, characterised by too much speculation and too many failed lines, was gripping the nation.

Certainly some of the stories, which survive from the early years of the railways, border on the surreal. The House of Lords, for example, heard of a broker's clerk, the son of a charwoman, who earned twelve shillings a week and was the nominal owner of £52,000 worth of shares in the London and York Railway Company. Hundreds of lines were submitting their plans for approval to the Board of Trade and the competition was intense, with rival groups being quite capable of employing violent means to prevent their competitors' plans reaching the Board. It was not unknown even for coaches to be wrecked or horses stolen. In fact one company got its plans through to the Board of Trade by secreting them in a coffin surrounded by mourners!

The rising star of Sir Robert Peel's administration was William Gladstone, a highly principled, intelligent and hard-working politician who had been making a tremendous success of his first Government post as President of the Board of Trade. Gladstone, acutely aware of the dangers of unfettered expansion on the railways, set up a select committee in February 1844 with the aim of regulating the railways 'for the public benefit'. George Hudson, determined to have his say, appeared before the committee on 18 March. He told Gladstone:

> I think there will be a reaction in the course of two or three years, and the anticipation of shareholders will be disappointed. Many of the railways will not turn out productive, and there will be a reaction as violent as the other, even supposing the money market to continue in its present state. Competition in railways must lead to compromise, but I think the public would rather be in the hands of companies than of the government.

When the Bill appeared in June, it was not to Hudson's taste at all. Such was his current pre-eminence in the railway world that he was immediately asked by his railway peers to lead the opposition to Gladstone and his attempts to impose state control on Britain's rail network. Hudson adopted, for once, a softly-softly approach and told the President of the Board of Trade: 'If there be defects in the system of management of railways, the companies will cordially unite with the Government in their correction, and in framing any Bill which, on full inquiry, and after a fair hearing on both sides, shall be considered necessary for the correction of every such abuse proved to exist, or likely to arise.'

The significance of these words lies in their tone, rather than their content. George Hudson was famous for his short temper, his sharp wit and his cutting words, as Recorder Elsey and other foes back in York could testify. But here, when faced with a politician as canny as Gladstone, Hudson was content to play a subtler, gentler game. It came as no surprise, to Hudson at least, that the 1844 Railway Act was a drastically watered-down version of the Bill and had little effect on the way in which Hudson, and his fellow railway entrepreneurs, ran their companies. The Act, tellingly, is now chiefly remembered for introducing the concept of third-class travel.

Hudson's major achievement in beating such a consummate politician as William Gladstone at his own game in the House of Commons was recognised by leading railwaymen such as George Carr Glyn, who remarked that 'the defeat of the Government was due entirely to the exertions of Mr Hudson'. Indeed, Hudson's besting of Gladstone was one of the finest moments in his extraordinary career. It also gave him a taste for the cut and thrust of debate in the House of Commons, and a sharper appreciation of the nature of power and how it could be used to his advantage. The parochial debates in the York Council chamber suddenly seemed strangely inconsequential.

The summer of 1844 was one of the happiest of George Hudson's life. Fresh from his triumph over Gladstone, he opened the thirty-nine miles of line which formed the Newcastle and Darlington Junction Railway on 18 June, which just happened to be the anniversary of the Battle of Waterloo, ideally suited to the patriotic, tub-thumping and self-congratulatory nature of the day. A stream of special trains converged on Darlington, which then linked up with the 'grand opening train' – carrying Hudson and the two Stephensons – on its journey to Gateshead. A superb dinner, which featured no less than twenty-seven toasts, was then held in Gateshead, and Hudson, clearly in his element, spoke seriously about the Christian duty that every railway magnate and shareholder had towards his employees. In view of the savage treatment meted out to employees of the loss-making North Midland railway, this was a trifle hypocritical. The Railway King, however, had his eyes on posterity.

When his own toast was drunk, as the evening staggered towards its close, Hudson paid a warm and heartfelt tribute to George Stephenson, saying: 'I am only a tool in the hands of a genius – and probably a very pliant one in carrying out the plans of the Messrs Stephenson.' That wasn't strictly true, as Stephenson needed Hudson almost as much as Hudson needed Stephenson, but such modesty struck a welcome chord in a night of hubris and Hudson was cheered to the rafters.

The significance of the opening of the Newcastle and Darlington Junction Railway was immense, underlined that very day by the arrival of a flying train from Euston with copies of the morning papers. The journey from Euston to Gateshead had taken eight hours eleven minutes at an average speed of 37 miles an hour. That was a distinct improvement on the speed of 21 mph which had been achieved by the first train on the York and North Midland line seven years earlier.

The momentum that George Hudson had now built up was unstoppable. The opening of Gateshead station meant that the link with Newcastle, Berwick and Edinburgh was even closer, and the west coast connection to Scotland was now looking like a very poor second option. Hudson capitalised on this by supporting George Stephenson's plans to build a bridge across the River Tyne in

Newcastle and to form two companies to link Newcastle to Berwick and Edinburgh. He also bought the Brandling Junction Railway, one of the small industrial railways in the north-east, in September 1844, receiving 1,600 free shares into the bargain, and the Whitby and Pickering Railway a month later.

By now George Hudson was a very rich man indeed. Attractive and spacious as 44 Monkgate was, it did not accord with his new status as a king. A king needs a palace, and Hudson set about finding one. In August 1844 he bought the Octon estate, near Bridlington, and a considerable piece of land at Baldersby, near Thirsk, for £100,000 from the Duke of Devonshire. Within a year he had added Newby Park, by the lovely River Swale and next door to his Baldersby estate, and the 12,000-acre Londesborough Park in East Yorkshire, to his magnificent portfolio of country properties. Londesborough alone cost £500,000, a huge amount of money in mid-Victorian Britain.

George Hudson did not collect country houses and estates simply for fun, as some people collect stamps or butterflies. He wanted each of his sons, George, John and William, to inherit a country estate when they grew up and he viewed both Octon and Londesborough as strategic investments. Octon was close to the Bridlington branch line, which Hudson was proposing for the York–Scarborough railway, while the acquisition of Londesborough effectively blocked his bitter rival George Leeman's plans to build a railway from York to Market Weighton.

As Hudson was slowly metamorphosing from the magnate of Monkgate into the nabob of Newby and the lord of Londesborough, moves were afoot which were to cast an ominous shadow over the summer of his years. The formation of the London and York Railway company in May 1844, chaired by William Astell MP and backed by Edmund Beckett Denison, MP for Doncaster, and Hudson's old enemy Recorder Charles Elsey, posed a huge threat to the Railway King's sovereignty over the rail network in the north and the midlands. It was proposed that the new line would run from London, due north to York, via St Neots, Peterborough, Lincoln, Grantham and Doncaster. This was an obvious and serious threat to Hudson's lines, which ran to London via the circuitous route of Normanton, Derby and Rugby. Hudson believed he would be in deep trouble if the London–York line were built.

In October 1844 he spelled out the dangers of this line to the fifteen directors of the Midland, the company which would be the most affected. He asked for £2.5 million to build rival lines to foil the opposition and, almost unbelievably, he got it. This is how he put his case:

> The directors have a very heavy weight on their shoulders, but it is much lessened when they are aware that they have an influential and an active body of shareholders to back and assist them. Gentlemen should bear in mind that in the list of shareholders are to be found widows and orphans, who depend on their dividends for a scanty existence, and whose interests claim their protection. The question which Parliament will have to determine is whether it will permit gentlemen who have yet never conducted a railway, many of them who have never travelled on railways, some of whom have never seen a railway; whether it will allow these gentlemen to reap the reward of the labours of this company, who have a better scheme than their opponents.

This might have been wonderfully overblown rhetoric, with only a nodding acquaintanceship with the truth, but it went down a storm. The Railway King sat down to tumultuous applause – and with the

£2.5 million, metaphorically at least, in his pocket. Incidentally, those historians who argue that Hudson was a poor public speaker should study all the impassioned speeches he made during the bitter and drawn-out struggle to destroy the Astell and Denison's London to York line. It was a struggle that was to have significant consequences for his empire.

The year 1845 began with a very public argument with the aggressive Doncaster MP Denison at Derby Station. Hudson suggested that Denison was raising capital for his London to York railway by foul means rather than fair, to which Denison retorted: 'Have a care, Hudson. I have warned you before now to restrain your language. You are a blackguard, and I have done with you. Go, go away!' This brief encounter whetted Hudson's appetite for battle and his personal distaste for Denison was to fuel many a memorable clash.

While Denison, who had emerged as the power behind the London and York Company, lurked disconcertingly in the wings, Hudson continued to piece together his magnificent railway jigsaw. In the spring of 1845, he bought the Selby and Hull railway at last, while the Newcastle to Berwick line was approved by the House of Commons two months later. The Midland then acquired the lines between Birmingham, Gloucester and Bristol, stretching the tentacles of Hudson's empire even further, and a new company was formed to connect Manchester and Derby. Finally, rounding off six months of intense activity, the York to Scarborough railway was officially opened on 7 July.

Although George Hudson was not a man given to introspection, he would surely have dwelt on the symbolic importance of the opening of the York to Scarborough line. The inaugural train, which was hauled by two engines called *Hudson* and *Lion*, passed by a tiny station he had built at his birthplace of Howsham, through Castle

Howard, to Malton and Scarborough. The conquering hero had returned to his roots – and the crowds cheered and cheered, as the train steamed through some of Yorkshire's most peaceful and picturesque countryside to the sea.

It was inevitable, given the amount of time that he was spending in London and the House of Commons, that George Hudson should have considered the possibility of standing for Parliament. Ideally he would have liked to have represented York or Whitby, but time was of the essence. The struggle over the London and York Bill in the Commons was reaching its climax and Hudson believed that his presence was needed in the House to consign the Bill to the dustbin of history. Fortuitously, a vacancy for an MP had suddenly occurred in Sunderland – and Hudson's name was very much in the frame.

Prior to the summer of 1845, it has to be said, Hudson knew little about Sunderland and cared even less – mainly because it wasn't on any strategically important railway route. But that was no bar. MPs then, unlike now, were not required to show much allegiance to their constituencies either before, or after, their election. Leading Sunderland Conservatives were happy to fish outside their waters for a new MP, and even happier when they hooked Hudson.

The Sunderland by-election had been caused by the death of Earl Grey, the Whig architect of the great Reform Act of 1832. His eldest son, Sunderland MP Henry Grey, was elevated to the peerage, leaving the town unrepresented in the Lower House. Sunderland had voted Whig, mainly in deference to the Greys, since 1832, but Hudson was determined to change all that.

These were tremendously exciting times in British politics. The rise of the Anti-Corn Law League, which was ultimately to destroy the new-look Conservative Party that Sir Robert Peel had so carefully fashioned, was causing passions to run high. The League had only one objective – the repeal of the Corn Laws which kept the price of corn artificially high – but this objective changed the political landscape of Britain for ever.

The Sunderland Tories knew what they were doing when they selected George Hudson in July 1845. They believed he would rescue the two most important commercial projects in the region, the Durham and Sunderland Railway and the Wearmouth Dock, as well as striking fear into his opponent, the quaintly named Anti-Corn Law campaigner Colonel Perronet Thompson. Thompson, not the most popular of men, told the voters that 'Hudson had no chance of being returned to Parliament for Sunderland', but Richard Cobden, the leader of the Anti-Corn Law League, was not so sure – nor so complacent. In typically perceptive fashion, he wrote:

> Hudson will go into the contest with an intangible bribe for every class. The capitalists would hope for premiums, the smaller fry would look for situations for their sons in the vast railway undertakings over which he rules so absolutely and the iron, rope, coal and timber merchants will all bid for his patronage. His undetectable powers of corruption at this moment are greater than the prime minister's. I would rather face any man than Hudson in a contest for Sunderland.

The Railway King himself, of course, was leaving nothing to chance. He gave two rousing speeches in the town, heartily applauded by his supporters from York, which contained an excellent resumé of his political convictions and a withering appraisal of his opponent. As he told a huge crowd gathered outside the George Inn in the High Street:

> I am charged with being a railway speculator and in favour of the Corn Laws. To both I plead in some measure guilty. It

is all very well to talk about the poor, but I like to act for the poor. My opponents preach about the poor, while I give employment to the poor – without which many of them might starve. Away, then, with the charge of being a railway speculator! I say, if results such as the world believes flow from railways, I have been a benefactor to my country. Is it a charge against me that I have made a fortune?

Meanwhile the repeal of the Corn Laws is demanded by manufacturers to enable them to employ people at less wages. If repeal were to come about, a great portion of the land of this country would be thrown out of cultivation. Yes, gentlemen, these fruitful valleys and fields which are at once the delight and pride of this country – and which is the best cultivated country in the world – would soon become a desert. Those mansions which have been the residences of our aristocracy for centuries will be destroyed; and the return for all this will be the great advancement of some of our great manufacturing districts. But the home consumers are the best customers the manufacturers have and, if those are sacrificed, the manufacturing interests will share in the ruin.

These were powerful words, mainly because they came straight from the heart. George Hudson had not forgotten his farming roots, nor his comparatively impoverished upbringing, and he was scathing of middle-class 'radicals' like Richard Cobden and his henchman John Bright. Cobden and Bright, he suggested with some justification, knew little about being poor.

Hudson also displayed some lighter touches, so beloved of today's politicians. He took his wife Elizabeth, daughter Ann and younger sons John and William on the election trail in Sunderland and flattered the town's 'fairer sex, whose beauty surpassed those of any other town in which he had been'. These days Hudson would have been pilloried for such a display of political incorrectness, but his flattery evidently worked. On 14 August 1845, George Hudson defeated Colonel Perronet Thompson by 627 votes to 497 and was duly elected the new MP for Sunderland. It was the happiest day of his life.

It is doubtful that Hudson would have broken off from the huge celebrations which took place in York the following day to see what *The Yorkshireman* had to say about his victory. Had he done so, he would have read the following ominous words:

> It is quite clear to us that Mr Hudson's return to Parliament is quite the worst thing that could have happened to that gentleman. Out of Parliament he was a great man, and wielding immense influence. In Parliament he will be nobody, and destitute of all influence. He will discover this himself, by and by. It is quite a different thing to address a meeting of railway speculators panting for 10 per cent . . . and the congregated intellect, learning and gentlemanly accomplishments such as the British Parliament contains. Men find their level in the House of Commons and Mr Hudson will find his. Perhaps, too, it may do him some good.

The Yorkshireman was no friend of George Hudson's, and had its own motives for attacking him during his moment of glory, but this warning was strangely prophetic. The seeds of Hudson's downfall may be traced directly from his greatest hour.

CHAPTER EIGHT

London Calling

*There were rumours of Hudson, the Railway King,
and his wife in the 1840s; but they were never
in society, which, however, was amused by the
reports of their doings which reached it*

Lady Dorothy Nevill

By the autumn of 1845 George Hudson was a millionaire, as well as
an MP. Although he had bought two of Yorkshire's loveliest estates,
and had other property liberally dotted around the county, he needed
a *pied à terre* in London for his work at the House of Commons. He
moved characteristically swiftly and, by the time he travelled down
to the capital to take his seat on 22 January 1846, a palace was
awaiting the Railway King. It was called Albert Gate.

Albert Gate, which stands on the north side of Knightsbridge
by Hyde Park, had been built as a speculative development by
Thomas Cubitt in the early 1840s. It was one of two houses, which
were known sarcastically as the two Gibraltars, because it was
thought no one would ever take them. The five-storey Italianate
mansions reeked of wealth and ostentation – and were made for the

Hudsons, who believed that wealth was something to be proud of. Hudson paid £15,000 for Albert Gate and spent another £15,000 on furnishings and decoration, without batting an eyelid.

Albert Gate East, to give the Hudsons' new home its full title, was probably the largest private house in London. It had a very grand staircase from the ground to the third floor, with a dome of wrought iron and glass above, and a number of large marble fireplaces. One critic, scathingly referring to its height and brashness, called Albert Gate 'a tall bully determined even in its vulgarity to lord over its fellows'. Hudson might have been amused by this description, because the words 'bully' and 'vulgarity' were not entirely unknown to him!

It was the perfect place to hold court, and since George Hudson was the first provincial millionaire ever to settle in London, there were plenty of people waiting to be entertained – both out of curiosity, and in the hope of advancement. The aristocracy, which had elevated snobbery to an art form in the mid-nineteenth century, were fascinated by the nouveau riche George and Elizabeth Hudson. Everyone else, meanwhile, was keen to pay homage and worship at the court of King George – in the hope that some of his magic, or money, might rub off. Hudson, however, was shrewd enough never to grant favours unless he got something in return.

It is doubtful that he minded very much about the malicious gossip which circulated about his dear Elizabeth. Whereas other men would have been mortified by the ridicule to which Elizabeth was subjected, and the contempt in which she was held by so-called polite society, Hudson was too busy with the House of Commons and his railways to worry unduly. He had never regarded his wife as either a great beauty or a great intellect, so he did not expect others to, either.

Elizabeth's ill-educated Malapropisms and extravagance aroused both mirth and scorn. She came out with some wonderful *bons mots*, especially when she tried to lace her conversation with a little French. Their trips to France, too, were packed with hilarious incidents. Mrs Hudson, it was said, had refused to stay at the Hôtel de l'Amirauté because its sign 'Ami Roti', literally translated as 'roast friend', was 'so thoroughly disgusting that I could not think of patronising such a hotel'. On another occasion, when she arrived in Paris, she ordered her maid to call upon Messrs Droit et Gauche because 'they must be the most fashionable shoemakers in Paris, for their names are in every pair of French shoes'.

Elizabeth Hudson's social and intellectual clangers mattered not a jot while her husband remained wealthy and influential. He was subject to an orgy of flattery as he settled into life at Albert Gate and the House of Commons, and he loved every minute of it. On the evening of 21 March 1846, he was one of the principal guests of the Marquis of Northampton, the President of the Royal Society, at his Carlton Terrace home. An eyewitness recorded the scene for posterity:

> Amid the constellation of celebrities, there were two men round whom the crowds circled, let them turn which way they would – bright particular social stars each with revolving satellites, and both receiving the deference of the great and noble as their right. One was the Prince Consort, the other was George Hudson. They looked rival monarchs, each with his obsequious courtiers round him, and divided pretty equally the honours of the evening.

Hudson, meanwhile, had entered the House of Commons at a crucial time. Sir Robert Peel, the leader of the Conservatives, had been converted to the principle of free trade and was preparing to repeal the Corn Laws. He would split the Tories, many of whom were strongly Protectionist, right down the middle. Hudson had already declared himself in favour of the Corn Laws during the Sunderland election campaign and he joined Lord George Bentinck and Benjamin Disraeli in the anti-repeal camp. He genuinely believed that British agriculture needed to be protected, even if that kept the price of corn artificially high. Clearly he had not forgotten his farming roots.

Unfortunately, the high price of corn, combined with the failure of the Irish potato crop and an ensuing famine, left four million people starving. In February Hudson made a speech in the House, which suggested that this famine had nothing to do with the Corn Laws and could be solved by a public subscription. It was neither the cleverest, nor the most sensitive, thing to say. *The Yorkshireman*, which could hardly wait for its own prophetic words of the previous year to come true, attacked his speech as 'an aggregate of the veriest rubbish which ever mortal uttered' and referred to Hudson as 'a sort of political Lilliputian in the land of Gulliver's adventures'. It added:

> The mind, which in 20 years had raised its possessor from the homestead of a yeoman to an equality with princes, and from a draper's shop to a rivalry with legislators, does not deem a high education is required to make its influence felt on topics affecting the welfare of England.

These were frantically busy days for the Railway King. As well as being a prominent member of the Tory Protectionists, who were a small but vocal band of dissidents, he was always looking after his ever-growing railway interests. Here is a record of his activities during one day, 8 May 1846. He left the House of Commons at two o'clock in the morning and went home to bed. He rose between seven and eight, took a walk in Hyde Park, returned to breakfast, then attended four consultations, gave evidence before the Commission on the Metropolitan Termini, attended another committee and was in the House of Commons by four. He then dined with the Duke of Buckingham in the evening, before attending the Sheriff's ball in the city, which he did not leave until two in the morning.

He must have had the constitution of an ox to maintain this punishing schedule. However, he did allow himself one form of relaxation, as he was fond of recalling in his old age:

> I do now, what I did when I lived at Albert Gate: I always go down to Billingsgate and buy my own fish. I never allowed a servant to do that for me when I could do it for myself. So when I was a great man in London, no matter where I'd been the night before or what grand people had been to my house – and nearly everybody was glad to visit me in those days – I used to get up early and go down in Billingsgate and choose my fish there for the day's use. I did it, because I liked it then.

And then there was the drinking. Alcohol was certainly an integral part of the Railway King's lifestyle, and kept him going through those long and dizzy social nights; but it was now beginning to take its toll on his health. He had become exceptionally fat and he suffered badly from gout, a terribly painful disease which tends to afflict heavy drinkers. Hudson had always been partial to a glass or two in York, and his public argument with Recorder Elsey was directly attributable to alcohol – on both sides! But there is every reason to believe that Hudson's love of fine champagne and wines slid into dangerous dependency as he became embroiled in the London social whirl. This, in turn, may explain why his magical touch with the railways – based on a sober and exhaustive assessment of all the issues – would soon desert him.

Certainly Hudson had soon established a reputation for himself in the House of Commons as, shall we say, a man of high spirits. One MP called Brotherton remarked that proceedings in the House would 'beget additional respectability if Mr Hudson would join a temperance society', while he was in the habit of rudely interrupting dull debates. That prompted Joseph Hume to complain of Hudson's 'nightly habit of coming down to the House, flushed'. *The Yorkshire-man* followed these exchanges with interest, and took great delight in reporting a spat between Hudson and Hume, when the latter accused his rival of labouring under 'Bacchanalian influence'. Hudson, befuddled with drink and struggling for a witty riposte, could only complain lamely that Hume 'never even gave dinner to a friend'. He then resorted to a wide range of insults, before being told to shut up.

Elsewhere, his drinking was causing both merriment and concern. Lord Macaulay, who loathed Hudson with a passion, called him 'a bloated, vulgar, insolent, purse-proud, greedy, drunken blackguard'. Thomas Carlyle, who wasn't impressed by the Railway King either, spoke of his habit of 'drinking largely of champagne, with other wines, eating nothing at all, before tumbling into bed worn out with business and madness'. The writer F. H. Grundy, who paid Hudson a visit in York, was subjected to 'six hours of champagne, port, sherry, claret and tobacco'.

Lady Martin, meanwhile, one of the few aristocrats who were sympathetic to Hudson, told a friend she was 'quite sorry to part with the old gentleman, having shared a carriage with him'. The 'old gentleman' was only forty-seven at the time. Clearly Hudson had a problem with alcohol, but it is hugely to his credit that he did not succumb to the temptation of drinking himself into oblivion when his empire began to crumble and he was faced with ruin.

There is no doubt that George Hudson loved his early days in London. The acquisition of Albert Gate, the challenging environment of the House of Commons and a brand-new social circle, all combined to create a rich and varied lifestyle. His family, moreover, were a constant delight. When the Hudsons moved to London, George junior was sixteen, Ann fifteen, John thirteen and William eleven. George and John were already at Harrow, where William would join them, while Ann was being educated privately. When she arrived in London, Ann was sent to a finishing school in Hampstead.

There is a touching story about Ann and the Duke of Wellington, which is worth repeating not only because it sheds new and gentler light on the 'Iron Duke', but also because it underlines how much the Railway King loved his little princess. Soon after the Hudsons had arrived in London, Wellington approached George and asked whether he might help his (the Duke's) sister, who had invested heavily in some rapidly depreciating railway shares and was in danger of losing a fortune. Hudson's solution was simple. He bought some shares in the same railway company, told everyone what he was doing and watched the value of the shares soar. He then advised the Duke's sister to sell – which she promptly did. The Duke was tremendously grateful and asked what he might do in return. Hudson's request was simple: 'Go and visit my daughter at school.' He was concerned that Ann was being teased by her fellow pupils, because of her northern accent and humble origins. A visit from the Duke, who presented Ann with a bouquet in front of the whole school, sorted this ugly situation out at once. If Ann was a friend of the Duke, her schoolmates reasoned, then she could be a friend of theirs, too.

If only Hudson's other problems, beginning to loom ominously on the distant horizon, could be solved as easily as this. In particular, if only the complex issue of the proposed London to York line could be unravelled, then the Railway King might regain his peace of mind. He had tried various means, some fair, some foul, to block the London to York Bill in both the House of Commons and the House of Lords, but he failed. On 28 June the Bill became law, on the same day, incidentally, that the Corn Laws were eventually repealed.

Hudson, though, was not one to grumble or fret over what might have been. It was crucial to prevent a direct line from London to York being built if his great railway empire was to remain intact – and time was extremely tight. So, with desperation beginning to creep in, he searched around for allies, strategies and solutions, and his eyes alighted on the notorious Eastern Counties Railway, whose lines ran from London to Colchester and Cambridge.

The Eastern Counties Railway was notorious because it was so unreliable and dangerous. The satirical magazine *Punch* suggested that every criminal waiting to be executed should have his sentence changed to a journey on the Eastern Counties. That did not worry Hudson too much, for he was pretty sanguine about accidents on his lines, as the troubled history of the Midland suggests. He was more interested in running trains from London to Cambridge, and then onwards to Doncaster and York. The cost of that, he estimated, would be £4 million, while the London to York line would cost more than double that. The figures looked good, and that is why the Railway King added the Eastern Counties to his empire in the spring of 1846. As chairman, he immediately ordered a half-yearly dividend three times larger than the shareholders had ever previously received. He was an immediate hero.

He was a hero, too, in Sunderland, where he committed himself to providing the town with a new dock and a new railway. He was a hero in Bridlington, where the long-awaited branch line was finally opened; he was a hero in Durham, where he was the deputy Lord Lieutenant; and he was a hero in York, where he was given the freedom of the exclusive Merchant Adventurers Company.

The plaudits came pouring in. When the Filey and Bridlington branch of the York and North Midland Railway was opened in the autumn of 1846, Sir Thomas Legard adapted Alexander Pope's epigram about Sir Isaac Newton thus:

> When railways and railway shares were dark as night,
> Men said that Hudson ruled, and all was right.

In Sunderland, where he was regarded as a saviour for promising a new dock (a promise, incidentally, that he would keep), Christopher Bramwell, the chairman of the Durham and Sunderland railway, was ecstatic. He commented: 'One attempt after another has been made to improve the town and yet all of them have fallen to the ground. No sooner did Mr Hudson appear than the cloud which had so long hung over the town was instantly dispelled.'

At the same time, however, more and more dissenting voices were beginning to make themselves heard. *The Times*, furious that Hudson was giving his support, if not his money, to its rival, the *Daily News*, wrote:

> When Majesty is loquacious, it naturally excites attention.
> The words which it vouchsafes to utter may be as puerile as
> the garrulity of children or old women; but the world will
> not let them die so soon out of recollection. The tide of the
> age is setting very strongly against unlimited sovereignty and
> his powers of life and death must be confined to his stokers
> and shareholders.

He was mocked frequently in cartoons and Charles Dickens had taken a passionate dislike to him. In a violent outburst which could have come straight from the mouth of one of his nastier villains, he wrote to his friend, the Count d'Orsay:

I find a burning disgust arising in my mind – a sort of morbid canker of the most frightful description – against Mister Hudson. His position seems to me to be such a monstrous one, and one so illustrative of the breeches pocket size of the English character, that I can't bear it. There are some dogs who can't endure one particular note on the piano. In like manner I feel disposed to throw up my head and howl whenever I hear Mr Hudson mentioned. He is my rock ahead in life. If you can let me know of anything bad about him, pray do. It would be a great comfort. Something intensely mean and odious would be preferred, but anything bad will be thankfully received.

The depth of Dickens's contempt is difficult to understand, but the eventual fall of the Railway King must have afforded him the most sublime pleasure. It is surprising that he didn't celebrate with a novel dancing, metaphorically, on Hudson's grave.

More ominously, his old friend George Stephenson was complaining that Hudson had grown 'much too grand for him'; and questions were being asked, with increasing urgency, about his accounting methods – if 'methods' is not too formal a word for what were little more than hastily drawn-up sums on the backs of bits of paper.

Such questions were asked most vehemently about George Hudson's acquisition of the Leeds and Bradford Railway for the Midland in the summer of 1846. This was a somewhat delicate situation because Hudson happened to be chairman of both the buying and the selling company. In whose interests was he acting, the Leeds and Bradford's or the Midland's? Or, as some angry shareholders suggested, purely in his own? It did not matter that the opposition to this deal had been drummed up by enemies of Hudson, railwaymen whose motives were far from disinterested. The Railway King's financial dealings were now going to be placed under increased scrutiny and his integrity was in doubt.

As long as the railway mania persisted, however, the king would remain on his throne. As long as dividends were seven per cent or more, most shareholders would ignore any doubts lurking at the back of their mind about Hudson's financial probity. And as long as the Great Northern Railway remained just a project and not a cast-iron reality, his empire would remain untouched. Had Hudson been able to gaze into a crystal ball, he might have seen that these three conditions of his future prosperity were built on foundations of sand.

As it was, he could enjoy the present. On 17 July 1846, the Hudsons celebrated their silver wedding anniversary. It had been a happy union, and there are no accounts of infidelity on either side. Young George's sowing of his wild oats at Howsham, for which he had paid a heavy price at the time, had not prompted him to follow a life of sexual adventure or excess. He loved his Elizabeth, for all her faults, because she supported him in all his enterprises. Just as Charles Dickens saw Hudson as the rock ahead of him in life, so Hudson regarded Elizabeth as the rock behind him. She was also a loving mother to their four children, all of whom had grown into fine and upstanding teenagers.

Although the Hudsons had enjoyed the novelty and the glamour of their first year in London, they never forgot their roots in York. George's power base with the York and North Midland was there, while Elizabeth's beloved brother Richard, growing rich on the back of his brother-in-law, was now an influential businessman in the city. Moreover, despite the flattery and the attention they received in London, they both felt more at home and more at ease in York. York, in return, loved them.

So it was not altogether surprising that, in November 1846, George Hudson was asked to become Lord Mayor of York for the third time. On nomination day, Sir Stephenson Clark, the surgeon who had succeeded him as Lord Mayor in 1839, described Hudson as 'the man whose name is lisped by the inhabitants of every clime and country upon the face of the earth'. The city of York clearly agreed and, in marked contrast to the previous occasion, he took office amid unanimous approval.

Well, almost unanimous approval. James Meek and George Leeman, the two men who most hated Hudson, were biding their time. They had both invested in the London to York Railway, possibly to spite Hudson, and were as committed to making the direct London–York link work as Hudson was to destroying it. They bargained on the likelihood of Hudson's third term as Lord Mayor throwing up some controversies they could exploit, but they were keeping quiet until the time was right. That was why *The Yorkshireman* regretfully remarked, as Hudson returned to York in triumph at the end of 1846, 'His enemies murmur gently – very gently – sometimes, and that is all.'

They would eventually be heard – with devastating results. The Railway King might have returned to his home city as a conquering hero, fresh from the House of Commons and meetings with royalty, but Meek and Leeman were unimpressed. Meek might have been a jealous, small-town businessman, but Leeman was in a different league altogether. A shrewd, quick-witted and hard-working lawyer, he was George Hudson's intellectual equal and was determined to destroy the Railway King. Hudson's return to York gave him the opportunity.

CHAPTER NINE

Storm Clouds over Paradise

*A man cannot be too careful
in the choice of his enemies*

Oscar Wilde

It was George Hudson himself who had suggested, albeit surreptitiously, that he was more than happy to become Lord Mayor of York for the third time. He felt that he was able to combine the duties of representing Sunderland in the House of Commons and the city of York in the Guildhall without compromising his effectiveness in either venture. He told friends, and, indeed, anyone who would listen, that he was delighted to be of service to the city he loved. But there lay a more significant reason behind his decision. He was desperately keen to revive his pet project of building a bridge over the River Ouse at Lendal, in the centre of the city.

The significant progress that was being made by the London and York Railway, which threatened the heart of the great Hudson enterprise, was a constant source of worry and distraction to the Railway King. The fact that it would be a direct competitor to his flagship company, the York and North Midland, was even more significant because many of Hudson's other concerns – notably the Midland and the Eastern Counties – were in the doldrums. The days of the ten per cent dividend were receding fast. It was crucial, therefore, that the York and North Midland continued to prosper – and a new bridge at Lendal would help considerably.

Hudson wanted his station to be more attractive than the one proposed by the London and York Company at Trinity Gardens in Micklegate and a brand-new bridge over the historic River Ouse would certainly enhance its beauty. Moreover, it would also be a bold statement about the ambitions and the capabilities of the York and North Midland, consolidating its position as the finest railway company in the land. Hudson's desire to mark his third term as Lord Mayor with both an extravagant and a permanent gesture to the city of York also came into the equation. A bridge, which might even be named after him, would be an impressive epitaph.

Whatever Hudson's motives in promoting the idea of a new bridge at Lendal, his attempts to raise capital for the project were ill-conceived and insensitive, laying himself wide open to criticism. Originally he suggested that the considerable cost of the bridge would be borne jointly by York City Council and the York and North Midland. However, when the details of the Lendal Bridge Bill were announced, there was no mention of the York and North Midland's contribution. George Leeman was incandescent with rage, arguing that Hudson was getting the council to finance the project on behalf of the York and North Midland, and the Railway King had to back down. It was agreed that Robert Stephenson would produce the designs – and Hudson would pay for them.

The *Yorkshire Gazette* could not wait to attack George Leeman, and it did so in style. 'Is it not pitiable?', an editorial sneeringly asked, 'to behold his [Leeman's] eyes always open for abominations? His nose, with an unctuous sound, snuffling for grievances? And the sole object of all this anxiety and painful sensitiveness is the career of the Hon. Member of Sunderland'. Certainly Leeman loathed Hudson with a passion by now, and his hatred would have been inflamed by public onslaughts such as this.

Although Hudson was preoccupied with the London and York, he did not forget how to entertain. On 17 December 1846, as this pivotal year in his life neared its end, he hosted a lavish reception at York's Guildhall for five hundred guests. These included the Archbishop of York, the Duke of Leeds, George Stephenson and Lord George Bentinck, his new best friend. The *Railway Times* called this reception 'a high festival in honour of the railway system'.

The *Standard* went even further:

Mr Hudson gave a dinner on Thursday to some happy hundreds at the Guildhall of York. But was that all? No, Mr Hudson was yesterday giving, and has for months and years of yesterdays been giving dinners to hundreds and thousands not less happy than the guests by whom he was surrounded in the Guildhall. He has found the labourers standing to be hired when no man hired them and he has given them employment and good wages and, we repeat it, good dinners. Two hundred well-paid labourers representing, as heads of families, nearly one million men, women and children, all feasting through the bold enterprise of one man and enjoying abundance from year's end to year's end. Let us hear what man, or class of men, ever before did so much for the population of a country?

That last point is one which George Hudson's many detractors, try as they may, can never counter or obliterate.

Hudson's friendship with Lord George Bentinck, the louche

aristocrat who was instrumental in the fall of Sir Robert Peel over the Corn Laws controversy, was blossoming. Bentinck, a political opportunist, was now a leading figure in the Protectionist rump of the Conservative Party and saw his friend George as a most useful ally. Hudson was exceptionally rich, a committed Protectionist and knew a thing or two about the railways. The combination was alluring.

In February 1847 Bentinck introduced a Bill in Parliament to stimulate employment in Ireland, which was still suffering from the ravages of the potato famine. It advocated a brand-new railway network for Ireland, which would revitalise the country's ailing economy. Alas, the Government would be required to lend two-thirds of the capital necessary to build the new railways – and that was a major stumbling block. George Hudson tried his very best to sway the House of Commons by declaring: 'Ireland has been to this country a constant source of anxiety – Government after Government has declared it to be their great difficulty. We have been cobbling and peddling with Ireland, but we have attempted ineffectually to develop its resources'. He was right, but the Government was understandably reluctant to commit £16 million to a new railway infrastructure for Ireland. Had the money been forthcoming, then the course of George Hudson's life might have been very different because he would have masterminded the whole project. But Bentinck's Bill was heavily defeated.

One of the main causes of the Bill's ignominious failure was the growing perception that the great railway bubble was about to burst. Already the precarious economic climate in Britain, which was in the throes of a serious trade depression, was being blamed on the over-promotion of railway building and irresponsible speculation in railway shares. If Hudson was disappointed by the failure of Bentinck's Bill, he had every reason to be terrified by the reasons behind this failure. If the railway bubble was going to burst, then the main victim would be the Railway King himself.

Nevertheless George Hudson was not a man to be too concerned about 'ifs', especially if the 'if' was unpalatable, and he continued to plan for the future. In the spring of 1847 he sold 44 Monkgate (or, to be more accurate, 42 and 44 Monkgate, for he had bought No. 42 and knocked the two houses into one) and made Newby Park his permanent Yorkshire home. Newby was, and is, the most beautiful retreat and it provided solace and escape when the storm clouds began to gather in. Built in 1721, it was one of the earliest Palladian villas in England, featured a magnificent double staircase and boasted a former Prime Minister, Lord Goderich, among its owners. Newby Park, unlike 44 Monkgate, was a constant reminder to Hudson of what he had achieved. Monkgate had been the base from which the embryonic Railway King had plotted and planned his many triumphs: Newby Park, alas, would have different memories.

Although the fortunes of Hudson's Eastern Counties and Midland railway companies were declining alarmingly, the Railway King had two reasons to be cheerful in the summer of 1847. First, the Newcastle and Berwick railway opened, leading to the formation of the York, Newcastle and Berwick Railway Company, giving him control of the main lines from York to the Scottish borders. Secondly, Queen Victoria and Prince Albert travelled by the much-maligned Eastern Counties Railway from London to Cambridge. Mr and Mrs George Hudson, of course, accompanied them. The royal couple, by all accounts, enjoyed their journey, but this public relations coup could not save the Eastern Counties from sinking deeper and deeper into the financial mire.

The main event of the summer, however, was the general election. The Railway King's political ambitions were growing daily, fuelled no doubt by the leading role he had found himself playing with Bentinck's Protectionists. He was not only aiming to hold on to his own seat in Sunderland, but also to ensure that Protectionists were returned in both Whitby and York. Sunderland was no problem because the Monkwearmouth Docks project had been an unqualified success (the foundation stone was laid during a glittering ceremony that autumn) and because the town enjoyed having a high-profile and influential businessman to represent it in Parliament. During this campaign, which he won in a canter, Hudson was asked how he found time to be an MP. It was a good question, to which he replied: 'I apply the hours which ought properly to be devoted to recreation to the duties of Parliament, because I prefer to indulge the honest ambition to serve my fellow countrymen.' It was a good, though not wholly truthful, answer. Whitby was ultimately no problem either, where Robert Stephenson was returned on the Protectionist ticket.

There was, however, trouble in Hudson's heartland of York. His protégé John Lowther, a Peelite rather than a Protectionist, was not seeking re-election (possibly after some strong Hudsonian influence had been exerted) and he was replaced by George Smyth of Wakefield. Hudson had already confided in his friends that Smyth would be keeping the York parliamentary seat warm for George Hudson Jnr, who was still at Oxford, and it was assumed that Smyth – together with the Whig candidate Henry Redhead Yorke – would be returned unopposed. Hudson's opponents, however, had other ideas and the election degenerated into farce and abuse.

These opponents, led by the ubiquitous Leeman and Frederick Hopwood, whom Hudson had once memorably dubbed as an 'itinerant teetotal lecturer', were determined to challenge Smyth and suggested that Lowther might, after all, be prepared to stand. At this point Hudson completely lost his temper, saying that 'he would spend £10,000 before he would be beaten'. Then the Sheriff of York, George Andrews (who built Hudson's stations for him), declared that Smyth would be returned as a Tory candidate, unless a £200 deposit for Lowther's candidacy could be found at once. Not surprisingly, it couldn't. An indignant eyewitness commented on the 'burst of indignation with which this unjust decision was received, and read in that general execration the fate of that petty dynasty which would fain trample on the rights and independence of the citizens of York'.

Meanwhile George Leeman, hiding behind the anonymous disguise of 'A Lover Of Freedom', wrote in *The Yorkshireman*: 'Within the last few years, a power has arisen, colossal in its proportions, and all but infinite in its ramifications, before which many of your citizens are bent with abject and mercenary servility. I allude to the great Railway Empire, on the absolute throne of which sits George Hudson'. *The Yorkshireman* itself vowed to 'destroy this tyranny' and urged the voters of York to petition Parliament against the 'illegal' return of Smyth.

There were two drawbacks to this course of action. First, John Lowther did not want to return to politics, especially in a hothouse like York. He had no wish to be a pawn in Leeman's and Hopwood's game. Secondly, the Whigs were not particularly keen to rock the boat. If Smyth had been elected illegally, then so too had their candidate Henry Redhead Yorke. They were happy to leave matters well alone; much to the disappointment of the anti-Hudson camp, who had to wait until the council elections in November to try to gain their revenge.

In the event the council elections were a bitter disappointment to Hudson's opponents. *The Yorkshireman* ran editorial after editorial criticising the power, the vulgarity and the corruption of the Railway King and even dragged Mrs Hudson into its columns, claiming that she had delayed the express from Darlington to York by twenty-seven minutes so that she could pick up a pineapple she had ordered. Ah, the prerogatives of royalty! Such vitriol was wasted, however, when George Hudson and his allies could spend heavily to ensure the election of their chosen candidates. It was alleged, for example, that it cost Hudson £1,000 to get his bank manager B. T. Wilkinson elected in Castlegate. And although he was known by his enemies as 'this pompous fragment of supercilious humanity', Richard Nicholson, George's brother-in-law, held the Goodramgate ward in the palm of his hand. The radicals, if that is not too official a label to attach to Hudson's enemies, were routed.

It was at this stage, when the Railway King was the master of just everything he surveyed, that he promised the shareholders of his various railway companies a period of peace and prosperity. The York and North Midland 'had now got all that at present it is expedient to attempt'; the Midland was in 'an improved and safer position'; and, as for the York and Newcastle, 'no railway company has prospects equal to our own'. Significantly, George Hudson did not mention the performance of the Eastern Counties in this particular round-up, but three out of four success stories did not appear to be bad. Except that they were not quite as successful as Hudson seemed to think.

No matter – for the time being the Railway King still believed that he was secure upon his throne, and the two portraits of him, which were painted in 1847 by Francis Grant RA, depict a man at the height of his powers. He was never to be the most handsome of men, with his pug-like face and large stomach usually encased in a white waistcoat, but his piercing, confident eyes brooked no dissent. Today one of these portraits hangs in the Mansion House in York and provides a fascinating insight into a complex and powerful personality. One enemy described Hudson as a 'greasy, butcher-looking fellow', while another called him a 'vulgar brute'. He might not have been an Adonis, but he wasn't that ugly!

It is difficult to pinpoint exactly when the railway bubble finally burst. The combination of the failure of the Irish potato crop, which led directly to the repeal of the Corn Laws, and the shortness of the American cotton crop precipitated a deep depression in Britain. The Bank of England increased interest rates from three to five per cent and money was in short supply. The Chancellor, Sir Charles Wood, blamed this depression on railway speculation, which had siphoned off huge quantities of money out of the economy.

George Hudson, quite naturally, was having none of this. In a speech which he made to the House of Commons in November 1847, after it had reassembled following the General Election, he declared:

> We cannot construct railways and import corn to a large extent, for in each case the bullion will have to be sent out of the country. But instead of putting a stop to railway proceedings, which employ such a large number of men and enable them to live in comfort, I ask whether it would not be much better to stop the great importations of foreign goods which throw so many out of employment and drain all the gold out of the country?

It is worth noting that, in 1847, more than 300,000 people were employed on Britain's railways.

Whether Sir Charles or the Railway King were right is, to some extent, immaterial. The depression was biting anyway. Firm after firm was going bankrupt, credit was less freely available and there was an almost complete suspension of ordinary commercial and financial transactions. Ominously, one of the cities worst hit was

Liverpool, where there was already a strong anti-Hudson lobby because of his dictatorial behaviour at the Midland. The Royal Bank of Liverpool closed its doors and the Midland shareholders who either distrusted or despised Hudson began to sharpen their knives.

This was exactly the time that George Hudson needed his friends but, as fate would have it, two of his closest colleagues in his great railway and parliamentary enterprises passed away in 1848. Both were crucial losses. George Stephenson, arguably the greatest railway engineer that this country has ever known, died in August. Stephenson's support for Hudson had been crucial, especially in the early days, and even though they had fallen out over the Railway King's 'grandness', this was a grievous blow. So, too, was the death of Lord George Bentinck at the untimely age of forty-six. His successor as leader of the Protectionists, Benjamin Disraeli, was less well disposed to the Railway King, partly because of Hudson's anti-semitic tendencies. Never again would the Railway King play a leading role in the House.

The rumblings of discontent among railway shareholders, meanwhile, were growing louder. George Hudson tried to gloss over the consequences of the economic depression when he addressed the half-yearly meetings of his four companies in February 1848, but he could not shield shareholders from the truth for much longer. He told the York and North Midland shareholders, who were receiving their beloved ten per cent for the last time, that their dividends might be smaller in future. This warning was repeated to the shareholders of the Midland and the York, Newcastle and Berwick, but they received seven and nine per cent respectively. The dividend for the hapless Eastern Counties shareholders was substantially less, and even though they had been feeding off scraps for a couple of years now, voices were raised and questions were asked.

Hudson, taking his cue from Dickens's Mr Micawber, promised that something would turn up.

Something, indeed, did turn up, but revolution was the last thing that George Hudson was expecting. The year 1848 saw uprisings across Europe, with France, Austria, Germany, Italy and Poland all experiencing varying degrees of upheaval. It mattered not that Britain remained relatively quiet (the 1832 Reform Act had taken the sting out of the middle classes' grievances), because trade with Europe was badly disrupted. The British economy began to contract even further, and railway travel – for the very first time – began to show a decline. This was a disastrous development that Hudson, with his heavy liabilities, was simply not equipped to deal with.

On top of all this, the Railway King's robust constitution, which had taken a tremendous battering over the years, began to show signs of wear and tear. Richard S. Lambert puts it quaintly:

> Hudson had led for years a life which, by no stretch of the imagination, could be called temperate. Night after night he had entertained at Newby Park or Albert Gate, consuming enormous banquets washed down with copious wines. In between whiles he was travelling long railway journeys or sitting up late in the stuffy atmosphere of the House of Commons. Not even the strongest constitution could forever withstand such ill-treatment; and now ill-used nature began to take her revenge.

During the early summer of 1848, as the revolutionary fires blazed across Europe, George Hudson was concerned about more mundane matters. He was confined to bed with a digestive disorder, which later affected his heart and caused painful angina attacks. He was already suffering from gout, and the combination of these debilitating illnesses dramatically reduced his energy and capacity for work. They could not have come at a worse time.

Apart from a couple of speeches in the House of Commons, where he was badly missing Bentinck, Hudson did comparatively little in 1848. A new branch line of the Midland, between Peterborough and Syston, near Leicester, opened in May, followed by Robert Stephenson's great High Level Bridge over the Tyne; and the York, Newcastle and Berwick company took over the Newcastle and Carlisle Railway in the autumn. This was the final piece of the jigsaw of Hudson's railway empire, which was soon to be shattered into tiny fragments. At the end of 1848 there were just over 5,000 miles of railway lines in operation in Britain, and Hudson controlled nearly 1,500 of those miles. His empire stretched from Berwick-on-Tweed in the north and dominated the whole of the north-east down to York. It spanned Sunderland in the east across to Maryport in the west. It came down to Rugby in the midlands and Bristol in the south-west. And it reached across to Cambridge and Colchester in East Anglia.

Although the depression was hitting railway speculators hard, the trains themselves were making impressive progress. The rival east and west coast routes to Scotland were now both open and an express could reach Glasgow from London in just ten hours, twenty minutes, travelling at an average speed of 46 miles an hour. It was just that fewer people were able to afford to travel on the railways.

The extent to which George Hudson had curtailed his involvement in public affairs, especially those of his beloved city of York, can be gauged by his reaction to the sudden suicide of the Whig MP for York, Henry Yorke, in the summer of 1848. Poor Yorke, who had been suffering from unnerving delusions, swallowed some prussic acid poison in London's Regent's Park and died instantly.

Hudson took absolutely no part in the ensuing by-election in York, a course of non-action which would have been unheard of just twelve months previously.

Two unrelated incidents, meanwhile, must have brought a smile to Hudson's fevered brow and eased his gout-ridden physique. The first was the engagement of his daughter Ann, who had blossomed into a young lady of rare beauty, to George Dundas MP. Ann was just eighteen, Dundas was twenty-eight. It was a match made in the higher echelons of society, if not in heaven, as the groom was a leading member of the famous Dundas family, part of the Zetland dynasty, and was MP for Linlithgowshire.

The second was the revelation that Frederick Hopwood, 'the itinerant teetotal lecturer' and perennial thorn in Hudson's side, had been drummed out of York for fraud. No doubt the Railway King permitted himself an especially regal smile when he heard the news, in view of the insults that Hopwood, and George Leeman, had thrown at him during the tempestuous York election of 1847. Hopwood had been guilty of breathtaking hypocrisy and was never seen in the city of York again.

These incidents, however, were dwarfed by a gathering storm. An increasing number of shareholders within all four of Hudson's railway companies were asking urgent and pressing questions about his arbitrary system of accounting and paying dividends. They were also concerned about certain overtures that Hudson had been making to his old rival Denison of the Great Northern. In exactly whose interests was George Hudson working? His shareholders? Or his own?

It was a pertinent question – and the answers brought the Hudson empire crashing down.

CHAPTER TEN

The Time Bomb Explodes

Mockery is the fume of little hearts

Alfred, Lord Tennyson

During the summer of 1848, a pamphlet with the innocuous-sounding name of *The Bubble of the Age or The Fallacies of Railway Investment, Railway Accounts and Railway Dividends* was published by Arthur Smith. It was dynamite, though its full impact was not felt for more than a year. The central allegation made by Smith, that dividends in George Hudson's companies had been paid out of capital rather than revenue, could not be ignored. Indeed, Hudson was forced to go public with his accounts for the first time. In his usual blustering way he was able to put a fine spin on his activities, which was faithfully reported by the *Yorkshire Gazette*. But these accounts were now in the public domain and that was extremely bad news for someone whose accounting methods owed everything to expediency and nothing to logic and figures.

At the same time Hudson's preoccupation with Edmund Beckett Denison's Great Northern Railway was seriously compromising his relationship with the Midland shareholders. He was showing signs of relaxing his attitude of unbending opposition towards Denison as the line itself came closer and closer to York. By the winter of 1847 it had reached as far north as Askern, beyond Doncaster, and was within forty miles of the Railway King's own city. It had become obvious that Denison's more direct route from London to York was going to be much more popular than Hudson's, which meandered around the midlands. He needed to be part of Denison's plans, whatever his Midland shareholders thought.

In fact, some of the Midland shareholders were very unhappy indeed. One, the Liverpool shipowner J. H. Brankner, had always disliked Hudson – possibly because he had a vested interest in the success of the west coast route, rather than the east coast route, to Scotland. Brankner wasted no opportunity to attack Hudson and, in February 1849, blamed the Midland's woes on his policy of leasing small lines. In reply, the embattled Railway King let slip that the Midland's half-yearly dividend would have been five per cent rather than six per cent, had he not taken into account the better prospects that were expected during the next year. That was a both a foolish and dangerous admission, which revealed that the shareholders were being paid a dividend that had not been earned.

The Railway King, once such an assured and confident operator, was now walking on a tightrope. Faced with an economic depression, dwindling rail traffic and angry shareholders on the one hand, and a predatory competitor in Denison on the other, he hardly knew where to turn. Eventually he turned to Denison and reached an agreement, whereby Great Northern trains would run into York (and beyond) via the Knottingley Curve, near Wakefield. Therefore, on condition that the Great Northern abandoned its intention to build an independent line from Askern to York, the York and North Midland would allow its rival to use the track between Knottingley and York, including York Station itself. The terms were £1,000 a year and sixty per cent of all gross earnings on the Knottingley–York track. This suited both men, and prevented them wasting thousands upon thousands of pounds building new, competing lines. But it did not suit the Midland, whose London to York route was now twenty-nine miles longer than the Great Northern's. They believed, with some justification, that they had been sold out.

Their fury was exacerbated by the plummeting value of their shares (though in this they were not alone). Only yesterday, it seemed, the round of half-yearly meetings with the shareholders of his four railway companies had been a pleasurable exercise for George Hudson. Now it was becoming a distinctly uncomfortable experience. Had he taken time out to do his sums in detail in the spring of 1849, he would have had a nasty shock. He had been borrowing money, at a high rate of interest, to keep his weaker companies afloat. When he had to repay £400,000 of that money to the banks, it left all his companies in a parlous position – with falling revenues and precious little scope for the payment of future dividends.

Alarm bells were also ringing in York. The city council were ready to push ahead with the Lendal Bridge project, but the money which Hudson had said would be forthcoming from the York and North Midland, under pressure from Leeman, was simply not there. Indeed a distress warrant had been taken out against the York and North Midland by the city council for its failure to meet a modest rates demand in Huntington, a suburb of York. At the same time Hudson's favoured candidates fared badly in the city council elections, which would have been unheard of two years previously. Indeed William Hargrove, the Hudsonian owner of the *Yorkshire Gazette*, was unseated.

It is crucial to remember, though, as we embark on the harrowing journey of George Hudson's catastrophic fall from grace, that many of those men who were so ready to destroy him were the self-same men who had praised him so fulsomely a couple of years earlier. As the diarist Monkton Milnes noted:

> Hudson has done exactly what the shareholders all the time wanted him to do, and which plan, if it had succeeded in making the branch lines remunerative, would have been regarded as a measure of courageous prudence, but which, having failed, is now called swindling. The truth is that it was neither one nor the other, but merely gambling; and the shareholders, having lost, are now kicking over the table and knocking down the croupier.

That, though, did not cushion the Railway King's fall. It was both spectacular and heart-breaking, and the zeal with which Hudson's enemies destroyed him and his family is deeply disturbing. In the face of such unbridled antagonism, he could so easily have become depressed and suicidal (like his brother-in-law Richard Nicholson) but he maintained an amazing serenity and humility, enabling him to cope with the vicious attacks to which he was subjected.

Let Richard S. Lambert, in his idiosyncratic prose, introduce the beginning of the end:

> And now the end was coming. No more capital could be raised; no new attractive schemes of extension could be dangled before the half-yearly meetings. The long-awaited turn of the tide of national trade had failed to materialise. Creditors were clamorous, and open rebellion was breaking out among the duped shareholders. Worst of all was the fatal division of interest between the constituent elements of Hudson's kingdom, brought about by the intrusion of the Great Northern. Hudson had come to realise the untenability

of his position as chairman of four railways with such divergent interests as those of the Midlands and Eastern Counties on the one hand – irreconcilable in their rivalry with the Great Northern – and the York and North Midland and York, Newcastle and Berwick on the other hand already moving towards an alliance with the Great Northern.

It was inevitable that Hudson would have to make a choice between the two groups – and he had already decided on the likely outcome. He would jettison the unproductive and troublesome Eastern Counties and find a plausible excuse to withdraw from the Midland. That would leave him with a streamlined operation and a coherent strategy, based on the London to Scotland east coast route, which just might provide an escape path from his ever-increasing problems. Inevitably this massive change of direction would require detailed planning, great sensitivity and exceptional hard work. There is every reason to believe that he might have pulled it off ten years previously, but the ailing Railway King was now in low spirits and he wondered whether he had any energy left for the fight ahead.

Indeed, as he struggled through the York and North Midland's half-yearly meeting in February 1849, he was overcome by world-weariness, saying: 'So sick and tired am I of this thing, and so difficult have I found the negotiations with parties about land and everything else, that I would not care if I never had another landowner to deal with, nor another railway to construct.'

The four meetings with shareholders that February brought home to Hudson both the strength of the opposition he faced and the depth of the mess he was in. Once he had presided over these meetings like a kindly doctor on his rounds. Now the doctor was sick, his medicine was unpalatable and his patients were rising from their beds in anger.

The first half-yearly meeting was with the Midland shareholders in Derby on 15 February and it promised to be the most difficult of the four. There had always been a strong and articulate anti-Hudson faction within the Midland, led by Brankner and his Liverpudlian friends, and this time they had the Railway King well and truly in their sights. Before the meeting Brankner circulated a letter to all shareholders, criticising Hudson's performance and methods, and when Hudson declared that the dividend for the half year would be just five per cent, Brankner's ally A. H. Wylie called for a committee of investigation to be set up to look into the company's affairs. He attacked the Midland company statement as 'most unsatisfactory – a more bald account I have never seen issued by any public body', and contrasted it unfavourably with the London and North Western's, which was open and complete. Under pressure, Hudson threatened to resign, which battered the shareholders into submission.

Bloodied but unbowed, George Hudson moved on to York, where he was to chair the meetings of the York and North Midland and the York, Newcastle and Berwick, at the De Grey Rooms in Exhibition Square on 20 February. The former meeting passed off without incident, despite the fact that the dividend was a comparatively paltry six per cent. Nor was the Railway King expecting much trouble from the York, Newcastle and Berwick shareholders, whom he felt had many reasons to be grateful to him. However, his confidence was badly, and dangerously, misplaced.

Unbeknown to George Hudson, two shareholders called Horatio Love and Robert Prance had been taking a particular and detailed interest in the financial affairs of the York, Newcastle and Berwick company. These were no ordinary shareholders, however; they were members of the Stock Exchange. Their interest in Hudson's financial activities had been awakened by an anonymous letter which had appeared in the *Railway Times* two months earlier. It concerned the purchase of shares in the Great North of England railway company and suggested that these shares had been bought at prices well above their market value. As a result, Love and Prance made a methodical and minute examination of all purchases of Great North of England shares that figured in the York, Newcastle and Berwick accounts. They soon discovered that some of the shares worth £15 had been sold at £23 10s. Prance, feigning innocence and mock puzzlement, revealed his findings to the meeting, saying: 'The total number of shares bought by the York, Newcastle and Berwick was 3,790. I am sure that no more than the odd hundreds were bought by the public, so that someone has received great benefit by selling them at this extravagant price to the company.'

That someone was George Hudson, and all eyes in the packed De Grey Rooms turned towards the chairman. For once he was caught completely off guard and could only stammer that he did not have the full facts and figures in front of him. That was clearly not good enough for the meeting, and Hudson was forced to explain himself further. He admitted that there might have been an 'overcharge' for the shares, and blamed Nathaniel Plews, a fellow Great North of England director, who had been responsible for valuing these 'rogue' shares. He concluded: 'If I have disposed of them to the company at a larger price than I ought to have done, I shall be disposed to do whatever the shareholders think will be most just and fair.'

Hudson was hoping to escape with either a vote of censure or with having to pay back the profit he had made on the shares with interest – and he would have done twelve months previously. But the mood of the meeting was turning ugly, and Robert Prance had more than a vote of censure in mind. He insisted on a committee of inquiry and he carried the day. The time bomb, which had been ticking more and more loudly during the past three months, had finally exploded. *The Yorkshireman* could hardly contain its glee, writing:

> The accusation against Hudson is the absorbing topic of conversation in the city. His former familiars shrug their shoulders, and confess to be quite confounded with amazement . . . the present situation is comparatively a bagatelle; but it will lead, or we are much mistaken, to disclosures more disastrous and more startling to the shareholders and the public.

The newspaper, of course, was not very much mistaken. Robert Prance's telling intervention at the De Grey Rooms was the first serious breach of George Hudson's defences. Prance himself became the chairman of the committee of inquiry, so if Hudson was hoping for leniency from the committee, those hopes were brutally dashed.

There was little respite for the embattled Railway King as his roller-coaster ride to hell gathered pace. The half-yearly meeting of the Eastern Counties Company, the meeting he was dreading the most, was looming on 28 February and he simply could not face it. He decided to take shelter (or should one say cover?) in the comforting surroundings of Newby Park and wrote a doleful letter to David Waddington, the vice-chairman of the Eastern Counties, excusing himself from the meeting.

He told Mr Waddington:

> I hope, if any attack is made on me, you will, if you can, defend me with reference to your company. I unfortunately hold a very large share, bought at a very great price, and lose terribly by the concern: they invited us – they were in a

ruined condition, both as to stock and credit. I shall resign whenever it may suit you and the board.

The grammar might have been wayward, and the sentiments poorly expressed, but Waddington was now convinced that Hudson had no intention of turning up to the half-yearly meeting. An urgent telegram sent to Newby Park, imploring the Railway King to attend, went unanswered – and Waddington and his fellow directors were left to face the music themselves. They were not amused.

A report of the meeting, which was attended by almost all of the company's shareholders, went thus:

At the appointed hour the directors entered the room, but Mr Hudson MP, the chairman of the company, not being amongst them, they were received with prolonged and indescribable expressions of dissatisfaction, groans and hisses, mingled with cries of 'Hudson! Hudson!', 'Why is not Hudson here?' and similar indications of the overflowing discontent of the shareholders. What a contrast to the meeting of September 1845, when the same mass had cheered Hudson, as if he had been a god descending amongst them!

The meeting was a disaster. David Waddington not only had to announce a paltry dividend, but also explain why George Hudson had stayed at home. Inevitably he attempted to divert all the attacks on himself and his fellow directors into the path of his absent chairman, who was unable to defend himself. The shareholders were beside themselves with rage – and another committee of inquiry was set up to investigate the Eastern Counties' accounts and exactly what had been going on behind the scenes at this troubled company. It would be chaired by the Quaker William Cash.

These committees of inquiry were clearly contagious. The shareholders of the Midland, many of whom were much less well-disposed to Hudson than their counterparts at the York and North Midland and the York, Newcastle and Berwick, began to press for an investigation of their own. Led by the persistent Mr Wylie, they demanded an inquiry into the running of their company. They especially wanted more details of the chairman's negotiations with their rival, the Great Northern, which appeared to be directly opposed to their interests. Within a month an inquiry had been set up, and Hudson had resigned.

Things were going from bad to worse for the embattled Railway King, whose crown was now perched extremely precariously upon his head. The three inquiries were bad enough, but now society – which had once welcomed him with open arms – was beginning to turn away. Towards the end of February, Hudson made one of his now increasingly rare visits to London for a meeting of Protectionist MPs at the house of their new leader, Lord Stanley. When he arrived, Stanley's secretary turned him away, saying that the charges levelled against him over the York, Newcastle and Berwick Railway, were so serious that he could not come in. This was acutely embarrassing and a chastened Hudson returned to Newby Park on the first possible train, too hurt and ashamed to visit any of his London friends.

Meanwhile there was now no way that the high-profile, high-society marriage of Ann Hudson into the Zetland dynasty could take place. The shame and opprobrium which was being heaped on Hudson reflected terribly badly on his beloved daughter and her engagement to the eligible George Dundas was quietly broken off. This, more than any number of committees of inquiry, brought home to Hudson the nature and the extent of his fall from grace. The family unit, once so strong, was now in danger of disintegrating.

These were dark days, so dark, in fact, that even *The*

Yorkshireman found a little sympathy in its anti-Hudsonian heart. 'We must confess', ran an editorial, 'that the repeated betrayals of Mr Hudson by his former truculent friends excites a sympathy in our minds for the humiliating position in which he is now placed.' This 'sympathy', however, did not prevent the paper twisting the knife viciously in the days and months to come.

Indeed, once the Prance Report was published in April 1849, *The Yorkshireman* could not contain itself. In a nasty, self-congratulatory piece, the paper wrote:

> Hudson's whole life has been one vast aggregate of avaricious and flagitious jobbing for the accumulation of wealth . . . We are, and have been, right for years. Single-handed, and contrary to the tone and disposition of the whole press of the kingdom, we have endeavoured to drag Mr Hudson to the bar of public inquiry and opinion, and there to leave him to the mercies of the duped shareholders.

The Prance Report was damning. It confirmed that Hudson had fixed the price of the Great North of England shares, which he then sold to the York, Newcastle and Berwick, at more than their market value. It also confirmed that he had broken company law by being financially involved with two companies who had been in economic negotiations with each other. Hudson admitted that he had done wrong, but his polite, measured replies to the Prance Report were in stark contrast to *The Yorkshireman*'s unsavoury gloating.

On the day after the Prance Report was published, George Hudson defended himself in these terms:

> It is not my wish to impugn the reasoning or question the conclusions of the committee, but I must be allowed to state

that this opinion of the position which I occupied in connection with the company, is now presented to my mind for the first time . . . I have never thought myself restrained from entering into personal engagements, either with the company or with others, by reason of the position I stood in towards the company, any more than if I had been an ordinary proprietor. I have never hesitated to take upon myself any amount of personal responsibility that the interests of the company might require.

It will be in your recollection that in a period of great difficulty I took upon myself the responsibility of giving personally the guarantee then necessary for raising the funds requisite to extend the railway communication northward to Newcastle. The risk was mine and I was entitled to the advantages which ultimately arose to myself and the other guaranteeing parties. When the interests of the company required, in my opinion, that those advantages should be relinquished, I did not hesitate to become a party to an arrangement with the company for surrendering them; and by that surrender I sacrificed a considerable annual income.

In other words, Hudson assumed personal responsibility for his companies, had worked extremely hard and had taken decisions purely in their interests. He genuinely believed that he had done nothing wrong. Nobody complained when the dividends were ten per cent; it was only when the railway bubble burst and shares plummeted that a scapegoat was needed, and the Railway King – with his ostentatious lifestyle and grandiose manner – fitted the bill perfectly. He might have been guilty of sharp practice, and the cutting of a number of financial corners, but his ultimate aim was the success and profitability of his companies and, as a consequence, his shareholders. Did he really deserve the following vituperative broadside from *The Yorkshireman*?

> Mr Hudson shall not escape us. The thousands he has duped, and the breaking hearts from whence spring against him curses both loud and deep, shall have ample satisfaction for the injuries they have suffered and the torments they have endured.

The intemperate nature of this attack says more about the newspaper's petty vindictiveness than Hudson's misdemeanours, while the flowery language, conjuring up a Hudsonian hell where George is playing the devil, is both inappropriate and insensitive. The paper's satisfaction at the dethronement of the Railway King is understandable, since its radical agenda was totally at odds with Hudson's traditional Conservatism, but its tone was becoming increasingly petty and vengeful. In the face of such persistent attacks, Hudson remained outwardly calm and philosophical. Inside, however, he was hurting badly as his personal nightmare deepened.

George Hudson was trying, as best he could, to tackle his problems one by one. But, just like his companies, they were all inextricably linked, and no sooner had he dealt with one tricky situation, than another raised its ugly head. So, having paid £30,000 to the York, Newcastle and Berwick at the end of March to cover his controversial share dealings, he found himself giving evidence in front of his Eastern Counties shareholders at the beginning of April. They were in an unforgiving mood, especially since Hudson's answers to the Cash committee of inquiry were vague and evasive. The Eastern Counties company had always been a thorn in the Railway King's side. Now it was more like a dagger in his heart.

Once again, Hudson tried to defend himself and, once again,

his words fell on deaf ears. Writing to members of the committee of inquiry from Newby Park, having failed to satisfy them orally, he maintained:

> I am aware that some of the current expenses of the railway were carried to capital, or rather to a suspense account. I did not expect that sum was large. If the committee will call to their recollection to the peculiar position of the railway when I joined it – that accidents were of daily occurrence, and that it was necessary to go to a very large expenditure to meet this extraordinary state of things – I think it was unfair to charge on the revenue the whole of such a state of things. I therefore feel we were justified in putting a certain amount to capital, or leaving it to be discharged on future years of success.

The *Railway Chronicle* put the situation more succinctly, defending Hudson thus:

> What shareholders said in 1845 was intelligibly and manifestly this: 'Hudson, do as you please, don't stick upon trifles! Benefit yourself, like a wise man, and we are content if you will; but let us share some of the benefit along with you. As to details and trifles, we will not stick upon them. We shall gain infinitely more by your attention to your own interests.' Such were the men who now ask the same Mr Hudson to account for his travelling expenses.

It was all to no avail. The Cash Committee's report was even more damning than the Prance Report. It revealed how Hudson had taken over the Eastern Counties and paid dividends to shareholders out of their own capital. It mattered little that the Eastern Counties was bankrupt when Hudson took control and it mattered even less that the shareholders, the very men who were now attacking their chairman, had approved everything he did. The Eastern Counties shareholders were pursuing Hudson like the Greek furies and were even suggesting that he, and his vice-chairman Waddington, had bribed MPs to support railway Bills. His belated resignation failed to pacify them.

On 19 April the Railway King was dethroned again, this time by the Midland. In a lengthy letter to shareholders, he did his best to defend himself, explaining:

Forming parts of one great line of communication, the Midland, the York and North Midland, and the York, Newcastle and Berwick railway companies have hitherto had one common interest to promote, and in watching over the development of them it has always been to me a pleasing reflection that I was contributing to the prosperity of each of the other companies. It was this which enabled me to discharge the duties of chairman, confided to me by the shareholders of three different lines; and it is because I am apprehensive that circumstances have now arisen which must render it impracticable for any one person to preside over all these companies that I felt it requisite to make the present communication.

It must be obvious to everyone that the Great Northern Railway, when opened, must of necessity materially affect the existing lines of railway in the district through which it passes. To the formation of that railway I gave my most uncompromising opposition. I believed its formation to be unnecessary, and felt that the benefits to be derived from it were not sufficient to justify the immense capital requisite for its construction. It pleased the Legislature to view the question otherwise, and the consequence is that this line will very shortly be brought into operation. The existence of that company cannot now be disregarded, and it may be that the interests of these three different railways may not be found to be identical. Therefore . . . I have thought it right to resign.

This detailed and honest resumé of the Midland's difficult relationship with the Great Northern was greeted with boos and hisses from the shareholders, who immediately launched a further investigation into the management of the company during Hudson's chairmanship. Clearly, hell hath no fury like shareholders whose dividends are falling.

George Hudson's friends (and there were still a few around) did their best to cheer him up in these dark, depressing days. He remained immensely popular in Sunderland and eight hundred of his constituents, including the Mayor and eight magistrates, travelled down from Wearside to Newby Park on 1 May to lend support to their embattled MP and to stress their confidence in his integrity. Hudson, grateful for their kind words, thanked them, saying: 'A sense of conscientious rectitude sustains me, and when the excitement has passed away, I fear not the calm judgment and the indulgent consideration of an intelligent and right-judging British community.'

He was being over-optimistic. It was inevitable, meanwhile, that the disintegration of the Railway King's great empire would have a human – as well as a financial – cost. While Hudson himself displayed remarkable courage in the face of considerable adversity, some of his colleagues and employees were not so strong. One, in particular, found the public dissection of his affairs and the vilification of his name too much to bear.

CHAPTER ELEVEN

The Fall of the Man 'Who was Everything'

George Hudson was the William the Conqueror of railways, and his system of government and equity was rather intuitive than legal

The Times

On the face of it, Richard Nicholson had every reason to be thankful for the day that young George Hudson walked into Nicholson and Bell's drapers' shop in College Street, York, and changed his life. Despite his rustic upbringing and demeanour, Hudson had proved to be a good husband to Nicholson's sister Elizabeth – and an even better businessman. As Hudson's fortunes soared, so did Nicholson's. By 1849, Richard Nicholson was a very wealthy man, able to indulge in his favourite hobbies of collecting fine art and drinking fine wines. He was an amiable, if rather pompous, man, who was perfectly happy to bask in the reflected glory, and wealth, of his famous brother-in-law.

The fall-out from the Prance Report, however, began to worry Nicholson deeply. On 4 May 1849, George Hudson resigned as chairman of the York, Newcastle and Berwick railway company, leaving the field open to his York enemies. James Meek and George Leeman duly stepped forward as members of a fresh committee of inquiry and Hudson's fellow directors braced themselves for a most unwelcome witch-hunt. Already rumours were flying around York – and beyond – that Hudson's two right-hand men, James Richardson and Richard Nicholson, were both heavily implicated in the controversy over the York, Newcastle and Berwick shares. Specifically it was alleged that the Great North of England shares which Hudson had bought to resell to the York, Newcastle and Berwick had been transferred in Nicholson's name as well as Hudson's.

On 7 May, meanwhile, attacks on Hudson began in earnest in the House of Commons. An MP named F. W. Charteris, following up the Cash report into the running of the Eastern Counties, raised the question of the possible bribery of MPs by Hudson and his fellow directors. He demanded an inquiry, and got one, into the way in which members of the Eastern Counties board had used, and possibly abused, their expenses.

That evening a weary and severely depressed Richard Nicholson sat down to dinner at his house in the smart Clifton area of York. He had cut a sorry figure in the city of York since the revelations of the Prance report and he was finding it increasingly difficult to look his friends, let alone his enemies, in the eye. Over dinner he drank half a pint of port, before setting out for a walk along the River Ouse towards the city centre. No one knows where he was bound, but he never got there. Having been spotted by three youths as looking 'dejected', he was never seen alive again. On the following morning, his body was pulled out of the Ouse by two boatmen at Scarborough Bridge, ironically the bridge which carried his brother-in-law's favourite York to Scarborough railway line over the river. The subsequent inquest concluded that he had killed himself.

Elizabeth Hudson had never taken a great deal of interest in her husband's business affairs, but the suicide of her beloved brother made her confront, for the very first time, the consequences of the collapse of the Hudson business empire. The atmosphere at Newby Park, to which Hudson was retreating more and more, was desperate and it cannot have been easy for him to watch his wife grieve over something for which he was at least partly to blame. He himself had loved Richard Nicholson like a brother, and his death was a terrible blow. If there was any fight still left in Hudson by the early summer of 1849, it was knocked right out of him by his brother-in-law's tragic demise.

If George Hudson could have bolted the doors at Newby Park and lifted up the metaphorical drawbridge, he would have done so. But he couldn't. Within days of Richard Nicholson's suicide, he was forced to face his enemies in the House of Commons and answer the charge, first raised by the Cash committee, that he had bribed members of Parliament. On the evening of 17 May, he rose in the House to defend himself.

Richard S. Lambert describes the scene:

For some moments he was so deeply affected by his position that he was unable to start his speech. There he stood, with his large head scantily covered with grey hair, his broad mounting forehead, and his penetrating grey eyes – his expression harsh and rugged as ever, yet softened, not this time by the usual flashes of benevolence, but rather by a pathetic and almost childlike consciousness of inability to explain the secrets of his own conduct. There had always been something of a great over-grown schoolboy about Hudson – a schoolboy who had played the unaccountable mountebank before his fellows. Now the tricks had lost their fun.

Indeed they had. Hudson's imposing presence and his swaggering self-confidence, often enhanced by a drink or three, had always lent a certain style to his oratory in the House of Commons. Stripped of this presence and self-confidence, this oratory was halting, disjointed and weak. He mumbled a few excuses, which the House heard in stony silence, before rallying a little and saying: 'I endeavoured to do my duty. I may have taken too sanguine a view of the undertaking, but I am a sufferer along with the rest in that sanguine view.'

Had Hudson been a born orator, a Disraeli for example, he could have launched a much more effective defence of his actions. Indeed, it is tempting to think that a barnstorming speech might have prompted the House of Commons to take a much closer and more informed look at the nature and consequences of railway mania, rather than throwing him unceremoniously into the dustbin of history. But that kind of speech was way beyond the country boy from Howsham, and it was left to *The Times*, once so critical of the Railway King, to put his case for him. The following editorial, which appeared at the height of the anti-Hudson campaign, is a brilliant piece of analytical journalism and essential reading for anyone who believes that Hudson was ultimately a victim of circumstances rather than a Maxwellian fraud:

Neither the other officials, nor the shareholders (of the Eastern Counties), must hope to escape censure under the cover of a personal onslaught upon Mr Hudson. The system is to blame. It was a system without rule, without order, without even a definite morality. Mr Hudson, having a faculty of amalgamation, and being also successful, found himself in the enjoyment of a great railway despotism, in which he had to do everything out of his own head, and among lesser problems to discover the ethics of railway speculation and management. Now we do not hesitate to say that it is a severe trial to anybody to be placed in a novel situation of great power and varied opportunities . . . Now Mr Hudson's position was not only new to himself, but absolutely a new thing in the world altogether. His subjects exalted him to the position of those early kings who knew no difference between their own purses and the public exchequer, between their private secretaries and the Lord Chancellor. Hudson was the William the Conqueror of Railways, and his system of government and equity was intuitive rather than legal. His colleagues knew this. His shareholders knew this. They would have tolerated it to this day, without the smallest objection, but for the unlucky circumstance that Hudson had outlived their success.

Their shares have sunk to their previous value, and many are ruined in consequence; so they now begin to discover that things were not quite as they should have been. We think the King and his subjects are much of a piece. If they deserve indulgence for their losses, he may also be excused for his difficulties. Mr Hudson found himself everything at once – a large shareholder, a comprehensive projector, a chairman, a trustee for shareholders, an agent for particular transactions – a broker, a contractor, a banker, a confidential friend of landowners, and a good deal more besides. Had he discharged all these functions with perfect fairness, he would have been little less than an angel, and that he certainly was not.

In one sense *The Times* was fighting a lost cause, because George Hudson was already doomed. In another sense, however, *The Times* was raising a number of very important questions. The paper was suggesting, with complete justification, that there was a spider's web of corruption and deceit in the Railway King's empire and beyond and that Hudson was just one of the players in a very dirty and very complex game. He himself was an easy target, and everyone was taking aim, but there were others just as culpable as he. The ramifications of railway finance ran deep and a number of senior political, social and business figures were deeply implicated in the scandal.

A classic example of the double-dealing and barefaced hypocrisy that characterised the so-called golden age of railways soon emerged. As the committee of inquiry delved ever deeper into the affairs of the Eastern Counties Railway Company, its members uncovered a startling fact. The inquiry's focal point was the company's dubious Sise Lane Committee, which had been set up to intrigue against the new London and York Company in 1845. How strange it was, therefore, to discover that a prominent member of this mischief-making committee was none other than William Cash, the pious Quaker whose report had hounded Hudson out of office. And how ironic that Cash seemed to remember even less about the Sise Lane Committee than Hudson did about the Eastern Counties' accounts. No wonder John Roebuck, the MP for Sheffield and a member of the investigating committee, wrote in amazement: 'The scene is a most remarkable one . . . the rascality now brought to life is astounding.'

The Cash episode encapsulated the problem facing Hudson's inquisitors. Should they concentrate solely on his guilt, and make him pay accordingly, or should they spread the net wider and investigate the whole rotten system of railway corruption? The first option was undoubtedly the easier, but the second was the responsible and the moral way forward. Unfortunately, responsibility and

Sir Francis Grant's famous portrait of George Hudson shows the Railway King at the height of his power

Insert: This poster, advertising prints of Sir Francis Grant's portrait of George Hudson, is a telling example of Hudson's popularity during the 1840s

GRANT'S
FULL LENGTH
PORTRAIT OF GEORGE HUDSON, ESQ.,
M.P.

Mr. SUNTER (of York) begs to announce to the Friends of

MR. HUDSON
THAT THE
SPLENDID FULL LENGTH

PORTRAIT,

(NOW ENGRAVING BY G. R. WARD, ESQ.)
FROM THE
PICTURE PAINTED BY FRANCIS GRANT, ESQ., A.R.A.,
EXHIBITED AT THE
ROYAL ACADEMY
LAST YEAR, IS NEARLY READY for PUBLICATION.

∵ Persons wishing to secure early Copies of this very
EXCELLENT PORTRAIT,
are respectfully requested to send their Names without delay to the following address, in order to prevent
disappointment.

YORK: PUBLISHER
ROBERT SUNTER,   IN ORDINARY
No. 23,   TO HER
STONEGATE.   MAJESTY

SIZE OF THE PLATE, 22 INCHES BY 16 INCHES.

Price to Subscribers.
PRINTS £2.2. LETTERED PROOFS, £4.4. INDIA PROOFS, £6.6.

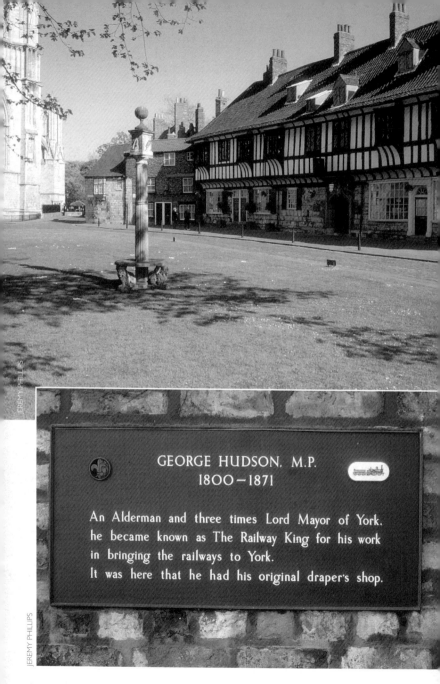

GEORGE HUDSON. M.P.
1800 – 1871

An Alderman and three times Lord Mayor of York.
he became known as The Railway King for his work
in bringing the railways to York.
It was here that he had his original draper's shop.

JEREMY PHILLIPS

Above: College Street, York, was the home
of Nicholson and Bell's drapers shop,
where Hudson started his working life

Below: This plaque in College Street is
one of the few examples of the city of
York honouring its most significant sor

Right: Monkwearmouth station in Sunderland was a grand symbol of Hudson's power and influence. Now it is a museum which honours the Railway King

Below: The picturesque port of Whitby was very close to George Hudson's heart. He so nearly became the town's MP in 1865

Monkwearmouth Station

A Brief History.

THE NEW RAILWAY STATION,
MONKWEARMOUTH,
OPENED ON MONDAY, THE 19TH DAY OF JUNE, 1848.

(PUNCH LTD.)

OFF THE RAIL.

(PUNCH LTD.)

LEPORELLO RECOUNTING THE RAILWAY LOVES OF DON JOHN.

Erina . . BRITANNIA. *Leporello* . . MR. G. HUDSON, M.P. *Don John* . . MR. JOHN BULL.

Top left: Cartoonists had much fun at George Hudson's expen when he fell. Here Leech make mock of the dethroned Railwa King in *Punch* in 1849

Bottom left: Punch likens Georg Hudson's railway empire to th amorous conquests of Don Jua

Below: Some of the Hudson fam happiest years were spent at thi lovely York town house in Monkgate. Ironically it is now h to a firm of chartered accountan

Top right: 'I remember, I remem the house where I was born.' Th sweet cottage in Howsham is still called Hudson's Cottage

Bottom right: Newby Park, nea Thirsk, was Hudson's pride an joy and his retreat during his darkest hours. It is now a girls boarding school

Crowquill, the cartoonist, found Hudson's spectacular fall the perfect subject for his humour. In these six cartoons, he dissects George's turbulent life with relish

He shows the Queen how to manage a train.

He does an extraordinary number of Lines!!

He is crowned!!
The world is at his feet.

The way he keeps his accounts

Public confidence is shaken
"Small profits but quick returns"

"The Fiend departs!!!"

Above: The York to Scarborough line passes through some of the most beautiful countryside in the north of England, including Hudson's birthplace

Left: This statue of George Leeman, Hudson's greatest enemy, dominates the station precinct in York. Many mistakenly think it is of Hudson himself

GEORGE LEEMAN

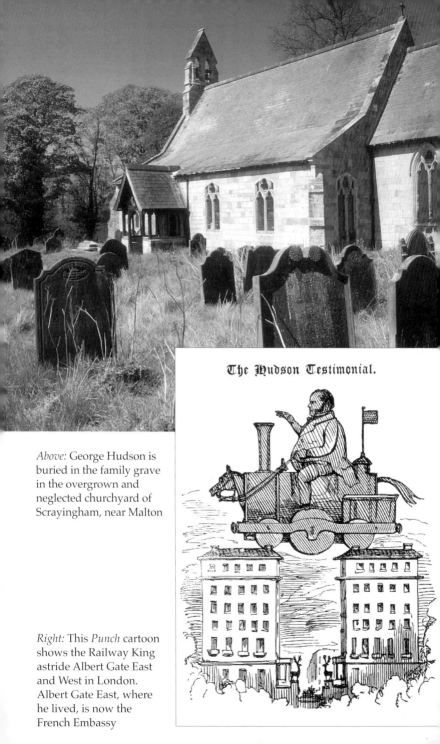

The Hudson Testimonial.

Above: George Hudson is buried in the family grave in the overgrown and neglected churchyard of Scrayingham, near Malton

Right: This *Punch* cartoon shows the Railway King astride Albert Gate East and West in London. Albert Gate East, where he lived, is now the French Embassy

morality were alien concepts to many of Hudson's enemies, who were content purely to bring the Railway King to his knees.

The focus of attention now moved to York, the city most affected by Hudson's fall. Hitherto the York and North Midland, his power base, had been the only railway company not to condemn him. But it was only a matter of time, with a viper's nest of enemies in York, before he was thrown out in disgrace. A hurried letter of resignation on 17 May avoided the ignominy of sacking, but the appointment of two of his keenest adversaries, James Meek and Joseph Rowntree, on to the York and North Midland board, showed the direction in which the wind was blowing. A committee of inquiry was duly set up, after it was alleged that Hudson had built a private station on his magnificent Londesborough estate out of York and North Midland funds.

If the embattled Railway King suffered from nightmares during this desperate period, and it is most likely that he did, one of the most recurring images must have been the terrifying proliferation of committees of inquiry and investigation. They seemed to be springing up all over the place, although in reality there were only three: one on behalf of the Midland, a second on behalf of the York and North Midland and a third on behalf of the York, Newcastle and Berwick. There was also the House of Commons investigation into the running of the Eastern Counties, but the revelation of William Cash's duplicity had slowed this down considerably. Throughout the long summer of 1849 these committees produced monthly reports, each adding considerably to the Hudsons' distress with further lurid revelations of corruption and false accounting.

Whereas the inquiry into the affairs of the Midland concluded that George Hudson was not guilty of any gross impropriety, the committee looking into the running of the York, Newcastle and Berwick company was less forgiving. The affair of the Sunderland

Dock Company, a concern extremely close to Hudson's heart, was especially worrying. In January 1846, Hudson had persuaded the York, Newcastle and Berwick shareholders to agree to invest in 3,000 shares at £25 each in this project. In the following year he bought another 2,000 shares in his own name (and in the name of Richard Nicholson) and charged them to the railway company – without telling the board.

Things got worse. In the summer of 1849 it transpired that large sums of money had been paid into George Hudson's personal account to enable him to pay off the landowners who stood in the way of the new Darlington, Newcastle and Berwick line. For example, the company had authorised payments of £10,000 to the Duke of Northumberland and £5,000 to Earl Grey, but these had remained in Hudson's account at the York Union Bank, accumulating a healthy amount of interest. A weary Hudson responded:

> With reference to all these sums, I would observe there have been periods at which I have been much in advance for the company than I ever had funds for them in my possession. For instance, I was for a long period in advance to them of upwards of £100,000 on account of the Brandling Road Junction, and it is hardly fair to take instances on the one side only, as done by this question ... It has frequently happened, in the course of my dealings with the railway, that I have been obliged, in order to obtain possession, to make myself personally responsible for payment to different landholders, and I had indeed to issue a circular to that effect, to enable the company to proceed at all. It was to a very great extent the practice for me to settle with all the large landowners, and I have no doubt that I saved the

company £5,000 or £6,000 in the Duke of Northumberland's case alone.

Ultimately it did not matter what George Hudson had to say, although he appeared genuinely keen to put the record straight and to defend himself against his detractors. He also believed that the immense amount of work which he had carried out for all his four companies entitled him to a number of perks. For example, when a somewhat shady deal involving the sale of a thousand tons of iron rails came to light, Hudson replied: 'I thought I had done so much for the company. I had a right to be paid.' It is also worth mentioning that, while George Hudson was coping with allegation after allegation of bribery and corruption, he never once betrayed either his friends or his business colleagues and acquaintances. That is the mark of a noble man.

One of the most significant findings of the York and North Midland inquiry was the revelation that the directors had secretly voted themselves an extra 100 shares each. One director, Robert Davies, echoed Hudson when he said this was entirely justified because of the 'serious personal responsibility that directors are called to enter into'. He could have been talking about today's share options, which are really just a legalised form of the same behaviour.

Overall, the York and North Midland inquiry had a very difficult time getting to the real truth, because the financial records of the company between 1845 and 1849 were terribly sketchy. As railway mania began to grip the country, and the York and North Midland's business increased dramatically, its accounts were a shambles. It was not until June 1849 that the board of directors passed a resolution that 'a cashbook be kept by the company from this day'. The inquiry concluded – and here one can envisage its members shaking their heads in despair – that 'Under Hudson's dictatorial rule, his own mind may be said to have been for the last few years the chief depository of very many of the company's affairs ... Mr Hudson lost his better judgement and moral rectitude when left with the entire control of the line.' But that begs the question: what were his fellow directors doing all the while?

Autumn brought no respite for the troubled Railway King. It was estimated that his liabilities, mainly to the York and North Midland and the York, Newcastle and Berwick, totalled nearly £750,000 – a huge amount for the time. There were demands for instant repayment and threats to drag Hudson through the courts. The magnificent Londesborough Park estate was hastily sold to Lord Denison, a cousin of Edmund Denison, who had been such a thorn in Hudson's side with his Great Northern Railway. He had never lived there, but today the overgrown avenue through the park, which once led from the house to the railway station, serves as a reminder of his grand plans for this grand estate.

The city of York, meanwhile, was turning its back on its once-beloved son. The council elections in November were a disaster for Hudson and his ever-dwindling band of supporters and the Tories began to distance themselves from their former leader. In a disgraceful act of cynical betrayal, they proposed that George Hudson's name should be erased from the aldermanic roll and suggested that his portrait should be removed from the Mansion House. The first proposal was accepted, but the second was rejected (mainly because George Leeman, in an uncharacteristic act of generosity of spirit, abstained). Soon afterwards Hudson Street, of which the Railway King had been so proud, was renamed Railway Street. The ungrateful city of York had removed just about every trace of its former benefactor from public view.

George Leeman, in his meticulous way, began to pick up the

pieces of Hudson's shattered empire. He had become the chairman of the York, Newcastle and Berwick and was intent on taking Hudson to court for the money he owed the company. However, once it transpired that Hudson's overdraft at the York Union Bank was nearly £250,000 and that Hudson himself was prepared to make a financial settlement to avoid costly and lengthy court proceedings, a compromise was reached. He agreed to pay £200,000 to end the matter, though he strenuously denied this implied an acceptance of guilt.

Indeed, his attitude throughout this ordeal, which had already led to the death of one man, was remarkably brave and stoical. He did not deal in shame or self-reproach, and did not pine for what might have been. He did not even say, in public at least, that he would have still been one of the richest and most popular men in England had the railway bubble not burst. Inside he may have been bleeding, but he wasn't going to give his enemies the satisfaction of seeing his pain.

Richard S. Lambert comments:

Physically, Hudson must have enjoyed the constitution and the nervous system of a Hercules. He was passing through an ordeal which was enough to drive a man to flee the country or kill himself. Yet his attitude was of genuine bewilderment as at some explosion of public wrath which he had provoked almost by accident. Hudson persisted in reiterating excuses for his actions – excuses which sounded utterly unconvincing, but which in fact came very near the truth. And though those excuses were scouted, he did not lose heart. He comforted himself with the thought that if there were any railway men better than he was, there were also many much worse; while, 'if he were called on to tell who had profited by him, names would appear of which the world little dreams'.

It was exceptionally ironic that, just as George Hudson's fortunes reached their lowest ebb, the magnificent High Level Bridge at Newcastle was officially opened by Queen Victoria in September 1849. This was just the kind of occasion that the Railway King would have loved, bursting with pageantry, back-slapping and excellent, unlimited food and drink. Instead of going to Newcastle to celebrate, however, Hudson stayed at Newby Park, with only his family and his demons for company. It must have been one of the most miserable days in a most miserable year.

As 1849 drew agonisingly to a close and the curtain came down on the first half of a turbulent century, George Hudson must have viewed the future with apprehension. He would be fifty within a couple of months, the prime of life for many men, but he was painfully aware that the best years of his own life were already behind him. No matter that he had achieved more than most people simply dream about. No matter that he had mixed with royalty and lived in splendour. No matter. The Railway King had been dethroned and his crown was lying, tarnished and discarded, in the gutter.

CHAPTER TWELVE

The Solace of Sunderland

When all have forsaken me,
Sunderland has remained firm to me

George Hudson

George Hudson celebrated his fiftieth birthday on 10 March 1850. It is doubtful that fireworks blazed across the sky over Newby Park or champagne corks popped on the rolling lawns. It is more likely that Hudson gazed morosely into space, wondering what horrors next year had in store and whether the two ladies in his life, wife Elizabeth and daughter Ann, would ever recover from the traumas of the past twelve months. Elizabeth was still coming to terms with the suicide of her brother Richard, while Ann's broken engagement to George Dundas carried its own emotional scars. Hudson himself, a loving husband and doting father, would have been only too aware of the role his disgrace and downfall played in both tragedies. He would, however, have derived some strength from the progress of his sons. George, the eldest, was in his last year at Oxford University, where he had been joined by John. William, meanwhile, was still at Harrow. All were remarkably well-adjusted young men.

One of his most pressing worries would have been the future of his beloved Newby Park. The sale of the Londesborough estate for nearly £500,000 had eased his most immediate money problems, but he was fearful that the three committees of inquiry would find him guilty of financial malpractice and demand huge sums of money in compensation. Already he had paid the York, Newcastle and Berwick £100,000 in instalments in return for the settlement of all claims against him. No doubt the other railway companies, of which he was so recently chairman, would have regarded this settlement as a precedent.

There were, of course, other assets apart from Newby. He still owned Octon Grange, near Bridlington, and Albert Gate, together with other smaller properties in Whitby and on the outskirts of York, which had been bequeathed to him by his great-uncle Matthew Bottrill. This was a substantial property portfolio, but there was no guarantee that it would meet all his debts. He was already under pressure to repay as many of these debts as he could from his wife Elizabeth, who although still reeling from the horrifying death of her brother, was desperate to recover the family's previous social standing.

Her husband was not especially interested in social niceties, but he remained determined to defend himself against every charge his enemies were hurling at him. Painfully aware that his settlement with the York, Newcastle and Berwick could be interpreted as an admission of guilt, he had written a long letter to the company's shareholders at the end of January. He said:

I am aware that transactions have occurred which are to be regretted, but in respect to which it is some consolation to me to reflect that the company have in no instance sustained pecuniary loss. Allow me to ask you to review those transactions with some remembrance of the excited period in which they occurred, of the multiplicity of concerns which I had to superintend and direct, of the brief opportunities I had for reflection, and of the impossibility of my giving sufficient attention to the public matters which then claimed my attention.

It was to no avail. As the influential *Herapath's Journal* commented: 'Reasoning with an angry man is throwing words away; and so it is with an angry public . . . Mr Hudson has indeed been most unfortunate in his choice of times. Prudence would have told him to remain quiet, for a child might have seen that the time was not come for him to justify himself if he could.' It was a cruel and harsh lesson to learn, but learn it George Hudson did – eventually. As he grew older, and wiser, he accepted the low esteem in which he was held by most people and became humble and (almost) contrite.

Yet he remained in a fighting mood at the beginning of 1850 – and there was plenty to fight about. Almost inevitably the spotlight had fallen on the York Union Bank, which Hudson had helped to found in 1833 and which had funded some of his more extravagant railway projects. The manager of the bank, Bartholomew T. Wilkinson, was also the treasurer of York City Council and he owed both these positions to Hudson. Unfortunately he was not the best manager in the world and he succumbed to the temptation of speculating in railway shares with the bank's money at the precise moment that the railway bubble burst. He was left with an embarrassing overdraft of £20,000, which he could not repay. Wilkinson was sacked from the bank and the city council in the autumn of 1849. Hudson, beset by his own problems, could only watch impotently from the sidelines.

The Yorkshireman could not contain its glee. 'Hudson', raged an editorial, 'is not only corrupt, but has corrupted everyone around him. It would certainly appear as if there existed a charter for mismanagement, artifice and defalcations in every joint stock company over which Messrs George Hudson and James Richardson have had control.'

James Richardson, in his capacity as Hudson's solicitor, obviously had an excellent overview of his client's business affairs. But that, in itself, did not make him corrupt. He immediately sued Thomas Wodson, the owner of *The Yorkshireman*, for libel. Wodson entered a defence of justification. A date for the hearing was set for July and Hudson had an anxious five months, waiting for a case in which he knew his character would – once again – be assassinated as well as dissected.

In the meantime, however, there was a tiny glimmer of light in this otherwise unremitting picture of gloom. The people of Sunderland continued to admire and love their MP, remaining loyal to a man who had served their town so well. He had, after all, remained consistently supportive of the shipping interest in the House of Commons and masterminded the provision of a brand-new dock on the south bank of the River Wear. This dock was officially opened on 20 June 1850, and George Hudson was the guest of honour as the chairman of the Dock Company and the town's MP. It was as if, for a day at least, the whole nightmare of the past two years had been erased and the Railway King's empire had been restored to its former glory.

An estimated 50,000 people gathered to watch the grand opening ceremony. At the banquet afterwards, Hudson – in a much happier frame of mind than of late – commented: 'Not even in London itself could they have produced a scene more magnificent than had been presented today.' In reply Joseph Wright, Hudson's political agent and the man who had once said that his MP was just the sort of person who 'ought to be rich', praised 'the extraordinary talents, the indomitable energies, the wonderful character and the mighty achievements' of the town's benefactor. How that must have been music to the embattled Hudson's ears.

Wright continued:

That remarkable gentleman has been known not only over this country, but over the world; and when they recollected the great works he had accomplished, and the immense benefits which he had conferred on the community, he thought they would all agree with him, that he was right in putting him among the remarkable characters of the age, and that he was right in ranking him with the best friends of Sunderland, he had almost said with the most eminent benefactors of mankind . . .

The construction of the Newcastle High Level Bridge and the Sunderland Docks had diffused a profuse expenditure of money in this district, and throughout the north of England, furnishing sources of employment to the trading and labouring classes, which, while other nations of the earth had been torn to pieces by devastating revolutions, had made this kingdom the scene of national quietude, general contentment and universal happiness.

How unfortunate that *The Yorkshireman* did not have a Sunderland correspondent, because the report of this grand opening ceremony would have made fascinating reading.

The Yorkshireman, however, had other things on its mind – notably the libel action brought by James Richardson. The case finally began on 17 July 1850, and it immediately became clear that it was George Hudson himself, rather than the radical paper, that was on trial. This was strange since it was the paper which had been charged with 'injuring Richardson's professional reputation and seeking the ruin the peace of mind of George Hudson'. Leaving aside the probability that peace of mind was the last thing Hudson had enjoyed for the past two years, this charge should have ensured that *The Yorkshireman* started the trial on the defensive. That simply did not happen.

Charles Wilkins, representing *The Yorkshireman*, decided that attack was the best form of defence and subjected Hudson to a two-hour grilling in the witness box, calling him, among other things, 'a stain upon the land' and a 'blot on the commercial honour of the nation'.

Wilkins was merciless, savaging Hudson for being the greatest enemy of mankind in his day, as one who had brought about more desolation, had effected more misery and had produced more ruin, than any man of his age.

The key accusations made by Wilkins at the trial were that both Richardson and Hudson were involved in the iron rails scandal, in which rails were bought and sold for huge profits, the withholding of landowners' compensation cheques and the illegal appropriation of shares in the Brandling Junction Railway Company. These mirrored the charges made by the York, Newcastle and Berwick inquiry reports. Once again Hudson defended himself by saying that he had always acted in the best interests of the company and that if he had made some money in the process, then that was his reward for working so hard.

In view of the widespread anti-Hudsonian sentiment in York at the time, the verdict of the libel jury was almost inevitable. They found that there had been no libel, but that there had been 'artifice, mismanagement and defalcation' in the companies over which Hudson and Richardson had control. Significantly they ruled that

Richardson himself was not corrupt, which implied that Hudson was. Nevertheless, his performance in court, where he had roundly rebutted Wilkins's charges, had boosted Hudson's confidence and prompted some admiring notices in the press. He had discovered, albeit temporarily, that life outside of Newby Park was not quite as horrible as he might have expected.

This prompted him to redecorate Albert Gate and to promise to resume his lavish Great Gatsbyesque banquets. There were even rumours that he wanted to become involved in the railways again, having made a killing on the Stock Exchange and repaid all his outstanding debts. They were, alas for Hudson, only rumours. His reputation was still desperately poor, and when he and his wife Elizabeth indicated that they might attend a Christmas Ball at the Assembly Rooms in York, *The Yorkshireman* warned they would be ostracised. They did not go.

Meanwhile Thomas Carlyle, the eminent historian and social commentator, was dipping his pen in vitriol. In 'Hudson's Statue', the seventh essay in his famous *Latter-Day Pamphlets*, he tackled the issue of the £25,000 which had been raised by public subscription to build a statue of the Railway King. Carlyle, a vain, self-important snob, had little time for Hudson, but he had even less time for those who had once worshipped him and had contributed £25,000 towards a testimonial.

In his usual flowery, rhetorical prose, he wrote:

I imagine him [Hudson] swinging from a gibbet as a tragic pendulum, admonitory to earth in the name of heaven – not some insignificant, abject, necessitous outcast, who had violently, in his extreme misery and darkness, stolen a leg of mutton – but veritably the Supreme Scoundrel of the Commonwealth, who in his insatiable greed and bottomless atrocity had long, hoodwinking the poor world, gone himself, and led multiples to go, in the ways of gilded human baseness; seeking temporary profit, where only eternal loss was possible; and who now, stripped of all his gildings and cunningly devised speciosities, swung there an ignominious detected scoundrel; testifying aloud to all on earth: 'Be not scoundrels, not even gilt scoundrels, any one of you; for God, and not the devil, is verily king, and this is where it ends, if even this be the end of it!'

It is doubtful whether Hudson himself worried unduly about this overblown flight of fevered fancy. He was more concerned about maintaining his profile and preserving his seat in the House of Commons, where he was immune from arrest for debt, and with settling his outstanding liabilities with the York and North Midland. He was a good deal more successful in the former than the latter.

The York and North Midland, where the Railway King had ruled like a benevolent despot for so long, offered a settlement figure of £50,000 for all liabilities. Since this was half of what the York, Newcastle and Berwick had demanded, Hudson would have been well advised to accept it. Stupidly, he rejected it. This was a bad error of judgement, presumably caused by over-confidence, and the York and North Midland directors immediately went to law and filed three suits against their former chairman.

Hudson fared better in the House of Commons in the run-up to the General Election of 1852. He spoke at length during the Budget debate on behalf of his Sunderland constituents who were campaigning on behalf of the repeal of duty on imported timber. This, apparently, had caused some distress to the shipbuilders and shipyard workers on Wearside and Hudson was anxious to lobby on Sunderland's behalf. A cynic might have argued that Hudson's

Protectionist views would have precluded him from supporting free (or freer) trade, but he had moved on from those heady Protectionist days of 1846 and was able to be more flexible in his views – especially if it suited his constituents.

He also spoke in the debate on the Corrupt Practices Bill, most probably unaware of the irony. He pledged to do his best to defeat the Bill, saying, 'until the leaders of both sides of the House declare publicly that henceforth they will dispense the patronage of the Government without favour or affection, and irrespective of political opinions, it is all nonsense, and purely absurd, to pursue the poor voter for taking a bribe'. He had a point, although *The Yorkshireman* could not resist attacking its old enemy for 'a consistency of iniquity unparalleled in our recollection'. This Bill never did become law, because it ran out of time as the General Election of July 1852 loomed.

Hudson was pretty confident of being returned as Sunderland's MP and he fought a belligerent campaign on the work he had done for his adoptive town and on the strong bond he shared with the town that had sustained him during the most difficult period of his life. He told an election meeting:

> You have supported me in many trials; you have comforted me when almost every comfort seemed to have forsaken me . . . When all have forsaken me, Sunderland has remained firm to me. I say again, in the presence of my own family, who may succeed me ere long; if that family were ever to be ungrateful to the town of Sunderland, I could almost rise up from my grave and curse them. My right hand shall forget her cunning, before I shall forget the favours I have received at your hands.

Whether Hudson's family were happy with this surreal threat we shall never know (though it is unlikely since both Elizabeth and Ann were still suffering the consequences of his downfall), but the electors of Sunderland were as putty in his hands, especially as a new and lucrative contract for Sunderland Docks, negotiated by Hudson, was announced on the eve of polling day. On 10 July 1852, he was re-elected, topping the poll by fifty-four votes. That was just as well, in the circumstances. Had Hudson failed, he would have lost the immunity afforded by the House of Commons and could well have been thrown into prison for debt.

Unfortunately, George Hudson now cut a somewhat forlorn and, on occasions, ridiculous figure in the House. Often the worse for wear, he tended either to misunderstand what others were saying or would deliver obnoxious witticisms, both of which upset the House. On one occasion in December 1852, when MPs were debating the amount of public money spent on the funeral of the Duke of Wellington, Hudson clashed with the leading Radical, Joseph Hume. Hume was attacking the proposal to spend £80,000 on the Duke's funeral and Hudson, most probably remembering the Duke's kindness to his daughter Ann at her Hampstead finishing school, was most indignant. Egged on by braying Tory back-benchers, some of whom were laughing with Hudson and some at him, he wasted no time in telling Hume exactly what he thought.

Hume, somewhat taken aback, then said he would withdraw his motion criticising the proposed expenditure on the Duke's funeral – provided Hudson would keep 'a check on his own party'. Alas poor George, who had clearly been drinking heavily, completely misunderstood this simple sentence and replied loudly: 'The hon gentleman talks about a check. I'll give a check for as much as he will.' This was too much for all sides of the House, which erupted into uncontrolled laughter for several minutes.

The Yorkshireman was not amused, commenting: 'It would be impossible to exaggerate the amazement, or the shrieks of laughter, with which this sally was received by the House.' Like so many drunks, Hudson did not learn his lesson and his behaviour in the Commons continued to cause hilarity and concern in equal measure. A few days later he made the mistake of emitting some strange and inarticulate noises, possibly indicating disapproval, during a Budget speech by the famed wit Ralph Bernal Osborne. Osborne rounded on Hudson and said, with just the slightest touch of sarcasm: 'I must beg the Member for Sunderland not to interrupt me; at this early period of the evening, he has no excuse for making a noise.' The implication was clear. Hudson was a renowned drunk, famous for his late-night exploits and senseless interruptions, but on this occasion he had begun to drink earlier than usual, making an even bigger fool of himself than normal. It was a savage slur.

Not surprisingly, Hudson was livid. He raised himself slowly to his feet, probably with some difficulty, and replied:

Sir, I have been personally alluded to by the hon and gallant member for Middlesex. I get up to answer the imputation he has cast upon me. I can understand the hon gentleman and the hon gentleman, or any other man, ought to be ashamed of himself to make use of such language. I tell the hon gentleman that there is no man more ready to meet an imputation than myself: and tell him that I am ready to meet him here or elsewhere. I have now done with the hon gentleman. I am sure that we have always had feelings of friendship towards each other and I am rather sorry that he should have cast such an imputation on me.

At this stage, as the House roared with laughter at the sight and sound of the hapless Hudson struggling with the complexities of the English language, Osborne cut in, saying: 'Sit down, pray. I accept your apology. Say no more.' The rest of Hudson's protest was then drowned by widespread hysteria. In the cold and sober light of day, these two incidents must have come back to haunt the poor man and it is not surprising that his subsequent interventions in the House of Commons were few and far between.

There is no doubt that Hudson's excessive drinking and sedentary lifestyle were now beginning to take a toll on his health. He had always been overweight, even as a young apprentice in Bell and Nicholson's drapers' shop, but his huge capacity for hard work, coupled with his nervous energy, kept this weight in check. As middle age tightened its grip, however, as Hudson's fortunes spiralled into decline, he piled the pounds on. In particular his gout, one of the most agonising of illnesses, began to worsen. Ironically, one of the most effective short-term remedies for gout is to drink more, because the alcohol soothes the excruciating pain. In the long term, however, this remedy is disastrous. Hudson discovered this to his cost.

So, as the year 1852 drew to its inglorious end, the once-proud Railway King was in poor physical, emotional and financial health. He had very little to look forward to, apart from the solid progress his children were making, and a great deal to look back on. He may now have finally realised that the fortune left to him by the generous great-uncle had become a poisoned chalice – and that an ordered life in a prosperous York drapers' shop would have been infinitely preferable to the turbulent existence he had experienced since his £30,000 inheritance. If he hadn't realised this by the end of 1852, he certainly did during the next twelve months. They were to be among the toughest and cruellest of his entire life.

CHAPTER THIRTEEN

The Creditors – and Fate – exact Revenge

I have been morally right, but legally wrong

George Hudson

The new year of 1853 began inauspiciously when, in January, the Master of the Rolls John Romilly delivered his judgement in the first of the three Chancery cases brought by the York and North Midland Company against George Hudson. The case involved the alleged appropriation of 12,500 East and West Riding Extension and Hull and Selby shares by Hudson for his own use. This had been facilitated by a shareholders' resolution of January 1846 which put these shares 'at the disposal of the board of directors'. This, argued Hudson's counsel, the acclaimed Fitzroy Kelly, allowed his client to use the shares as he wished. He also contended that as the shares belonged to the shareholders of the York and North Midland, and not to the company itself, the company had no right to sue his client for their return. Finally he suggested that the £500,000 Londesborough estate had been bought with the interests of the York and North Midland in mind, rather than Hudson's.

It sounded good. But Richard Bethell, the solicitor general who was representing the York and North Midland, was scathing in his response. He argued:

> The defence which has been made is as great an outrage on this court as the conduct of the defendant is an outrage on honesty... My learned friends have said nothing to extenuate the charges, but have adopted a course which aggravated the offence... The matter, to use a common phrase, had been brazened out. Mr Hudson said here, in effect, 'It is true that I took your property. I had a right to take it. I performed services for you, and I had a right to take it.'
>
> The delinquency and iniquity of the defendant consisted not merely in taking the shares improperly, but in corrupting the people about him, and appointing his own tools in the company for his own particular purpose. He has lost, in fact, that which is the last thing that anyone should lose – the sense of shame!

The Master of the Rolls clearly agreed. He ordered Hudson to refund, with interest, whatever profit he had made from the East and West Ridings and the Hull and Selby shares. This was a major blow, compounded by the unfortunate revelation during the case that Hudson had charged his erstwhile company ten times more for parts of the Londesborough estate than he had paid for them. This made the York and North Midland directors even more determined to extract every single penny it could from their former chairman and, if necessary, destroy him in the process.

The second case quickly followed upon the first, as Brian Bailey explains:

The York and North Midland sought a refund from Hudson of the proceeds from shares in the North British Railway, which he had kept after selling them on behalf of the company. He had already paid back £60,000 on account of this debt, but there was a further sum outstanding. The York and North Midland also wanted a lien on Hudson's estates, which the company alleged had been purchased with its money. This claim was dismissed, but the Master of the Rolls made judgement in February against Hudson in the matter of the shares. Hudson was ordered to repay with interest all the profit he had made from the sale of the shares.

Hudson appealed against this judgement, but he was still ordered to pay back his profits with interest in July. Within days, the third and final case against the disgraced Railway King came to court. This concerned the murky 'iron rails affair', which was declared completely illegal by the Master of the Rolls. These decisions in favour of the York and North Midland were body blows to Hudson and he now faced bankruptcy, if he ever left the House of Commons. He agreed to pay £20,000 immediately to his old company, while another £34,000 would be handed over at a later date.

Inevitably Hudson realised that further resistance would be useless (and how he must have wished he had settled for the £50,000 that had been suggested four years previously) and during the winter of 1853 he entered into further negotiations with the York and North Midland in an attempt to put a lid on his liabilities. It was, sadly, too late to save his beloved Newby Park. In January 1854 it was announced that the York and North Midland would drop all future legal proceedings against him, in return for £72,670 in settlement of all its claims. He had already paid more than £26,000 back to the company – and now he needed to find another £46,000. Newby Park would have to go.

This was one of the saddest moments of George Hudson's entire life. Newby Park had been his pride and joy in the good times – and his refuge in the bad. It had been the greatest symbol of his success, now its sale was a chilling reminder of his failure. As he walked through those lovely grounds towards the gently flowing River Swale for the last time, his poor heart must have been very close to breaking. Worse was to come, though. Viscount Downe, who bought Newby Park for £190,000, employed Hudson's old enemy George Leeman as solicitor for the sale. Albert Gate, meanwhile, was being leased by the French ambassador and Londesborough Park had long since been sold, so his magnificent property portfolio had disintegrated into nothing, just like his empire.

These were desperate days – and they became even more desperate when Hudson let slip, during the hearing of the third Chancery case, that he had distributed shares 'to certain persons of influence connected with the landed interest and Parliament, for the purposes of securing their good offices in connection with the operations of the railway company'. In other words, he had bribed them. The outcry was huge.

The Times, which had written such a temperate and thoughtful article on George Hudson's downfall, led the way with a savage attack, thundering:

> Will the House of Commons tolerate so base a stigma upon them in their collective and individual capacity, placed on the solemn records of the highest court of justice in the land, and attested by the oath of a member of the House of Commons, professing himself to be the agent and distributor of the corruption and refusing, from a sense of honour, to

reveal the names of those noble lords and honourable gentlemen whose hands were contaminated by his bribes?

Inevitably, Hudson's decision to incriminate his colleagues in the House of Commons, even if he did not name them, led to questions in Parliament. On 8 February 1854, he tried to justify himself to the House, knowing that if he did not, he could well be expelled and, consequently, be declared a bankrupt:

It is utterly impossible, during my long intercourse with this House and with society, for any gentleman to charge me with having said, directly or indirectly, that I have ever tampered with any Member of this House, directly or indirectly. My position has been one of misfortune; I have been morally right, but legally wrong ... I have known what it is to live in popularity, and to enjoy the smiles and the confidence of the world. And I have had a bitter reverse to bear. I hope I bear it with the fortitude with which a man who is conscious of his innocence should bear it ... I am ready to unravel and unfold everything . . . I have seen times, and had the opportunities given me when, if money had been my only object, I might have enriched myself to any amount. I have sat at boards when shares have been distributed, and have been offered to me, and on public grounds I have declined them, and they have been taken by my colleagues ... The House can take me from my cradle and follow me to this day, and if they can fix on me any charge of a dishonourable character, or which would render me unworthy of the confidence of my friends, or of a seat in this House, or any public position, then I shall retire.

This was a wonderful exercise in the art of evasion and self-justification, as well as being one of the better speeches he ever made in the House of Commons. It was also a veiled reminder to any MPs who had partaken of his generosity over shares that he knew exactly where the bodies were buried. This knowledge was to stand Hudson in good stead over the coming years, though, to his great credit, he never tried to bring any of his corrupt colleagues down with him. The House eventually decided to do nothing about 'Hudson's bribes', believing that the outbreak of the Crimean War was more deserving of their attention.

Meanwhile George Hudson's attempts to create some order out of the chaos of his personal finances were even more fruitless than rearranging the deck chairs on the *Titanic*. The sale of his three primary homes had eased the burden a little, but creditors were still knocking at his door on a regular basis and he was desperate to make some money to regain his independence. Unfortunately, he was too desperate.

He had entered into a business relationship with a French count called Seraincourt, who was keen to buy a substantial amount of iron. Hudson agreed to supply him with 20,000 tons of the stuff and a contract was signed. However, hardly had the ink dried on this contract, than the price of iron went up by five shillings a ton. Foolishly, Hudson tried to incorporate the new price into the deal and, when Seraincourt objected, he refused to deliver the iron. Once again he found himself in court and was forced to pay Seraincourt £4,000 in damages in the spring of 1854. This was a blow that he simply could not afford. Indeed he now found it impossible to meet his York and North Midland liabilities and was falling ominously into arrears. By the autumn of 1854, he was in serious trouble and only the fact that he was a sitting MP saved him from bankruptcy.

Nevertheless, there were a couple of reasons for George Hudson's sagging spirits to lift, albeit temporarily. In April 1854 his daughter Ann, now fully recovered from the trauma of her broken engagement to George Dundas, married Count Michael Suminski at the picturesque parish church of Topcliffe, near Thirsk. Ann was now twenty-three, the bridegroom thirty-one. They soon settled abroad, with Ann probably relieved to leave a country in which she had endured such contrasting and unsettling experiences during her short and eventful life.

The town of Sunderland, moreover, was still well disposed to its MP. In the summer of 1854 he presided over a meeting of the Sunderland Dock Company, where a dividend of four per cent was declared for the shareholders. This may not have been a massive dividend, in comparison to those heady railway dividends of ten per cent in the 1840s, but it gave Hudson 'great satisfaction'. He had never, he told the shareholders, addressed such a meeting 'with greater pleasure' and he promised great things in the future. He needed to keep these promises, because Sunderland would not necessarily continue to support an MP whose speeches and appearances in the House of Commons were becoming disturbingly rare.

The town of Whitby, too, retained a place for Hudson in its heart. In September 1854 he was the guest of honour at the twenty-first annual meeting of the Whitby Agricultural Society, of which his brother Charles was a prominent member. Hudson was received with 'loud and repeated bursts of applause', according to one observer, because he had done so much for the town.

These were, however, but rare shafts of sunlight in a predominantly gloomy year. *Punch* summed up Hudson's plights thus:

Full many a noble lord who once serene
The feasts at Albert Gate were glad to share.

For tricks he blushed not at, or blushed unseen,
Now cuts the Iron King with vacant stare.

Indeed, Albert Gate, although it was leased to the French ambassador Count Walewski for more than £1,000 a year, was causing Hudson problems. Albert Gate's builder Thomas Cubitt had agreed to carry out some work, costing £600, to make the house ready for the ambassador, and had not been paid. In April 1854 he wrote to Hudson:

> I think you will feel that I have a strong claim upon you for this money as the work was done when I was much pressed with business requiring attention and which was delayed to my great inconvenience so as to get the work on your house completed to suit the French Embassy so that you might get a tenant for your house and this could not have been done without considerable exertion by my people.

Albert Gate was eventually sold to the French government for £21,000 and this fascinating specimen of mid-nineteenth-century British architecture is still the French Embassy today. Opposite, Albert Gate West is the Kuwaiti Embassy, and both buildings retain the style and grandeur that made them such talking points when they were first built by Cubitt.

By now George Hudson was weary of England, the country that had made him a king and then destroyed him. On 12 August 1855 he set sail from Sunderland to Spain, hoping it would prove to be his Eldorado. It was his plan to build a brand-new trunk line near San Sebastian in the north-east of the country and, if this was successful, to repeat the process across Spain. Unfortunately, the change of climate played havoc both with his long-suffering digestive system and his gout. He was confined to bed for at least three months, which must have been purgatory in a foreign country where few people spoke English, and the brand-new trunk line never materialised.

His long-suffering wife Elizabeth did not accompany her husband to Spain, simply because she could not afford to. Alone and practically friendless, she languished in small lodgings in Burton Street, near Euston Square, in London. She would have been visited by her family from time to time, especially her eldest son George who was now studying law and William who was up at Oxford. Daughter Ann, as we have seen, had settled abroad and son John was serving with the 10th Hussars in the Crimea. Otherwise she had been all but deserted by her society friends, who no longer found her Malapropisms funny now that she lived in poverty.

The failure of George Hudson's Spanish railway project, which even today remains shrouded in mystery, was a huge blow. He was desperately keen to pay off the remainder of his debts (he now owed only £16,000 to the York and North Midland) and was banking on creating a network of lines, and companies, which would free him from the chains of poverty. It was a gamble, though, because he was still the MP for Sunderland and his constituents were not likely to take kindly to their parliamentary representative spending most of his time in Spain. When the gamble failed, he needed his parliamentary seat more than ever – and it had never been in so much jeopardy.

At last, in July 1856, fifty-six-year-old George Hudson felt well enough to leave Spain and travel to Germany, where he took 'the waters' in a vain hope to cure his gout, and then to France, where he met his son John in Marseilles. John was *en route* to India, to join his new regiment, the 6th Dragoon Guards, and was a source of great pride to his father. While in France in the spring of 1857,

Hudson heard the news which, although inevitable, he had been dreading. There was to be a General Election.

Hudson was no fool – and he knew that there had been rumblings of discontent in Sunderland about his lengthy spell in exile. The San Sebastian train project was of no interest to his constituents, and nor was his painful gout. True, when Hudson had been in Paris, he had tried to persuade the French Government to appoint a consul, rather than a vice consul, to Sunderland. But that could hardly be ranked as a major achievement and Sunderland's MP faced a tough task if he was going to hang on to his seat. He approached it with relish.

First, he issued a manifesto from Paris, apologising for the long absence from parliamentary duties which he attributed to illness and to 'unavoidable attention to a large undertaking with which I became connected in Spain'. Then he arrived in Sunderland itself on 19 March, destroying the widespread rumours in the town that he was not standing for re-election and discovering that his reputation, once so formidable, was on the wane.

The *Sunderland Herald* was especially sarcastic about Hudson's behaviour, writing in March: 'Wonders will never cease! Our truant representative desires re-election . . . Remember it was Mr Hudson who left the constituency, not the constituency who left Mr Hudson.'

Retaining the seat, however, was not totally a lost cause. He still had good friends in Sunderland, who were willing to work for him, and his political views were broadly in keeping with those of his constituents. Like the astute politician he was, he championed a scheme to make Sunderland a Harbour of Refuge on the storm-ridden north-east coast. He also promised to spend much more time in the constituency if he was re-elected. That was enough for the influential Shipowners' Society, which had been expressing doubts about Hudson's commitment to the town, to support him.

He told an election meeting: 'It is my decided intention, gentlemen, to make up the leeway and to do double work, to work over hours, and to endeavour to redeem everything that the proud constituency of Sunderland has the right to demand of me.' If he sounded anxious, he was. He was playing for high stakes, because defeat would almost definitely mean jail.

So it came as a tremendous relief, at least to George Hudson, when the election results were announced. He had come second, by some forty votes, and was returned to the House of Commons as one of the town's two representatives. He kept his word and immediately took lodgings in Sunderland (during the election he had given his address as Whitby). He also began to make more appearances in the Commons, and to devote himself to promoting the interests of the Sunderland Dock Company. It appeared that the Railway King was making a comeback, nearly a decade after his ignominious downfall.

It was then that fate intervened, delivering a series of crushing blows that all but broke George Hudson's indomitable spirit. Indeed, as Richard S. Lambert writes:

> Victory in the Sunderland election in 1857 was almost the
> last gleam of sunshine that shone upon Hudson's declining
> public career. For now fortune, as though she felt she had
> done more than enough for her former favourite, turned her
> back on him altogether.

First, news came from India that his beloved son John had been killed in action in December 1857. He was only twenty-five. John's death had a terrible effect on all the Hudson family, but George took it especially badly. He heard the news just before he was to address a meeting of the shareholders of the Sunderland Dock Company and an eyewitness described what an awful state Hudson was in. This state was exacerbated by the return of his gout.

At the same time Elizabeth Hudson was robbed of £200 worth of jewellery and clothes by a servant. She could ill afford such a loss, and her disposition – which was nervous at the best of times – was now teetering on the edge of despair. The death of a child is very hard to bear in the best of circumstances, but for Elizabeth, lonely and poverty-stricken, circumstances could hardly be worse.

The Yorkshireman, which had now softened its anti-Hudson line following the death of its editor John Duncan, was moved to write:

> The melancholy death of George Hudson's son in India appears to have deeply affected him. His appearance at the Sunderland Dock meeting, lame with gout, and hardly able to crawl into the boardroom, painfully affected those who knew him when he was the bluff and white-waistcoated George Hudson, to whom the railway world did honour.

Worse still, the shareholders of the Sunderland Dock Company were becoming restless. Hudson's prediction of better times ahead remained resolutely unfulfilled and dividends were falling sharply. The dock had cost a great deal of money to build and its earning capacity depended on the willingness of the North Eastern Railway Company (the product of an amalgamation of the York, Newcastle and Berwick and the York and North Midland in 1854) to use it for the shipment of coal. Unfortunately some of the great coal-owners of the north-east were jealous of the monopolistic powers of the North Eastern Railway and decided to boycott the docks. This was a disaster, especially as other docks, such as West Hartlepool, Seaham and Middlesbrough, were being built in the region. Even more ominously, the North Eastern Railway Company was building its own super-dock at Jarrow.

In these circumstances, it was hardly surprising that the half-yearly dividend of February 1858 was a meagre three and a half per cent. Hudson himself had a large investment in the docks, but it was heavily mortgaged and he found himself trapped. While shareholders, echoing their dissatisfied railway counterparts a decade previously, began to grumble that their chairman was pursuing his own interests and nobody else's, a desperate Hudson tried to find an escape route. There were precious few options.

In a last throw of the dice, however, Hudson devised a deeply flawed plan to induce the River Wear Commissioners to subsidise the Sunderland Dock Company to the tune of £2,000 a year, on condition that dock charges were reduced and a minimum depth of water was maintained. It was pointed out very forcibly, when the subsequent Sunderland Dock Bill came before the House of Commons, that it would be wrong to approve a scheme which meant using public funds to pay a private company to do what it should have been doing anyway. The Bill was defeated – and Hudson was desolate.

In August 1858 shareholders were told by their chairman, in a 'dolorous and lachrymose' speech, that their dividend had fallen again, this time to one and a half per cent. The meeting became heated and turbulent and ended with the shareholders walking out and Hudson's own salary being reduced. The shadows were closing in and our embattled hero, unable to face the unpalatable fact that his only remaining business concern was facing ruin, fled to France. That was hardly designed to endear him either to the shareholders of the Sunderland Dock Company or to the electors of Sunderland. Predictably, both camps were growing increasingly restless at the erratic and unproductive behaviour of their chairman and MP.

Occasional manifestos and bulletins, despatched from Hudson's Paris HQ, did nothing to pacify them.

Acutely conscious that another General Election was imminent, as Lord Derby's weak Conservative government struggled to make an impact in the Commons or the country, Hudson returned to England in February 1859. He immediately made a determined effort to raise his profile in the House and, on 3 March, spoke animatedly about the effect of timber duties on the shipping interest. He demanded that the Government abolished these duties, which were 'a blot on our statute book in an age of free trade'. In an age of free trade? Was this really George Hudson, the arch-Protectionist, talking?

Lord Derby's government, which was driven by its opportunistic and volatile Chancellor Benjamin Disraeli (no friend of Hudson's), was finally defeated on 31 March 1859, over Disraeli's attempts to introduce a second Reform Bill. Hudson, following the party line, voted for the Bill, but it was to no avail. It was thrown out and a General Election was called to put Lord Derby and his sorry administration out of its misery.

A General Election was the last thing that Hudson either wanted or needed, as his fortunes in Sunderland had plummeted in the last two years. Nevertheless, he dragged his gout-ridden body and battered reputation up to the north-east in a Herculean effort to convince the voters of Sunderland that he deserved one last chance. The stakes could not have been higher. If he failed to be re-elected, he would not just lose his seat in the House of Commons, he would also lose his liberty.

CHAPTER FOURTEEN

Lost and Lonely
in France

But I, being poor, have only my dreams

W. B. Yeats

If George Hudson had been a betting man, rather than just a gambler on the railways, he would have been offered extremely long odds on his chances of retaining his parliamentary seat in Sunderland at the 1859 General Election. The key to his fortunes, a prosperous Sunderland Dock Company, was but a dim and distant memory, the town was in a depressed state and the Conservatives were hugely unpopular throughout the country. Moreover, the *Sunderland Times*, the most influential paper in the town, had been bought by the Liberals and Hudson himself had hardly been the model constituency MP during the past two years. It was an immense mountain to climb.

The unpopularity of the Conservatives, which was one factor beyond Hudson's control, stemmed from their blatant opportunism since the party's damaging split over the Corn Laws in 1846 and the subsequent emergence of the Liberals from the ashes of the old Whig party. Some leading Tories were dismayed by the behaviour of their leader Lord Derby and his number two, Benjamin Disraeli, and one senior party member, Henry Drummond, complained:

> Lord Derby and Disraeli have led the Conservative party to adopt every measure they opposed as radical ten years ago. They have made the party the tool of their ambition and sacrificed everybody's public and private interest. I do not think it creditable to the intelligence or the honour of the country gentlemen of England to vote black to be white or white to be black at their bidding.

Drummond might have added the townsfolk of Sunderland to the country gentlemen of England. The town was no longer predominantly Conservative and the *Sunderland Times*, reflecting the public mood, urged voters to 'remove what was an unnatural tumour on a reform borough'. The paper added, with dubious logic, that 'George Hudson, from the day, now 14 years ago, since he made his appearance in Sunderland, attended by his 300 men of York, has been ever more representative of what may be called the county and agricultural, rather than what may be called the borough, commercial and trading interests'. That was not entirely true, because Hudson had fought hard to promote the Sunderland Dock Company, which was clearly a commercial rather than a county concern. The truth, however, was that the paper was much more in tune with its readers than Hudson was.

Nevertheless, he launched his vigorous campaign with the following battle cry:

> I have spent my time, money and labour for the working classes. I have given employment when labour was not abundant, and when no other man could have done it.

There are thousands on whom I have conferred happiness and prosperity, and if I have not made a fortune for myself, I do not regret it. When I look to the noble works which have been executed by my intelligence and industry, if I had not made a fortune, I have erected a number of monuments to my name in this district which will never be blotted out.

Tell it not in Gath that the liberal-minded people of Sunderland have forgotten the services and sacrifices rendered by an individual to her prosperity, for it would not be heard of in Sunderland.

Hudson's use of the phrase 'the liberal-minded people of Sunderland' suggested that he already knew the game was up. He gamely declared his support for electoral reform and free trade, both essentially Liberal policies, but his theft of the opposition's clothes was ruthlessly exposed by the Liberal candidate, William Shaw Lindsay. Meanwhile, as the Sunderland Dock Company's fortunes continued to sink, so did George Hudson's. There were rumours, in a throwback to those early elections in York, that he had tried to 'apply the screw' on Sunderland's tradesmen, but it would have had to have been a mighty big screw to have influenced the result.

Polling day was on Saturday 30 April and Hudson knew he had been beaten by lunchtime. He only polled 790 votes out of 4,000, trailing Lindsay by some 500. He had represented Sunderland in the House of Commons for fourteen years and the town, to be fair, paid tribute to him.

The *Sunderland Herald* wrote:

Even taking into account the influences consequent on the unhappy divisions amongst the Liberals, it is now made abundantly manifest that Mr Hudson was indebted to Whig support for his return in former years – a support which could not have been given because of his political views, but simply out of regard to the great service which he rendered the town at a time when the town could not well assist itself. And that service is assuredly not now forgotten, for in the hour of his fall, there is a tender and perhaps more genuine sympathy felt for Mr Hudson . . . than at any previous period in his later history.

Even the *Sunderland Times*, now staunchly Liberal, conceded: 'Mr Hudson has, as a man, the sympathies of many who have been compelled to oppose his pretensions as a legislator.'

George Hudson made his farewell speech amid a mixture of 'cheering, hissing and groaning' and, at times, struggled to make himself heard. But he bravely carried on, thanked his Sunderland supporters and wished them health, happiness and prosperity. He likened himself, rather forlornly, to an unsuccessful suitor, and elicited some sympathy from the noisy crowd.

Sympathy, though, was not much use to Hudson now. Having bidden his dignified farewell to the town that he had loved well, and served as best he could, he fled to France to escape his creditors. Shortly afterwards the Sunderland Dock Company was wound up and, on 10 August, the River Wear Commissioners assumed responsibility for the town's ailing docks. It was the end of an era for George Hudson. But would it be the end of his liberty too?

Hudson had only been in France for a couple on months when the news filtered through that his old friend Robert Stephenson, the son of George and the MP for Whitby, had died. In an ideal world, he would have leapt on to the next boat heading for his favourite Yorkshire resort and contested the ensuing by-election, but he wasn't living in an ideal world. There was every chance that he would be arrested for debt the moment he set foot on English soil. It was a risk which was simply not worth taking.

He wrote from Paris:

Unfortunately I have had to undergo a persecution of a most cruel and reckless character which ever befell a public man – a persecution which while it crushed my energies did not benefit the persecutor... I believe, indeed I know public opinion has vastly changed, and some who were my bitterest enemies have acknowledged their error, and have stated to me that the course pursued towards me was as unjust as it was cruel. I trust during these painful trials that I have done nothing to forfeit the good opinion of my friends, but that I have born them manfully.

It was especially galling for Hudson that the Whitby seat, which now he coveted above all others, was won by the Liberal Harry Stephen Meysey Thompson by thirty-nine votes. Thompson, who lived at Moat Hall in Little Ouseburn, near York, had superseded George Leeman as Hudson's greatest enemy. He was not only Whitby's MP, but he had also become the chairman of the York and North Midland Railway which, as mentioned, had amalgamated with the York, Newcastle and Berwick to become the North Eastern Railway. How cruel that one man had fulfilled two of George Hudson's greatest dreams. And how equally cruel that the two men who masterminded Thompson's successful Whitby campaign were none other than George Leeman and James Meek.

Nevertheless, Hudson made it perfectly clear that he would return to Whitby and contest the seat at the next General Election. After all, he had promoted the rail link to the resort, and taken over the Whitby and Pickering railway line, for both political and financial reasons. He believed that Whitby could become one of the finest tourist attractions in the north of England, given sufficient accommodation for visitors and good rail communications. He had endeavoured to provide both.

Thus the Whitby Cliff Building Company, which had evolved from the property left by Matthew Bottrill, had been founded in 1843 and Hudson himself had built and bought a number of houses on Whitby's attractive West Cliff. This endeared him to the residents of the town, who considered him their greatest benefactor, and in 1857 he had been asked to be the guest of honour at a special dinner. The invitation came from 100 merchants, ship-owners and tradesmen 'in consideration of the great services he has rendered to the town and trade of Whitby, particularly by the enterprise he manifested in promoting the erection of the magnificent buildings on the West Cliff'. He had been unable to accept the invitation, but was clearly touched by the affection in which he was held by the residents of the town he loved the most.

He had written to his friends in Whitby in May 1857:

The last two months have been marked by events that have afforded me unmixed pleasure. The kindness with which the people of Sunderland returned me to Parliament at the last election has made an impression on my mind which no time can efface. While it is still in my memory, I am called upon to acknowledge your warm and generous tribute to the efforts I have been enabled to make to improve your beautiful town. They are proofs . . . that gratitude is not always reserved for favours to come . . . the people of Whitby and Sunderland at all events are not found unmindful of past exertions – they are found faithful amongst the faithless.

Even when Hudson was MP for Sunderland, his advice had been sought by the great and the good of Whitby. For example, in February 1859, he had received a deputation at the Royal Hotel on the subject of the Permissive Bill about the liquor trade. The members of the deputation accepted that they had no right to seek an interview with Mr Hudson, because he was not their MP, but they wanted to talk to him as a 'great benefactor to the town, an owner of property and a personal friend'. Hudson agreed to see them because he 'appreciated the respect and kindness always shown to him by the people of Whitby'.

Then, in a startling attack on the evils of alcohol (startling, that is, in view of his own consumption of the stuff), he commented:

> The traffic in drink has become a monster nuisance . . . My own experience of drink is extensive, both in private and public works, and I have seen men of the finest genius debased and brutalised by drink. England sadly contrasts with other countries in this. In my travels in Spain, the only drunken man I saw was an Englishman. Englishmen have all the qualifications which can adorn and exalt the man, but for drink.

No doubt he had temporarily – and conveniently – forgotten those embarrassing times in the House of Commons when he had attracted the attention, and ridicule, of fellow MPs by interrupting at the wrong times, by misunderstanding what was being said and, now and again, by simply making unintelligible noises. Heavy drinkers, though, tend to enjoy the luxury of a selective memory.

There are conflicting stories of how wealthy and how happy George Hudson was as he bided his time on the continent, waiting for another chance to fight an election at Whitby. A. I. Shand, in his book *Old Time Travel*, published at the beginning of the twentieth century, recalled how he met the Railway King in exile at the Hôtel Meurice in Paris, a haven for the 'affluent English middle class'. He wrote:

> There was generally a lively group of English assembled for the evening, and for a time, Mr Hudson, the dethroned railway king, reigned there supreme. I took greatly to the philosophical old gentleman, who was always good-humoured and who could be easily drawn into reminiscences of the days when he kept open house at Albert Gate and had half the impecunious aristocracy for courtiers.

That contrasts sharply with the comments by the *York Herald*, which, incidentally, had amalgamated with *The Yorkshireman* in 1858, after John Duncan's death. The *Herald* wrote:

> What Hudson suffered in silence no one ever knew but himself. He was so miserably poor during the long years he languished on the Continent that there is good reason for believing that he not infrequently went hungry to bed; and at one time those staying at the hotel, where he lodged in what was called a garret at the top of the house, came to know, when his place was vacant at the table d'hôte, that the formula, 'I am preferring a chop in my own room today', was a figurative way of concealing necessities which the poor fallen monarch shrank from admitting.

Meanwhile Hudson's old adversary Charles Dickens reported a strange sighting in Boulogne. The fascinating story was recounted in J. Forster's *A Life of Dickens*, who quotes the novelist as follows:

I encountered an old friend of mine called Charles Manby, as he was stepping on to the boat at Boulogne, bound for Folkestone. Taking leave of Manby was a shabby man of whom I had some remembrance, but whom I could not get into his place in my mind. Noticing when we stood out of the harbour that he was on the brink of the pier, waving his hat in a desolate manner, I said to Manby: 'Surely I know that man.' 'I should think you did,' said he. 'Hudson.' He is living – just living – at Paris, and Manby had brought him on. He said to Manby at parting: 'I shall not have a good dinner again, till you come back.' I asked Manby why he stuck to him. He said because he (Hudson) had so many people in his power, and had held his peace, and because he (Manby) saw so many notabilities grand with him now, who were always grovelling for shares in the days of his grandeur.

So which account of George Hudson's state of body and mind are we to believe? Did the dethroned Railway King hold court in the affluent, quintessentially British ambience of the Hôtel Meurice, or was he to be found eating a single pork chop in a lonely garret or gazing out to sea at Boulogne wondering where his next meal was coming from?

Well, Dickens loved a good story – and, like so many novelists, was prone to exaggeration. Certainly a sighting of Hudson, looking a little shabby and shop-soiled, would have excited his writer's imagination and might well have led to his account of the fascinating conversation with Charles Manby. Whether that account is wholly accurate, however, is another matter entirely. Shand, who had no axe to grind and no imagination to take flight, might well have painted a truer portrait of George Hudson's circumstances. But then there is the report of the *York Herald*, which suggests that

Hudson was in really desperate straits. Could this be journalistic licence?

Quite possibly.

If George Hudson had been in terrible financial trouble, then there is little doubt that he would have returned to England – and faced the threat of jail. His wife Elizabeth, whom he still loved dearly, would have been delighted to see him, and his eldest son George, now a successful barrister on the north-eastern circuit, could have helped with some of the most pressing debts. If life was really as bleak in France for Hudson as Dickens painted it, then he would have come home.

It is more likely that he was living quietly and frugally, still dreaming those dreams of a better, richer life ahead. According to Frederick Leveson Gore, he spent a great deal of time in Calais 'where he every day awaited the arrival of the steamer in the hope of meeting some of his former acquaintances, to whom he might confide his misfortunes and his hope that he would soon retrieve his fallen fortunes by some new speculations'. Leveson Gore is assuming that Hudson still had some money tucked away, with which he could speculate, and that is a fair assumption. It is most unlikely that someone, who was as rich as Hudson once was, would not have made a small provision for a rainy day.

There were subsequent rumours, which were reported in the *Sunderland Times* in June 1864, that George Hudson, 'ex-Railway King and ex-MP for Sunderland', had reached a settlement over his controversial Spanish railways project. This settlement, said the paper, was worth £200,000 and apparently he was now in possession of a handsome fortune. The paper urged some caution, however, commenting: 'How far this may be correct we cannot say, but it is certain that his ex-Majesty is now in good circumstances.'

It is certain that Hudson did not receive such a large settlement, because that would have led to a radical change in his modest circumstances. But there is no reason to believe he lived in abject poverty. He was able to move around, living in boarding houses and small hotels in Germany, as well as in Calais, Boulogne and Paris. Monarchs and noblemen might not call at his door, but a good steak and a glass or two of wine was a good enough substitute. There is no evidence that his spirits sank too low – and it is probable that the chance of a parliamentary seat in Whitby, where he was still so popular, kept him going.

It is hugely to George Hudson's credit that he did not betray any of his rich and famous 'friends', to whom Charles Manby had alluded. Had he been as ruthless and grasping as his detractors would have us believe, then the odd spot of blackmail here, and extortion there, would have set him up nicely for his old age. It would, in fact, have been the perfect pension plan. But Hudson never succumbed to this temptation, which speaks volumes about his moral fibre.

It is worth remembering how railway mania had gripped the country in 1845 and how anyone who was anyone, from the Duke of Wellington and his sister downwards, speculated with shares in the railway companies which were springing up across Britain. Robert Wilson, in his exhaustive *Life of Queen Victoria*, describes this fever well:

> The mania, which produced some monstrous schemes during the close of 1845, began to bear evil fruits when holders of scrip, in face of falling markets, were haunted with visions of bankruptcy. It emerged that the oddest jumble of all sorts and conditions of men were involved. Vicars and vice-admirals elbow each other in the reckless race after ill-gotten gain. Peers struggle with printers, and barristers with butchers, for the

favours of Mr Hudson, the Railway King, who was the presiding genius of this greedy rabble. Cotton spinners and cooks, Queen's Counsel and attorneys, college scouts and Catholic priests, editors and flunkeys, dairymen and dyers, beer-sellers and ministers of the Gospel, bankers and their butlers, engineers and excisemen, relieving officers and waiters at Lloyd's, domestic servants and policemen, engineers and mail-guards, with a troop of others whose callings are not describable, figured in the motley mob of small gamblers.

George Hudson knew where those bodies were buried, and the more salacious of the Victorian papers would have been fascinated to know the names of all those vice-admirals, noblemen and bishops who were as guilty as Hudson himself in the rush for railway gold, but who had escaped public humiliation and financial ruin. It is ironic that Hudson's enemies then, and his critics today, gloss over the loyalty which he showed to his friends and colleagues in their bid to denigrate the poor, deposed Railway King.

While Hudson was living in exile in France, the controversial Lendal Bridge project was finally completed and the brand-new bridge opened for traffic in 1861. It was almost thirteen years previously that this bridge had been so vehemently opposed by George Leeman, and Hudson had been given such a difficult time by his enemies on York City Council. Now Leeman, occupying senior positions in both the North Eastern Railway Company and the city council, took all the plaudits and the credit. It is doubtful, given Leeman's intense dislike of Hudson, that his thoughts would have strayed across the English Channel to France to his old adversary during the bridge's opening ceremony. No doubt Leeman had conveniently forgotten Hudson's considerable role in the conception of a bridge across the River Ouse at Lendal.

If Hudson had been forgotten in York, he had certainly not suffered the same fate in Whitby. On 11 June 1864, the *Whitby Gazette* wrote:

The great topic of conversation for some days past in Whitby has been George Hudson. Among the many great and important undertakings of Mr Hudson, and the various railway and other schemes that owe their origin to the master mind of the ex-Railway King, the new town of West Cliff of Whitby stands as one of the boldest monuments to his fame. Many consider him to have been the means of setting Sunderland on its legs and raising it to its present position as a shipping port. And everyone must acknowledge that had it not been for Mr Hudson, whose foresight (comprehending what the town of Whitby might be made, and appreciating the capabilities of the port) led him to open a way through the barriers which pent up the place, it is very doubtful whether we should have possessed our present railway facilities and it is pretty certain that we should not have had those terraces and crescents of splendid and stately mansions with which our West Cliff is now adorned.

The *Gazette* continued in this fulsome vein:

For these reasons, Mr Hudson is respected and has the sympathies and good wishes of a great proportion of the public, who would be right glad could they once more behold his face among them. Rumour states that it is the intention of Mr Hudson to offer himself for the representation of Whitby at the next vacancy. We are enabled to add, on the authority of a letter received in Whitby from Mr Hudson this week that it is his intention to visit this town in a short time, and although the Sunderland people are desirous of his going to that place, both his inclination and duty lead him to Whitby.

It is not known which Sunderland people were desirous of having George Hudson as their MP once again, but there were hardly likely to be enough of them to get him elected. Whitby, however, was another proposition altogether. He was, as we have seen, hugely popular in the town, and the Whitby Conservatives were well-disposed to a high-profile candidate with a remarkable track record. Other Tories had put themselves forward for this attractive seat, but Hudson was the clear favourite. All that remained was for the General Election to be called – and it was imminent as Lord Palmerston's Government, an intriguing mixture of Whigs, Liberals and Radicals, was nearing the end of its six-year term.

In December 1864 Hudson's hopes received a setback when his brother Charles, an influential figure in Whitby's political world, died suddenly at the age of sixty-one. George returned to Whitby, despite the threat of arrest, for the funeral and used the occasion to remind the Whitby Conservative Registration Committee that he was very keen to stand as their candidate at the impending General Election. His interest was noted, and he was duly selected to fight Whitby for the Tories – defeating Arthur Duncombe, the son of Admiral Duncombe, by twenty-seven votes to eleven.

George Hudson was ecstatic. This was the opportunity that he had been waiting for during those long, lonely six years in exile. His beloved Whitby was offering to him a passport back into Parliament and, crucially, a chance to live in freedom and without fear of arrest in the country of his birth. Moreover, Whitby in 1865 was not going to be like Sunderland in 1859. This time he had every chance of winning.

CHAPTER FIFTEEN

High Noon
at Whitby

Harry Thompson, go away!
Whitby people like fair play.
You, dog-like, have had your day,
We'll hear no more you have to say

A popular refrain during the 1865 Whitby election

George Hudson returned to England – and Whitby – in excellent spirits in June 1865. Even though he was sixty-five, and his body was showing all the signs of a misspent youth and a self-indulgent middle age, he was ready for one last challenge. Two of his brothers, one older and one younger, might have died within the past six months, but George was determined that one Hudson at least should enjoy an Indian summer. His positive mood was further enhanced by the warmth of his reception when he arrived in Whitby on 19 June. He was greeted by cheering crowds at the station and, having repaired to the Angel Hotel by the harbour for refreshments, told his supporters from the window that he 'had risen from the ranks of the people and had always been the friend of the people, especially the poor'. Whether the second part of that statement was strictly true was debatable, but it was received with rapturous applause.

Harry Thompson was again the Liberal candidate and his six years as Whitby's MP had not endeared him to his constituents. Indeed, he had become extremely unpopular. He was held responsible, as chairman of the North Eastern Railway, for the failure to link Whitby to the main railway network in the north-east, and he was blamed for the rise of Scarborough, at Whitby's expense, as Yorkshire's premier seaside resort. His support of Lord Palmerston, the reduction of the national debt and non-intervention in Europe were all very worthy, but these policies had little resonance with his Whitby constituents.

Moreover, Thompson was fundamentally unsound on the vexed question of electoral reform – at least from the point of view of his fellow Liberals – and there was some disquiet within the party that their candidate was not the best representative of their cause. The *Yorkshire Gazette* reported:

> In fulfilment of a pledge he gave in 1859, Thompson had voted for the reduction in the franchise of boroughs to £6; but he would never vote for such a measure again, because he believed there was no principle in it. He believed that the suffrage might be extended to the most deserving of the working classes without disturbing the proper balance between all the classes of the country . . . he believed the working classes . . . did not want to have control and monopoly of the representation. He would vote for no measure which would swamp many classes for the sake of enfranchising one . . . These remarks seemed to startle his Liberal friends, who looked quite uncomfortable during their delivery, and there was some confusion in the body of the hall.

It is not surprising to learn, therefore, that George Hudson was determined to take advantage of his opponent's plight – and he did so in scintillating fashion. The following passage from the *York Herald* is worth quoting at some length, for it offers the best case for George Hudson's defence, as expounded by the great man himself, that we possess:

On Monday evening last (19 June), Mr George Hudson addressed a large meeting in St Hilda's Hall, when, in addition to explaining his political principles, he entered into an elaborate defence of his railway career. In reference to this subject, he said: 'Gentlemen, my character has been assailed. That attack was founded on a report of the Eastern Counties Railway, in 1849. My object in going into that undertaking was to consolidate the railway system. A man cannot always succeed in his object, and I did not succeed in accomplishing that. A committee was appointed, and the report they drew up was founded on utter falsehood. They stated that I had altered the accounts, but I, at this meeting, utterly deny it and in giving it the lie here, I not only speak to the meeting, but to the world at large. (Cheers.) These accounts were never altered by me, and I had nothing whatever to do with them. Now, I am in a position to bring up as evidence the late secretary of the company, who says that the accounts were not falsified by me. Founded on that report, a petition was presented to the House of Commons, of which I was then a member, asking for a committee of inquiry. I answered that petition by stating my readiness to vote for the inquiry. I denied the accusation against me in my place in the House, and in so doing I received the universal cheers of that august assembly. (Applause.)

'Gentlemen, I was prepared to defend my character and my honour as one of the members of parliament, if it has been allowed me; but the members of the house so warmly cheered me on all sides that it was clear they did not believe one word that was said against me. (Cheers.) At that time, gentlemen, I had not the evidence in my favour that I now possess; but as time has rolled on I have secured the authority of a person, no less than the secretary of the company, to state that I never altered the accounts, and that the charge against me was a complete and entire fabrication. (Cheers.) It showed the animus that actuated men's minds opposed to me at that day, for it was a time when men's consciences and judgements were warped, and when malice and all sorts of unkindness predominated against me. (Hear.) Before they published that report they ought to have asked me – "Did you alter these figures, Sir, are these altered figures, Sir?" If they had done so they would have received the answer of denial that was necessary. (Cheers.) But they did not. (Cheers.) The figures were not mine, I never made them in my life, and two excellent friends of mine who had seen them have told me, "I know your figures, and I know your writing; but these figures and this writing are not yours." (Loud cheers.)

'Then there was the Midland report. No blame attached to me with regard to the Midland line, but malice upon malice was heaped upon me relative to that concern. I was the principal and chief manager of this railway, and in the report of the Committee of Investigation not a single word of reproach was uttered against me. Then why should an attempt be made to injure my character as regards the Midland Railway after the enormous benefits which I conferred upon that company. When I entered upon the management of that concern it consisted of three rival companies – they were torn with distraction and with competition which was throwing the property away. I took a course which was new in railway management then; but which is now perfectly well understood, and generally adopted. I made them unite themselves together and become friends and not enemies. I have now the satisfaction of feeling that what I did was for the best; and that I was in the right – that the policy was characterised by wisdom and foresight; and if the railway world owes me no other debt of gratitude, at all events I can claim from it in the merit of founding a system which has worked so admirably in the consolidation of these great advantages, and has conferred not only great benefits on the companies, but also on the public at large. The Midland shares were then down below 50, and by my policy they rose up to 190. (Hear.) I will ask, was that no saving of property; did the widow and orphan suffer in that case? No, gentlemen, the widow and orphan were made to rejoice by the course of conduct which I took on that occasion. (Applause.) There were, gentlemen, upon that committee, gentlemen of first-rate integrity and intelligence, and Mr Arkwright was their chairman. They employed a public accountant, a man of ability, and he went through and over everything, fishing and ferreting about. He stated that such and such things ought to be charged to revenue which were put down to capital. Not having any malice or bad feeling against me the Committee repudiated the proposition of their account-ant as being untenable, and through their chairman, Mr Arkwright, they declared that the accounts were fairly and honestly made out, and perfectly correct. (Cheers.)

'Then there was the York and North Midland report, a report to which I entirely objected because the accounts were quite right. The company was properly managed, and in a prosperous condition when I vacated the chair. You are all well aware that persons connected with trade experience from time to time periods of prosperity and periods of depression or loss, and therefore how was it possible for me to ensure constant sunshine in these large railway undertakings any more than it is possible to secure continued prosperity in trade, and commerce. Railway must depend on the prosperity of the country. If the tradesmen, the manufacturer, the ironmaster and the artisan suffer, why the railways must suffer too. (Hear.) With regard to the Newcastle and Berwick line, I could weep on thinking how deeply painful the course of that company has been. One of the charges against me respecting it was that I was extending its unprofitableness and mismanaging it merely for electioneering purposes at Sunderland. I was accused of having fixed a tariff of rates giving to that place a priority over other ports, and I was charged with having done so to promote my political position as its representative. But what was the fact? The new management altered these rates but in less than twelve months they were obliged to revert back to my rates of charges, finding that otherwise they would suffer enormous loss of traffic and revenue. (Cheers.) There was another point. I had taken a large amount of dock shares for the company, and I had the foresight to see and believe that they would be exceedingly valuable in an indirect manner to the company. I wished the company to be a master of that dock, but the shares were repudiated by the Committee of Inquiry, and forced upon me, by which I lost a sum of at least £80,000. And what did the company gain? The effect of their policy was to admit a serious competition, which abstracted from the North Eastern Railway a revenue of at least £30,000 a year. The result has shown that I was in the right and that they were in the wrong with respect to the Sunderland docks, and they used me cruelly by forcing me to take £80,000 of dock shares, when they would have paid the company indirectly a very large dividend. (Applause.)

'Then there is the Newcastle and Carlisle Railway. I took that railway in hand and on an arrangement to pay its shareholders six per cent, and worked it as part of the North-Eastern system. The committee, men without any commercial experience and knowledge, said that they would have nothing to do with it, that I might take it and get rid of it, and I had to do so at a loss of £12,000 to myself. Since then, however, the line has been taken by them, and eight per cent is now being paid for it. I also took the Maryport and Carlisle Railway at four per cent for a term, with an increase of to six per cent ultimately. The committee advised the shareholders of the Newcastle and Berwick company to reject this beneficial arrangement, and they did so. From that contract I was relieved without loss. The Carlisle and Maryport line has had such an element of prosperity about it ever since that it has paid from eight to eleven per cent. (Hear.) This proves the wisdom of my policy. Instead, then, of oppressing me – a single individual, with an iron hand, and extracting from me the last drop of blood, they ought to have adopted an entirely different course towards me. They have thrown away, by their weakness, malice, and folly, hundreds of thousands of pounds, in pressing down one who had done them no harm, and in seeking to ruin and send me into poverty. (Cheers.)

'Then there is again the Stockton and Darlington line, which I had arranged for at five per cent, and is now paying nine or ten. These are the facts, I think, which will tell your minds that the course I pursued was the right one. Time has shown that my policy was wise, and that I have not been actuated by the motives which these men attributed to me. (Hear.) It has often been said how many families have been ruined by me; but I will ask how many families have been saved by my policy? How many think you? I have made upwards of twenty millions of property safe and secure, and thousands of families receive their dividends with as much certainty as if they had their money invested in the funds. No speculations of this class can be looked upon as blessed with complete success; and although loss may have been sustained by a few individuals, yet I look back with wonder and astonishment to find that all my schemes and plans have borne such rich fruit, and the railways with which I was connected have stood better than almost any other railway property in the kingdom. (Applause.)

'It is always disagreeable to speak of oneself, but I am obliged to do so in this assembly of my own friends to vindicate my character. I have longed from the bottom of my heart, for years to have the opportunity of telling the electors of Whitby of my wrongs, and, in doing so, to defend myself, and I am proud that I have had the chance of saying these few words to you. (Cheers.) It has been seriously said that I purposely depreciated the value of the property of which I had the management. Why, gentlemen, it is absurd to talk of depreciation. I am old enough to recollect well when the Great Western shares were at £180 premium, which were worth £60 paid, made them £240. What is the price of them now? They are 70, and I have seen them down at 47. They might charge the chairman of the Great Western with depreciation of the value of property with greater force than they do me. There is another line, the London and North Western. I remember when the shares were at 380, and afterwards they went down to about 100. Now they are about 120. Do they charge the London and North Western chairman with the same charges they bring against me? No. The Manchester and Leeds were at one time 180 to 190 per share; they are now at 120. Was the chairman of this company accused of depreciating the property? No. (Cheers.) The fact is, gentlemen, I have been made the scapegoat for the sins of the people, but I have borne all of the obloquy showered upon me with much courage and strength of mind, and my innocence has been a great support to me in the persecutions I have undergone. I can tell all my enemies and detractors that I can bear their malice, however intense, and however long continued, with the same sang-froid and with the same resignation as I have endured attacks from much abler men.' (Cheers.)

Harry Thompson found this storming display impossible to cope with, especially when Hudson turned his fire on George Leeman, Thompson's campaign manager. Hudson had waited a long time to attack his old enemy Leeman and he was determined to make the most of his opportunity. He was especially incensed over Leeman's role in the Lendal Bridge affair in York, which had rumbled on since the idea of a bridge at Lendal had been first mooted by Hudson himself nearly twenty years previously, and now he did not hold back:

It is the fate of some men to be powerful for mischief, and Mr Leeman takes a high rank in that class. Hence his saddling the old city [York] with a debt of £35,000 for the erection of a bridge, not a shilling of which would have been incurred had I been allowed to carry out my plans.

If Thompson was unpopular before this speech, he was positively hated and derided after it. 'It is impossible for parties at a distance to conceive the bitterness of feeling against Mr Thompson,' reported the *York Herald*. It mattered not that Hudson's stout defence of himself begged as many questions as it answered; it mattered not that he was still technically on the run from his creditors. The Whitby electorate was adamant that the Railway King, who had been so cruelly and harshly dethroned, should re-ascend his throne.

Placards appeared with 'Avenge Hudson's wrongs' written all over them, Thompson's main electoral address disintegrated into chaos, and a hard-hitting poem, entitled 'Hudson for Whitby', began to do the rounds. The poem was hardly in the league of Milton, Wordsworth or Keats, but it was effective political propaganda. Here are a couple of verses:

Hurrah for Hudson then – be united Whitby men
Bundle Thompson off to Scarboro' by train;
    That's where all his cheap trips went, and where brass was
        spent
And he'll do the same again.
Whitby lads, he'll cut you all again

Although it's 'two pluck one', bold Hudson is our man
The right man for the place is he
Send the others to their mothers, with their labour for

        Their trouble
    And vote Hudson Whitby's next MP
  Vote Hudson in MP.

The scanning, grammar, rhyming and content all needed a little
fine-tuning, but the sentiments were clear. George Hudson should
become Whitby's new MP and Harry Thompson should be shunted,
metaphorically if not literally, back to Scarborough. If Hudson
knew he was going to lose Sunderland in 1859, he was equally
convinced that he would win Whitby in 1865. With just a couple
of days to go to polling day, which was scheduled for the second
week of July, the Whitby Tories were already preparing to open the
champagne. Only a catastrophe could stop him now. And a
catastrophe duly did.

On Sunday 9 July, George Hudson was rudely awakened at his
Whitby lodgings by a loud knocking at his door. It was the Sheriff's
officer from York, and he had come to arrest Hudson for debt. A
shocked and angry Hudson tried to complain, but it was to no
avail. He was bundled on to the first available train to York and
taken to the gloomy debtors' prison in the forbidding York Castle.
There he was to languish helplessly while the Whitby election took
place. The glittering prize of a parliamentary seat, and with it that
priceless immunity from arrest, had been cruelly snatched away
from him only forty-eight hours before polling day.

Richard S. Lambert suggests that 'fate had dealt her final blow
to her old favourite'. In fact the truth was a great deal more prosaic
and less arbitrary than that. It was not fate, but George Hudson's
enemies who had 'kidnapped' him and thrown him into prison.
Although both Thompson and Leeman strenuously denied that
they knew what was going on, they were lying. They were both
heavily implicated in Hudson's arrest, which was designed to get

Thompson back into the House of Commons and to remove Leeman's greatest foe from public life forever. It was a highly cynical move, even in the cut-throat world of nineteenth-century British politics, and it outraged the Whitby Tories.

As Hudson, broken in body and spirit, lay in his cold and lonely cell in York, the Whitby Tories got to work. They only had two days in which to find another candidate, but they were determined not to allow this audacious *coup d'état* to succeed. A prosperous local businessman called Charles Bagnall, who lived at nearby Sneaton Castle, was immediately selected as Hudson's replacement and he took advantage of Thompson's ever-growing unpopularity to run a hugely effective two-day campaign. The final result was Bagnall 305 votes and Thompson 282, and the latter's six-year reign as Whitby's MP came to an ignominious end.

Although it was widely believed that Thompson was responsible for Hudson's arrest, he and Leeman issued a public denial. Even Dr Alf Peacock, hardly one of George Hudson's greatest supporters, suggests that both men were ultimately behind the coup, although they encouraged others to pull the trigger. They were fearful, for differing reasons, that Hudson would win the election and enjoy a happy ending to his turbulent life. That is why the arrest took place just two days before polling day.

It transpired that this arrest followed an action taken against Hudson by the York-based solicitors Newton, Robinson and Brown. They were acting on behalf of a Mr Sandeman, of the firm Sandeman, Sandeman and Company to whom Hudson, allegedly, owed a large debt. The solicitors explained that they had sought Hudson's arrest because, 'if the defendant had been allowed to get into Parliament without paying his debt, the plaintiff's remedy would be lost, or at least in abeyance so long as the Parliament lasted'.

Although this might have been technically correct, it does not satisfactorily explain the timing of the arrest nor address the charge that it was politically motivated. In a stinging attack, George Hudson's solicitors, Elmslie, Forsyth and Sedgwick of London, exposed this ridiculous charade and accused Sandeman's solicitors of 'violating the important principle which studiously exempts from public controversy and comment every legal proceeding which has not received final judicial decision'.

They continued in the same vein:

> Let us be frank. It is the misfortune of Mr Hudson to have found united in the person of Mr Thompson a political adversary and electoral competitor, and, as chairman of the North Eastern Railway, the representative of claims against him susceptible alike of liberal adjustment or of unlimited, stringent and harsh enforcement . . . Mr Hudson's popularity increases, with assured prospect of his triumphant return for Whitby at the ensuing general election. Long before the recent dissolution of Parliament the realisation of this anticipation could not be doubted . . . The enthusiastic return of Mr Hudson was inevitable, if not averted by some bold coup.

The assertion by Thompson and Leeman that they had nothing to do with Hudson's arrest was a bare-faced lie. As chairman of the North Eastern Railway Company, Thompson was already pursuing Hudson through the courts and he could not take further action against Hudson himself. Sandeman, however, could. Most significantly, Sandeman's claim was based on the fact that he had a financial stake in Hudson's West Cliff development in Whitby. So, too, did the North Eastern Railway Company. It is inconceivable that

Thompson and Leeman did not know what Sandeman was doing, especially since Thompson's court case was all about Hudson's debts and the ownership of Cliff Company, which had developed Whitby's West Cliff and which Hudson had allegedly mortgaged to the railway company. Thompson would have known all about the 'large debt' owed to Sandeman and would have primed this most useful creditor accordingly.

It says much about the arrogance and the duplicity of both men that they believed they could get away with orchestrating George Hudson's eleventh-hour arrest. They thought they had timed their coup to perfection because, although the warrant for Hudson's arrest had been taken out two months before it was executed, it was decided only to use it in an emergency. This emergency arose when it was apparent that Thompson was going to lose his Whitby seat. At that point the trigger was pulled – and Hudson was jailed. Justice was done, however, when Thompson still lost his seat.

This unsavoury episode is extremely instructive. One of the most nauseating traits of George Hudson's enemies is their adoption of the moral high ground. Hudson is consistently portrayed as unscrupulous and fraudulent, whose life was dedicated to exploiting and robbing other people in order to make himself the richest man in the land. Yet the behaviour of Thompson and Leeman in Whitby was no better; in fact it was worse. By lying and cheating to further their own ends, they sent a defenceless and ailing old man to jail. If that is not the politics of the gutter, then it is difficult to know what is.

CHAPTER SIXTEEN

His Friends in
the North

*I would have been a better man today,
if I had never left that little shop in York*

George Hudson

Today the Castle Museum in York provides a cheerful and illuminating window into the city's past. Olde worlde cobbled streets have
been imaginatively recreated and hundreds of visitors a day take an
enjoyable trip back in time, many of them blissfully unaware that
they are walking through what was once a gloomy and distinctly
uncomfortable debtors' prison. As Charles Bagnall celebrated
his unlikely victory, after just a two-day campaign, over Harry
Thompson at Whitby, George Hudson would have been staring
helplessly at his cell walls. It was bad enough for him to be locked
up in prison, but it was worse being incarcerated in the city of his
greatest triumphs.

Hudson remained in prison for three long months, on the
grounds that he was in contempt of court for not paying his debts.
His imprisonment was futile, because he did not have the money to
satisfy his creditors, and his plight soon attracted sympathy in York

and beyond. The idea of an elderly and infirm man being locked up twenty-four hours a day offended Victorian sensibilities, and Hudson was eventually released in October 1865 – thanks to the generosity of a colliery owner called George Elliot. Elliot, the president of the Association of Mining Engineers, paid off Hudson's debt to Mr Sandeman and the poor jailbird immediately left England for France again, just in case he was re-arrested.

Unfortunately for George Hudson, Sandeman's success was seen as an encouraging precedent by other creditors. So when he returned to England in June 1866, to continue his debilitating legal battle with the North Eastern Railway Company, he was immediately re-arrested for debt. This time he was detained outside his London club, The Carlton, in Pall Mall, and taken to the debtors' prison in Whitecross Street in the City of London, where he remained for three weeks. The creditor who was pursuing him on this occasion was a Mr Bartlett who was allegedly owed £13,000. Once again, this was money that George Hudson simply did not have.

Hudson was eventually released from prison on the grounds that he had a right to visit his solicitor and that a reasonable amount of time should be allowed to elapse between such a meeting and any potential arrest. This ruling went right back to the days of Magna Carta in 1215, which allowed MPs an allowance of time to get to and from Parliament. But Hudson was not interested in the legal niceties of his case; he simply fled back to France as quickly as he could.

In July 1866 the North Eastern Railway Company's case against George Hudson came to court (with Hudson himself safely en-sconced in France). It was heard by Lord Romilly, the Master of the Rolls, who needed all his wits about him to unravel the facts from the fiction in an extremely complex case. The Attorney General, Sir Hugh Cairns, represented Hudson and argued that the compromise settlement of £47,000 between his client and the North Eastern Railway was binding – even though Hudson had defaulted. The NER's counsel, Sir Roundell Palmer, disagreed and argued Hudson owed £73,390 minus the £33,000 which he had already paid. Lord Romilly ruled that Hudson was liable only for the outstanding £14,000 (£47,000 minus £33,000), plus interest. It was a victory, of sorts.

But the North Eastern Railway Company would not let the matter rest, even though Hudson was in no position to pay his debts in full, and lodged an appeal with the House of Lords. This heralded the beginning of a long and tortuous legal battle, which would not be resolved until March 1869.

In the meantime the General Election of 1868, which saw Hudson's old sparring partner William Gladstone and the Liberals sweep to power, came and went. Hudson followed events at Whitby from afar – from Germany, to be precise – but with a good deal of interest. He sent messages to the Whitby electorate, urging them to support the Conservative candidate. This was not going to be Charles Bagnall, who had indicated that he did not wish to stand for Parliament again. Significantly, Bagnall had some kind words to say about Hudson in his valedictory address, which were greeted with loud cheering and applause:

At the last election you had a leader, the darling of the people of Whitby, a man who, if he came here now, would be returned without any opposition. The chosen man of the other party hates a contest, and he won't come unless he feels certain of being safe. Let Mr Hudson come into Whitby, and Mr Thompson's name will never be mentioned again. It is perhaps to the misfortune of the party that Mr Hudson cannot come, but he sends his cordial good wishes to the candidate whom the Conservative Party might choose. You remember that within 48 hours of the last election that man was kidnapped. You were in the position of the men playing at a game of chess, when the King was snatched off the board, and there was an end of the game.

Despite this rousing speech, the Conservative candidate Major W. C. Worsley of Hovingham Hall, near York (the great-grandfather of the present Duchess of Kent), was defeated by the Liberal candidate W. H. Gladstone, the new Prime Minister's son. Whitby, however, never forgot George Hudson, the best MP it never had. Today the town's Hudson Street, near the Royal Hotel on West Cliff, proudly bears his name.

In March 1869 the House of Lords finally delivered its verdict on the North Eastern Railway versus George Hudson case – and it was a devastating blow to Hudson. The Law Lords ruled, despite some difference of opinion between them, that it had been the clear intention of the parties to the various agreements that if the conditions of the compromise were not fulfilled, 'the rights of the appellants to the whole of the debt originally due to them were to revive'. In other words, the conditions of the 1854 settlement were binding. As a result, the railway company's costs were added to Hudson's original debt.

If George Hudson's life had been a boxing match – and he certainly gave as well as received a number of hefty punches in his time – this would have been the knock-out blow. The judgement left him flat out on the canvas – with no prospect of being able to get up. He was sixty-nine years old, in ill health, in exile and bankrupt. Apart from the huge sum of money which he now owed the North Eastern Railway, estimated at more than £60,000, his good friend George Elliot believed there were a 'great many' other creditors. Whatever Hudson's crimes, and they were not nearly as heinous as some historians would have us believe, he did not deserve to end up like this.

There was, however, a glimmer of light at the end of this hitherto pitch-black tunnel. On 24 April, the *Whitby Gazette* carried the following paragraph, under the heading of 'The ex-Railway King':

> The result of the long litigation between the North Eastern Railway Company and Mr George Hudson was to confirm the reversal of the decision of the Master of the Rolls and reduces Mr Hudson to a state of penury. He is now in France and is said to be utterly destitute. In addition to a subscription to meet present wants, and in the belief that the Railway King was as much sinned against as sinning, a large shareholder has intimated his intention to ask his co-partners in the North Eastern Company to grant to Mr Hudson an annuity of £200 a year. An interesting discussion is looked for at the next general meeting and many believe the feeling will be in favour of the project.

In fact, it transpired that the shareholders of the North Eastern Railway could not grant George Hudson an annuity without the permission of Parliament, but the idea of helping Hudson financially had captured the imagination of his friends. They were becoming increasingly concerned about his mental and physical health, and George Elliot, having seen Hudson in Paris, said that he had been very much struck and very much hurt to see the destitute condition he was in. Apparently the clothes he was wearing 'were hardly such as any respectable man would like to be seen in'.

Elliot, who was now the Conservative MP for South Durham, and Hugh Taylor, a successful businessman with interests in shipping and mining in the north-east, therefore decided to launch a subscription fund for their friend. The subscription, which was agreed at a meeting of the Wearside Commissioners in May, was an immediate success.

Elliot told the Commissioners: 'With regard to the amount of the fund, it would not be proper to limit it. The amount should be considerable and, as such, would place Mr Hudson in a position of comfort for the rest of his life.' He added that he was glad that the subscription had been inaugurated in Sunderland because it was the right place. He hoped the people of the town would respond liberally and he had no doubt that contributions would be general throughout the country and that the movement begun in the town would be appreciated. The subscription list was then passed round and Elliot and Taylor gave 100 guineas each.

The *Sunderland Times* was in no doubt that this plan to help George Hudson out of his straitened financial circumstances was an admirable idea. In an editorial of 29 May, the paper wrote:

> Sunderland was the place which above all others has profited largely by the works which that remarkable man set agoing . . . He was the foremost in a mighty forward movement, which chequered the face of the land, with railway lines; and bowed down to and worshipped as he was, like Nebuchadnezzar's golden image on the plain of Dura, by all the inhabitants of the earth, save a momentarily insignificant, pragmatical few, no wonder if his head was turned, and he forgot that the chairman of so many huge amalgamated companies . . . was not altogether independent of such common moral obligations as are supposed to bind smaller men . . . Sunderland Docks will forever remain a noble monument to George Hudson. It would be scandalous

to the town had the old man been left to end his days in sordid pinching penury. He has suffered enough for his sins. Let him be made comfortable for the rest of his life.

Hudson himself, quite naturally, was extremely grateful for any financial help which came his way. An anonymous correspondent of the *Hull Express* described how he had been asked to deliver a letter to Hudson in Calais *en route* for Paris. This messenger eventually tracked Hudson down in the depths of Calais and delivered the letter. Tears rolled down the old man's cheeks as he opened it and discovered a banknote. He then provided his new-found friend with a modest meal in his lodgings and told him: 'I would have been a better man today if I had never left that little shop in York. Never aim, my dear sir, too high. Fortunes can only be secured by a steady plodding industry, which brings you at last an honourable reward.'

Meanwhile fate, at last, was beginning to smile on old George. The subscription fund had raised more than £1,000 in three weeks in York and a trust was formed which ensured that his creditors could not get their hands on any money.

On 14 July Hudson wrote to the Lord Mayor of York from Calais:

Amidst all the afflictions with which my latter days have been clouded, it is to me a source of deep gratitude that so many friends have united to express, in so substantial a manner, their sympathy towards me, and their acknowledgement of my services in the promotion of public works. Be assured, my Lord Mayor, that to you, and to all my other kind friends, I feel a gratitude which words cannot express, and which will ever remain deeply engraven on my heart.

The subscription closed on 31 and the *Whitby Gazette* wrote soon afterwards:

> The trustees who have been appointed for the investment of the fund are Mr George Elliot, MP for Westminster; Mr Hugh Taylor of Chipchase Castle, Northumberland; Mr James Hartley of Ashbrook, Durham; and Mr James L Foster of York. These gentlemen have just completed a contract with the North British Assurance Company for the purchase of an annuity of £520 by an investment of £4,000 at the rate of 13 per cent. Of the sum the York treasurer (Mr Foster) has provided £1,500 and the London, Newcastle and Sunderland treasurers have raised the remaining £2,500. The residue of the entire subscription, estimated to produce another £1,000, when realised, will be invested by the trustees. The timely provision thus made for Mr Hudson is purely alimentary, and is not assignable by him, nor subject or affectable by his debts or deeds, legal or voluntary.

And there was more good news. On 1 January 1870 the Abolition of Imprisonment for Debt Act became law, which meant that George Hudson could now return to England without the fear of being arrested. The Act stipulated that no person could be arrested or imprisoned for making a default in the payment of a sum of money. He was now safe from all his creditors, from the North Eastern Railway Company downwards, though he must have wondered what his latter years might have been like had this Act been law when he fought that fateful Whitby election campaign in 1865.

Hudson's return to England in the early spring of 1870 might not have been as triumphant as his entrance into Whitby in 1865, but it was equally satisfying. Having been in almost permanent exile since 1859, living in increasingly dingy boarding houses and poverty-stricken circumstances, it was a joy to arrive in London and be reunited with his long-suffering wife Elizabeth. He went to live with her at Churton Street in Pimlico and was able to resume his favourite habit of buying fresh fish from Billingsgate Market in the early morning, just as he had done at the height of his fame as the Railway King. He was also welcomed back by his club, the Carlton, and was delighted when he was elected to be the chairman of the smoking room once again. It was as if the clock had been turned back twenty-two years, though money was not in such plentiful supply as it had been in his heyday. Still, older and wiser, his needs were less now.

The smoking room at the Carlton Club provided old George with a platform and an audience to reminisce about his extraordinary life. It was here that he was reported as saying: 'The happiest part of my life was when I stood behind the counter, and used the yard measure in my own shop. I had one of the snuggest businesses in York, and turned over my £30,000 a year, five and twenty per cent of it being profit.' Although these were the same sentiments that he had expressed to the friendly messenger with the banknote in Calais the previous year, any objective assessment has to be that it was a good thing for Hudson himself, and for the city of York, that he had leapt over the shop counter in College Street and made an indelible mark on the Victorian age.

Although he was perfectly content living with Elizabeth in Churton Street and recounting his past exploits at his club, Hudson felt it was important to thank his friends in the north, who had rescued him from the ignominy of debt and exile. He might have been seventy years old, and riddled with gout, but his spirit was willing. So, in April 1870, he embarked on a tour of the north, visiting the scenes of his past triumphs and staying with the friends who had been so kind to him.

The first stop was Newcastle, where he was accompanied by the loyal James Foster, before travelling to Chipchase Castle, the home of Hugh Taylor, where he must have appreciated the comfort and splendour all the more after his depressing exile in Calais. The next stop was Sunderland, where he was greeted by the mayor, the town clerk and the chairman of the Wear Commissioners, who had played such an important part in promoting his subscription fund. On 16 April the *Whitby Gazette* reported:

> The South Dock presented an extremely gay and holiday-like appearance, streamers flying here and there, and bunting in profusion being observable whichever way the eye turned. All the ships in the dock were dressed with almost countless flags, and with a gentle breeze and bright sunshine, the scene was one of great brilliancy. Arched over and decorated with flags, the bridge at the South Outlet told the onpasser the whole place was *en fête* for the occasion, and noticeable at this point was a large blue silk banner bearing the words 'Success to the docks and Sunderland's prosperity'.

If George Hudson's confidence and self-esteem had been sapped by the persistence of his enemies, the debilitating effect of debt and the loneliness of exile, this wonderful reception brought a twinkle back into his eye and a swagger back into his gait. So, during a dinner in his honour at the Queen's Hotel in Sunderland on 16 April, he treated his audience to a rose-tinted trip down memory lane, saying, 'By some intuitive force or genius, I rendered railway property in the north profitable', adding that he had benefited Newcastle by refusing to cross the Tyne lower down the river and that he was proud of creating the docks at Sunderland. He also pointed out that the Newcastle and Carlisle line, which he had leased at seven per cent, had been taken over at ten per cent and he denied he had ever taken a 'sixpence' dishonestly. Whereas some of Hudson's deals could not be described as strictly honest and above board, only his hardest-hearted enemy could begrudge him this chance to draw attention to his achievements after languishing in the shadows for so long.

Meanwhile, his lengthy court case with the North Eastern Railway Company was finally drawing to a close. In June 1870 the Master of the Rolls heard that Hudson still owed the railway company more than £70,000 despite confirming that more than £50,000 had been raised by the combined sale of Newby Park (to Lord Downe) and Albert Gate (to the French Government). There was no chance that he could pay the outstanding amount back from his annuity, although this had now increased to £635 a year. In any case, the annuity was legally protected from the NER's clutches. As a result, a final arrangement was reached with the NER during the following year and Hudson was finally freed from the chains of debt which had bound him for more than twenty years.

There is some evidence to suggest that George was a happy, relaxed and fulfilled soul at this late period of his life. He had been through a terrible ordeal, which would have killed weaker men, and had survived to tell the tale. But it was the tales of his days as the undisputed Railway King of England that he liked to tell the most, as Richard S. Lambert recounts:

> At this stage his spirit was as fresh, sanguine and life-enjoying as a boy's. He was as fond as ever of talking about himself; of his speeches when at the height of his prosperity; of the

quiet family grave in the little Yorkshire churchyard which he used to visit from time to time; of old George Stephenson and the fun they used to have together; of his civic triumphs as the Lord Mayor of York and the famous wine coolers he used to bring out at his banquets; of the way in which the nobility and the great world of London used to run after him in the days of his greatness; of the respect with which he was listened to in the House of Commons – and of a hundred anecdotes and quaint episodes of his extraordinary career. He even began to save up and put aside a little of his income, saying – in reply to the playful remonstrances of his friends – that he had now more than he needed, and was yet hoping to re-enter Parliament. His debts were at last all compounded, and he had begun to plan a fresh development at West Cliff in Whitby.

He was also enjoying life with his wife Elizabeth again. They celebrated their golden wedding anniversary on 17 July 1871, no mean achievement in view of everything they had experienced together – and apart. There has been much speculation about the exact nature of their relationship following George's fall and the subsequent suicide of Elizabeth's brother Richard, but there is little doubt that they remained a close, if not loving, couple until the end. It is true that Elizabeth did not follow her husband abroad, but that was because of financial, rather than emotional, considerations. It is more significant that Hudson chose to live with his wife at Churton Street on his return from exile.

During the autumn of 1871 he went north again, spending a few days with the Earl of Lonsdale at Lowther Castle before moving on to Whitby and York. At Whitby, where he stayed at the Royal Hotel, the *Gazette* reported that he was in excellent health and devoted half a column to praising his role in the development of the Whitby Railway:

> Coming to Whitby by railway you branch off at Malton from the direct North-Eastern route, and proceed by a line for which, among other benefits, Whitby is indebted to the once well-known Mr George Hudson. The line was originally a horse-railway, constructed by George Stephenson, and is said to have been the third ever made in England (the Stockton and Darlington being the first and the Liverpool and Manchester the second) and was literally what the Americans would call a 'one-horse' concern until the Railway King took it in hand, laid down a double line of rails, made it applicable for steam traffic, altered its course, and finally developed it into what it is, one of the most picturesque lines in the country.

He moved on to York, where he dined with the Lord Mayor at the Mansion House, scene of some of his greatest banquets and triumphs, before returning to London. But the lure of Yorkshire was too much and he returned to his native county in early December 1871, visiting friends and family in his birthplace of Howsham and Malton, before moving on to York. There he stayed with his best friend James Foster, now owner of the *Yorkshire Gazette*, and he planned to attend a Sunday service at York Minster, before dining with the Lord Mayor (again!) on the following day.

Sadly, when the *Gazette* had said that old George was in excellent health in September, it was being somewhat economical with the truth. His gout was terribly painful, but it was his angina that was causing the greatest concern. He suffered a bad angina attack on Saturday 9 December and was advised to return home to London immediately by a Dr Matterson, the son of the doctor who had turned against him so shamefully at the time of his disgrace. George, however, was too ill and too forgiving to bear the doctor any grudge for his father's betrayal.

Desperately sick, he travelled back to London, and Churton Street, by train on the Saturday. By Monday he had recovered sufficiently to write to James Foster and tell his dear friend of his progress. But it was a false dawn. On the Wednesday he had a massive heart attack and he finally passed away, in the arms of his youngest son William, at 8.40 a.m. on Thursday 14 December. He was 71.

CHAPTER SEVENTEEN

Peace at Last

O death, where is thy sting?
O, grave, where is thy victory?

I Corinthians

Even when George Hudson was at the height of his fame and wealth, and entertained the aristocracy in lavish style at Albert Gate, he remained a countryman at heart. Like so many Yorkshiremen in exile, he remained fiercely loyal to the county of his birth and returned there whenever circumstances, or the authorities, permitted. So it comes as no surprise to learn that he had requested to be buried in Scrayingham churchyard, near his birthplace of Howsham, where generations of his family lay. He had, after all, regaled his friends at the Carlton Club with tales about the Hudson family vault at Scrayingham. It was where he wanted to be laid to rest. Thus his body was taken from Churton Street to Euston on Wednesday 20 December and then was transported up to York via the 'Midland route', arriving at 9.00 a.m. on the following day.

The *Yorkshire Herald* reported this sad occasion thus:

The body was transferred, in the presence of a number of friends, to a hearse for conveyance to its long home in the vault at Scrayingham. At half-past nine the funeral cortège set out from the Station Hotel. It consisted of a hearse drawn by four horses, the former being void (by request of the deceased himself as well as of Mrs Hudson) of those nodding plumes which give pomp to funeral pageantry. Four bearers walked on each side of the hearse, and following it came a mourning carriage, containing the deceased's two sons, and Dr Matterson, Mr W. Richardson and Mr J. L. Foster. Then came two other carriages, in the first of which were Mr Edwin Thompson, Mr Luke Thompson, Mr E. Oates and Mr Routledge; and in the next Mr H. Tennant (general manager of the North Eastern Railway, Mr Christison (passenger superintendent of the same company), Mr Cabry and Mr Close. The carriages of the Lord Mayor and Mr Ald Weatherley followed. The cortège passed along, to the solemn tolling of the minute bells of the Cathedral, and of the churches of St Michael-le-Grand, St Michael's, Spurriergate, and All Saints Pavement. As it took its way over Lendal Bridge, the spectator could not fail to be struck with its simple and unostentatious character, and in the mind to shadow in review the remarkable life of him who was passing so quietly away. The route taken was along Lendal, Coney Street, High Ousegate, Pavement, Fossgate and Walmgate, whence the cortège passed through the villages of Grimston, Gate Helmsley, Buttercrambe and arrived at Scrayingham. In all the streets mentioned above (though most generally in Coney Street) and in other parts of the city the tradesmen showed their respect for the deceased by keeping their shutters up and their window blinds down, and groups of spectators gathered in the streets and gave expression to their feelings as the mournful procession passed along. There were also a number of other gentlemen at the station who did not follow the body to Scrayingham, but were present to display a last mark of respect.

There were two notable absentees from this funeral procession: George Hudson's wife Elizabeth and his daughter Ann. There are those who have speculated that Elizabeth stayed away because the wounds opened by the suicide of her brother Richard had still not healed, but that does not match up with the facts. If Elizabeth was still furious with her husband, she would not have welcomed him back to Churton Street once his exile was over. No, the truth is more mundane. She was seventy-six years old and was thought to be too frail to make the long journey from London to Yorkshire. Ironically, she lived to be ninety-one! Ann, meanwhile, was living abroad and was unable to get back to England in time for the funeral.

Other absentees included George Leeman, Hudson's arch-enemy, who was in the process of stealing his glory both as a York politician and a railway magnate, and Harry Thompson, who had preferred to see Hudson in jail rather than lose his Whitby seat. It is unlikely that they would have been made very welcome by the other mourners, notably George's closest friends, James Richardson, James Foster, Thomas Cabrey, his former engineer, and John Close, who had worked faithfully for his master since those halcyon drapers' shop days. The young Dr Matterson, who had looked after Hudson at the end, was there too.

In the pretty little village of Scrayingham, in the heart of the Derwent Valley, the cortège was joined by more mourners from Howsham, Malton and Whitby. They gathered quietly around, as the heavy coffin, which weighed half a ton, was carried into the parish church.

The *Gazette* commented:

The whole proceedings were conducted free from ostentation and parade. As friends met friends, they expressed their warmest regret for the deceased gentleman, whose remains now rest in the substantial vault of his ancestors, overlooking the beautiful sequestered valley of the Derwent. Throughout the day the sun shone with a brilliancy rarely witnessed on St Thomas's Day (the shortest day of the year). Thus closed in calmness and in peace the last scene of one who, during his active life, had filled so prominent a position among his fellow men.

It is clear that the humility which had characterised the last few years of George Hudson's life, give or take a couple of speeches of self-justification, had accompanied him to the grave. Those grand-iose banquets and triumphal processions, which characterised the reign of the Railway King, had proved to be empty and worthless. The sober and restrained nature of Hudson's funeral procession, which he had requested himself, showed that he had learned the important lesson that the ostentatious trappings of wealth are but transient. It was a lesson which allowed him to be at ease with himself in his later years and to accept his difficult circumstances with a remarkable degree of equanimity.

The *Yorkshire Herald* underlined this point when writing:

Those who saw Mr Hudson in his later years since his return from exile were surprised to find how much innate simplicity of character he retained. It was amazing to find a man who had undergone such startling vicissitudes and to whom, it would seem, the hollowness of the world must have been thoroughly proved, enjoying life with a gusto, which never flagged, and cracking jokes and telling anecdotes with as much energy and enjoyment as the youngest diner out. Those who knew him best during the long and poverty-stricken sojourn he was compelled to make abroad, rarely found him down-hearted and there were few men who were better company.

George Hudson's will is an extraordinary document, bearing in mind that he was once one of the very richest men in England and the proud owner of the Londesborough estate, Newby Park, 44 Monkgate, Albert Gate, plus property in Whitby and on the outskirts of York. He left under £200. This is the text of the will, now in Somerset House, in full:

This is the last will and testament of me, George Hudson, of the Carlton Club in the County of Middlesex. I make this twenty-fourth day of February one thousand eight hundred and fifty eight. I give, devise and bequeath all my real and personal estate and effects whatsoever and of what nature or kind whatsoever subject to the payment of my just debts funeral and testamentary expenses unto my two sons, George Hudson and William Hudson, their heirs, executors, administrators and assigns in the following proportions namely two thirds thereof to my son George Hudson and the remaining third to my son William Hudson. But I hereby request that before the division of my said estate and effects as aforesaid they will endeavour as far as may be to carry out my views and wishes respecting my daughter Ann, the wife of Count Zuminski, and I also give to my said two sons for their own use and benefit in the proportions aforesaid all my estate right and interest in the Spanish Railway now in the course of construction by me in conjunction with George Mould and I request my said two sons to advise with my friends James Richardson and Henry Richardson of the City of York, Solicitors whenever they may have occasion for professional advice or assistance. Lastly I hereby appoint my said two sons George Hudson and William Hudson joint executors of this my Will and I declare that they shall not be answerable the one for the other of them and by no means for involuntary losses and that they shall be allowed their reasonable costs or expenses occasioned in or about this my Will for witness whereof I, the said George Hudson, the Testator and for his last will and testament in the presence of us present at the same time who in his presence and the presence of each other have subscribed our names as witnesses, James Richardson and Charles Edmund Gold.

This will was witnessed on 11 July 1872 on oath by George Hudson's two remaining sons, George and William, who – once upon a time – would have expected to have received rather more than £100 each and a stake in a worthless Spanish railway company. But their father had given them both the best start in the world by sending them first to Harrow and then to Oxford University. Neither were in the least ungrateful, or disappointed, that their final share of their father's worldly goods was not as lucrative as it once might have been. They had embarked upon their own careers and were more than happy to be independent and self-sufficient.

In Leslie Burgess's melodramatic play about George Hudson, *Sounding Brass*, the younger George is portrayed as a self-satisfied prig, who strongly disapproves of his father's rampant capitalism and refuses to follow in his footsteps, either as a railway magnate or as an MP. This, like most of Burgess's play, is an imaginative reworking of the truth. In reality George qualified as a barrister after leaving Oxford and practised on the north-eastern circuit, living at Monkwearmouth Grange in Sunderland. He then secured a safe position as an Inspector of Factories and led a peaceful, uneventful life – in stark contrast to his father's – until he died in 1909, aged eighty. He married Hannah Singleton, youngest daughter of the Rev. W. R. Griesbach, of Millington, near Pocklington in East Yorkshire in 1879, but they had no children. He is buried in Dorking, unlike his mother Elizabeth and brother William, who were buried at Scrayingham.

William, meanwhile, had trained and qualified as a doctor after leaving Oxford. He settled in London and lived near his mother in Hindon Street, Pimlico. Tragedy struck, however, only five years after his father's death, when he was hit and killed by a train at Victoria Underground Station in February 1876. The irony, given his father's role in the development of Britain's railways, of the manner of his death is immense and the symmetry is disconcerting. William, who loved both his parents dearly, never married.

Ann, the pretty little schoolgirl who had been befriended by the Duke of Wellington at her Hampstead finishing school, had grown up to be a countess, albeit a Polish one! She only lived to be forty-four, though, and died in Berlin in November 1874. Nor did she have children, which meant that George and Elizabeth Hudson had no grandchildren and, therefore, no direct descendants.

There are today, however, plenty of Hudsons living in Yorkshire and further afield who claim the Railway King as an ancestor and are exceptionally proud of their connection with the great man, as they should be. It is significant that there is scarcely a Hudson in North Yorkshire who does not believe that he or she is related (somehow) to George. Clearly the passage of time has highlighted his achievements and dimmed his mistakes and misdemeanours, so far as his relations are concerned.

David Hudson Smith, who runs a printing firm in the pretty little market town of Easingwold, some twenty miles away from George Hudson's birthplace of Howsham, is descended from the family of Susanna Smith. Susanna, who died in June 1810 and is buried at Scrayingham, was George's paternal grandmother. Susanna was eighty-six when she died and will doubtless have had memories of young George, playing in the Howsham fields and helping about the farm. David Hudson Smith says, with more than a hint of pride:

> Some people might think that my relationship with George Hudson is somewhat distant or tenuous, but I don't agree. I am very proud to be descended from the family of such an important and hard-working man, who achieved more than most people could even dream about in his lifetime. There is little doubt that he made York into the most important railway centre in the north of England and transformed its fortunes in the process. I would suggest that, if Hudson had not made all the railways come to York (which he did, even if he didn't actually say those very words), the city would now be a backwater like Lincoln.
>
> It is interesting that our family added the name of Hudson to our name of Smith in 1844 when George was just about to reach the height of his fame and fortune. I am sorry to say that we dropped it briefly when he fell from power and fled to France, but it is reinstated now. That is our way to remember a great man.

It is deeply ironic that David Hudson Smith, in his capacity as a respected and accomplished printer of local history books, has published the two volumes of *George Hudson: The Railway King* by Dr Alf Peacock: ironic because, as we have seen, Dr Peacock presents George Hudson in the most unflattering light. But as he points out:

It would have been wrong for me to have refused to print Dr Peacock's books because I disagreed with his conclusions. It is not the business of printers or publishers to challenge or censor what an historian says, however much they disapprove of what is being written. Personally I think Dr Peacock's dislike of George Hudson stems from their different political persuasions. George was an out-and-out capitalist and Dr Peacock is, shall we say, a little more to the left. That means that Dr Peacock sees my ancestor's behaviour from a more critical perspective.

In my view there is no way that George Hudson can be likened to Robert Maxwell, as one of two historians and modern commentators have tried to do. It is true that some of his accounting practices were somewhat suspect, but no one minded until the dividends plummeted. In any case, most railway entrepreneurs in the mid-nineteenth century behaved in exactly the same manner. Maxwell, meanwhile, was an unprincipled crook. More importantly, though, George Hudson left an amazing legacy behind him whilst Maxwell left only anger and debt.

That, in a nutshell, is why I am proud to be related to such an important man as George Hudson. I am delighted that there are now efforts in the pipeline to completely rehabilitate my famous ancestor, which is no less than he deserves. He wasn't perfect, but then who is? If the city of

York is finally going to acknowledge the debt it owes to him, then I, for one, would be so pleased. It is long overdue. A statue or a monument, for example, would be a fitting tribute.

Mrs Ivy Wilson (née Hudson), a sprightly seventy-eight-year-old who now lives at Camden, near Sydney, in Australia, is equally proud of her distant relation:

> I was brought up in York and I was well aware of the influence, both good and bad, that my ancestor was supposed to have had on the city. I was educated in Acomb, a suburb of York, and the school had a Hudson House. That was named after George and I was proud of that. My name was special because of him. That made me feel special in turn.
>
> I am well aware that I am not a direct relation – no one is – but the family is definitely descended from the Howsham Hudsons. My sister Dora, who was a keen student of our family history, had loads of cuttings all about George, together with a medal which he had been given by the city of York in recognition of all his work. Unfortunately Dora died recently and all her Hudson memorabilia was thrown away. I think the medal has gone too, which is an absolute tragedy. I don't suppose it was worth a lot of money, but it would have proved, once and for all, that the city of York did care for George Hudson, though not nearly as much as he cared for it. Either way, I think a lot of George's secrets have gone to the grave with Dora.
>
> But that does not mean that our family will forget all about George Hudson, the great Railway King. Far from it. We were all very resentful that his reputation has been

damaged and do not like the fact that George Leeman has got all the glory – and the statue. We believe that that statue should have been of George Hudson (indeed the money that was raised to build the statue in the first place was for a statue of George) and we think it is unfair that visitors to York are led to believe that Leeman was the more important man. That is clearly nonsense.

Ivy Wilson's granddaughter, Lindy Hymes, agrees. Mrs Hymes, who lives in York, and is a keen student of her ancestor, grew up among all sorts of rumours about the Railway King:

One of the most interesting was that he had a huge sexual appetite and had a string of mistresses throughout his life including, believe it or not, when he was in exile in France. I have tried my very hardest to substantiate this and I cannot. I do know that he was expelled from Howsham when he was 15 for fathering an illegitimate child and I often wonder what became of this child. Could the child, for example, have had children? If so, then there may well be some direct descendants of George Hudson after all, although they most probably don't know it.

It is quite possible that the 'bastardy incident' in Howsham led to these rumours about his promiscuity. But I am also fascinated by the relationship he had with his wife Elizabeth. Although he came back to her at the end, once his exile in France was over, he spent a long time away from her when he was in exile. I know he wasn't in the best of health in France, but I cannot see him declining some kind and comforting female companionship. We were always told that our ancestor had mistresses, and there's no smoke without fire. On the other hand, there's no proof and the unfortunate loss of my great-aunt Dora's documents probably means that there never will be.

However interesting his sexual habits might be, though, I think it is more important to dwell on his achievements and his influence on the city of York, which was immense. As I was growing up, my family used to say that the influence of our ancestor was everywhere in York, and they were right. The city might have tried to airbrush him from its history, but no one can completely rewrite or obliterate the past. York is a major railway city because of him, it is as simple as that. Personally I don't think that's anything to be ashamed of.

I have also found evidence that George Hudson, contrary to rumour and legend, was a very generous man. For example, in 1845 a committee was set up to start a Ragged School for the poor in York and two rooms were hired in Bedern, the area where a lot of the city's poor lived. The school opened in 1847, but not very many people came at first, especially in the mornings. As a result the committee started to give the children breakfast, and the bill for this was met by George Hudson out of his own pocket. This piece of selfless generosity enabled the school to flourish and it was transformed into an Industrial School, housed in the old workhouse in Marygate. I like to think that this streak of generosity remains in our family today. We all enjoy giving, and I certainly enjoyed discovering that George had a kind and generous side to his character.

I think it is very important to take this side of his character into account when discussing and analysing him. If he was an out-and-out crook and blatant fraudster, then he would not have been interested in helping the Ragged School in York. But I suspect the Ragged School reminded him of his comparatively poor origins and he was happy to help those less fortunate than himself. Now I am not for a moment saying that his main motivation in setting up all those railway companies was to help others. But, by the same token, it wasn't simply to make himself rich. He had a wider vision – and it is that vision which has been forgotten, or ignored, by all his opponents. I don't think George deserved that and I'm not just saying this because he's family. He wasn't perfect, but neither were those who attacked him. I think it is now time to put the record straight and for York to properly honour the man who made the city great. Come on, York City Council, it's over to you now.

The final word, however, must go to Henry Hudson of Clifton in York. When Mr Hudson retired from a life of working on the railways in York in December 1968, he brought to an end a family association which stretched all the way back to that fateful meeting in Mrs Tomlinson's Hotel in 1833. Of his great-great-uncle, Henry Hudson said: 'From a commercial point of view, he was the greatest railwayman who ever lived.'

Now you should not, indeed you cannot, argue with that!

CHAPTER EIGHTEEN

The Verdict is Delivered

George Hudson was no mere speculator,
but a projector of great discernment,
courage and rich enterprise

William Gladstone

Although George Hudson had slipped out of public life, and out of the public's consciousness, since his spectacular fall from grace more than twenty years previously, his death did cause the obituary writers to sharpen their pens and jog their memories in an effort to pay a proper tribute to a great entrepreneur. It is refreshing to report that most of these writers were as fair and as kind to Hudson as he had been to both his friends and his enemies following his demise.

The most balanced, and accurate, obituary of George Hudson appeared in *The Times* on 16 December 1871. It read as follows:

We have to record today the death of one whose name has long been used to point the moral of vaulting ambition and unstable fortune. A new generation has arisen since George

Hudson was the Railway King. Those to whom his face and figure and voice were familiar, who added to the crush at his entertainments, and listened to or retailed the anecdotes respecting him, are to be found only among the middle-aged members of the House of Commons or the most seasoned frequenters of London society. There was a time when not to know him was to argue one's self unknown, now he is only a tradition.

The first tide in his affairs led on to fortune, but he was afterwards stranded, and neither he nor his schemes could float. A quarter of a century ago he turned all that he touched to gold; in after years his name was enough to wither the prospectus on which it was printed. The world which blindly trusted him, which cringed to him and flattered him, avenged itself by excessive and savage reprobation . . .

He was a man who united largeness of view with wonderful speculative courage. He went in for bigger things than anyone else and was for two or three years looked upon as having the key to untold treasures.

The *York Herald* (23 December), which had swallowed up Hudson's old enemy *The Yorkshireman*, was far fairer than the latter paper would ever have been, saying:

Mr Arthur Halps has just told the world, in his Thoughts Upon Government, that if he was asked to point out the men in his experience of public affairs who have shown the most remarkable competency for the conduct of business, they would, in several instances, prove to be men of very limited education. That George Hudson was one of these men is impossible to doubt. His history and the influence he exercised without apparent effort over the hard-headed money-getting men of his generation proved the general belief in his competency; and you could not talk with him or note his singular mixture of shrewdness and simplicity without finding that his education had been limited indeed. He never lost the broad Yorkshire accent, and never affected greater refinement of manner than is appropriate to the provincial shopkeeper of the old school.

But the *Herald*, inevitably, could not compete with the *Yorkshire Gazette*. In an editorial written by James Foster, the paper commented:

The mental and moral nature of Mr Hudson, as proved by deeds which, never meant to be known cannot be specified, is as necessary to a conception of his character as his public acts. He did great good by stealth; he availed himself of his riches to assist the needy; he helped scores of persons through improvident or unfortunate undertakings; he made loans to many without the least prospect of payment. Much of his benevolence was spontaneous – many a one has benefited who never knew from where the favour came. Many an afflicted widow and embarrassed family were relieved who never knew the alms giver. The public charities of York and Yorkshire found in him a munificent benefactor. Such was the man for whom future days of adversity and gloom were in store.

For half a century we have possessed the friendship and regard of him of who we now write. Whether in sunshine or in cloud, we ever found him the same generous hearted man – one who scorned a mean action – was not inflated and lifted up by flatterers in his prosperity; and in his adversity he ever relied on the rectitude of his own heart for consolation, and bore all his adversities with a fortitude becoming a Christian.

The *Sunderland Times* of 19 December was equally gracious:

The death of George Hudson is an event which recalls many memories of what are now long by-gone days, but days pregnant with vital, lasting consequences for the world. The Railway King, who rose suddenly like a splendid meteor in the commercial horizon, fell again after a few years with the same startling velocity.

During his splendid reign he originated, forwarded and completed many gigantic public works which might otherwise never have been undertaken or finished yet and which, though in most cases the reverse of remunerative to the original shareholders, have now for a long time been highly lucrative and, indeed, desirable.

George Hudson's whole career was a romance and whenever his life shall be written by someone able to do the man and his work justice, it will be one of the most entertaining, suggestive and useful books in the language . . . Mr Hudson, though an old Tory, was practically a revolutionist. His name will forever be associated with a gigantic forward movement which is fast changing the physical, social and moral face of the world, bringing all tribes and nations together and going far to annihilate distance . . . The foibles of such a man ought to be buried in his tomb. In George Hudson's case, we are sure they will be.

The *Railway Times*, seemingly oblivious to Hudson's role in the rapid development of Britain's rail network, recorded his death with fourteen bland lines on 23 December. There was no hint of comment, either positive or adverse, and the obituary writer dwelt purely on the blindingly obvious. Hudson deserved better than this anodyne account of his life and death.

The *Daily News*, thankfully, provided it with the following obituary which was printed in several provincial newspapers, including the *Yorkshire Post*, within a week of Hudson's death.

This is scarcely the time to be dwelling upon the fever which beset the nation during railway mania, or for analysing the part played in it by George Hudson. If he was one of the chief offenders, he was assuredly one of the chief sufferers, and it is tolerably notorious now that some of the practices for which he was so heavily punished have not always been held sufficient to ostracise the commercial people who have been guilty of them. 'Hudson never split on his friends,' once remarked an authority in the railway world, 'or there might have been some curious stories to hear about people whose fingers you'd think were incapable of being soiled.'

Punch, which had poked fun at Hudson ever since his spectacular fall from grace, could not refrain from some poetic sarcasm at his expense, although the real targets of the magazine's satire are the men who worshipped the Railway King in his heyday and then attacked him in his decline. The poetry is marginally better than the Whitby street ballad which sung Hudson's praises in 1865, but it remains pretty ropy stuff (apart from the last verse):

He moved a monarch, blunt and bluff:
To hear was to obey!
Who of us could bow low enough,
On his gold-paven way?
Lords, Cits, Respectable and Rough,
Church, Court, all owned his sway!

So he we fawned on so, and feared,
With curses down was cast,
King Hudson had no statue reared,
But forth to exile past,
To climb the stranger's stairs, and beard
Penury's bitter blast.

Faint tidings of his lot we had
From far across the main,
A fat old man, poor, shabby, sad,
Of casual dinners fain:
Their doubtful recognition glad
To give men back again.

Till some on whom he smiled when king
Though shame that this should be,
And clubbing their alms-gathering
Bought an annuity.
They said it is a sorry thing
A Beggared King to see!

And poor KING HUDSON clutched the gift
And grateful was therefore,
The weight of poverty to shift,

The Wolf keep from his door;
His pittance used, they say, with thrift,
Till int'rest's fruit it bore.

Now, from his ups and downs not loath,
He rests, where Kings and churls are one;
He scaled heights, sounded depths, with both:
As basely fawned as spit upon.
Should men who hailed his mushroom growth,
Cast at his humble grave the stone.

This final verse, which addresses the Railway King's turbulent life and the different emotions that he aroused, underlines the complex nature of the man and his achievements. It is, therefore, hardly surprising that Hudson's biographers have been unable to agree on whether he was one of the greatest Englishmen of the nineteenth century or a fraudster on a gigantic scale. Significantly, there is little love lost between those who have faithfully chronicled his life.

The first attempt to make some sense of the Hudson hurricane, and to put it into historical perspective, came from D. Morier Evans in his essay *Facts, Failures and Frauds*, in 1859. While taking a dim view of some of the Railway King's accounting practices, Evans does recognise that Hudson was a railway pioneer in nineteenth-century Britain and accepts that his vision, courage and drive were crucial in the early development of the railways in this country, well ahead of our European rivals.

He sums up Hudson, who was still MP for Sunderland at the time of writing, thus:

The wisdom of his policy of amalgamation has since been justified on the material evidence of prosperity which have attended the working of the system. Taking a retrospective glance at the whole of his career, there are many features in it deserving credit . . . He has done the state some service.

It was pitiable to notice the rapid alteration in the robust alternation and the rotund form of the great railway magnate a few months after these discoveries [of fraud] and although he evidently endeavoured, with the natural force of his character, to brave out the mighty hostilities waged against him, the proof was there in the individual that they were not without strong influence on his constitution.

A massive pillar, as he was, centred on himself, but yet keenly susceptible to external influences, he was tormented by every contending element. He nevertheless sustained himself with an apparent amount of fortitude which was truly astonishing and, except to those personally acquainted with him, almost passing belief.

Curiously, Evans's stimulating essay is largely ignored by Hudson's subsequent biographers, possibly because it was overshadowed by the first definitive work on the man. This was *The Railway King: A Study of George Hudson and the Business Morals of His Times* by Richard S. Lambert, published in 1934.

This highly readable book has attracted some ferocious criticism, notably from Dr Alf Peacock of York. Certainly Lambert's book has its faults, the language is somewhat flowery and facts – on occasion – are treated in cavalier fashion, but I believe it is a formidable achievement. Written quickly, with mountains of original source material to sift through, it is an intelligent and sympathetic appreciation of Hudson set against the backdrop of hypocritical mid-Victorian morality. Lambert admits that Hudson made errors of judgement, and accepts that his financial methods were dubious, but believes that his achievements outweighed his faults and that many other Victorian entrepreneurs would have behaved in exactly the same manner to achieve their objectives. The end, in other words, justified the means – and Hudson's shareholders heartily agreed with this approach, so long as dividends from his companies remained at ten per cent.

It is not Lambert's errors of facts which annoy Dr Peacock so much as his sympathy for his subject. It transpires, as one reads Dr Peacock's own well-researched volumes on Hudson, that he loathes him. It is intriguing that a historian should devote such a huge amount of time and effort to writing about someone with whom he has such a natural antipathy, both politically and intellectually.

Dr Peacock explains his interest in Hudson as follows:

He was an important person in York's history, but that does not stop him from being a scoundrel and a knave. I have devoted some 10 years of my life and I've got to know him pretty well. But that does not mean that I have grown to like him. He was a bully and a swindler in his heyday and treated people badly.

I do have a sneaking respect for him in his old age, however. He took his punishment and his exile extremely well and never complained or betrayed anyone once. That showed a very different side to his character and makes him a more rounded human being. A cynic might say that he never betrayed anyone because he was paid off, but there is no evidence for this.

Nevertheless, George Hudson ultimately was a deeply flawed person and I would not agree with any move to rehabilitate him in York, or anywhere else, for that matter. You might as well erect a monument to Hitler or Dr Crippen.

The plot thickens, meanwhile, when Dr Peacock launches into an attack on a book entitled *George Hudson of York*, published by Clapham in 1971. He writes in his essay 'George Hudson and the Historians' (York History, 1974) that 'a limited study of Hudson's career appeared in 1971, rushed out to meet the centenary of his death, and, because of that, was marred by a locust-plague of printers' errors, like a war-time novel'. Elsewhere he writes: 'A short, unsatisfactory book on George as a York figure appeared in 1971.' How strange to discover that this short, unsatisfactory book was written by David Joy and one Dr A. J. Peacock!

Nor is Dr Peacock too keen on the most recent biography, *George Hudson*, by Brian Bailey, published in 1995. This workman-like effort, which charts, with a steady if uninspired hand, Hudson's rise and fall, provoked an interesting reaction from the good doctor:

> I'm afraid that this book does not add very much to anyone's knowledge of Hudson. A lot of it appears to be based on my research, but the author never approached me personally. In fact, I don't even know who he is, although I gather he edits children's books. Certainly it is not a very good book at all. Mr Bailey has tried to argue that Hudson is some kind of hero, but his facts simply do not support his case.

In a review of Bailey's book, entitled *Hudson, Goodrick and Glory* by J. P. Johnson and published by York History in 1996, the author writes of a 'new book on George Hudson by P. Bailey, which has been reviewed in the *Yorkshire Evening News*'. This was an inauspicious start, since the book was by B. Bailey and reviewed in the *Yorkshire Evening Press*. No matter. J. P. Johnson soon gets into his stride:

There is a great difference in the presentation of Bailey's work and that of Dr Peacock. The latter uses proper foot-noting whereas the former is sparing in this respect – a fact to be regretted surely. Bailey's text is short for a study of a man who lived to be 70 and had numerous careers. What has he added to Peacock's account? A few corrections, it is true, but his work comes out as something like a précis of Peacock's two volumes. They were written because Lambert's work was the only study of the old Railway King in existence and because it is so bad. There is in a public collection a corrected version of Richard Stanton Lambert's work and it is incredible to look at. Peacock never missed an opportunity to go for Lambert, Bailey wrote. Well, given his intentions (to put the record straight) he could hardly leave him alone. Historians should be grateful for that monumental piece of putting the record straight. Bailey, incidentally, neglects to use the first of Peacock's corrective articles – that in the *Journal of the Railway and Canal Historical Society*, an excellent publication.

Clearly J. P. Johnson is a great fan of Dr Peacock and has an intense (if not obsessive) interest in his work. Well, that is not really surprising, since J. P. Johnson and Dr Peacock are – believe it or not – one and the same person! Dr Peacock admitted this, a little shamefacedly, when I inquired about the origins and whereabouts of Mr Johnson.

In the light of this information, the rest of this acerbic and disparaging review – with its constant references to Peacock's excellent biography of Hudson – makes perfect sense. Here is a sample:

So *The Rise and Fall* (by Bailey) uses the same sources as Peacock, the same local newspapers, the same secondary publication and the documents, articles, government papers etc. Missing from this section is Peacock's 'York in the Age of Reform', and in it is a misleading note about York History . . . But why did not Bailey build on Peacock's work? How could this be done? Probably by using company records. Why did Bailey not use these to test the Peacock contentions? Why go over the same ground? Why, indeed. Why also use familiar quotations (frequently the same as those called on by Peacock) so often – and why at such length? Bailey's predecessor as Hudson biographer said why he did so (it had to do with correcting the hold the dreadful Lambert work exerted). But in a short work like Bailey's it seems excessive. The hard work sorting out Hudson and Lambert had been done when Bailey's work appeared. A considerable number of sources have been overlooked . . .

There is much more in the same vein, extolling the virtues of Dr Peacock and denigrating Brian Bailey. J. P. Johnson (aka Dr Peacock) even draws upon that well-known publication, the *Bulletin of the American Fern Society* (Vol. 20, No. 2), to attack Bailey over the spelling of Count Suminski, Hudson's son-in-law. I accept that Bailey's biography is a trifle pedestrian, but it does not warrant this ferocious and sustained attack from a fellow historian who blows his own trumpet whilst hiding behind a pseudonym.

There is an even more serious point to be made. Dr Peacock never tires of telling us that it is his duty to tell the truth and expose George Hudson as a fraudster and a villain for the sake of posterity. That is as may be. But if Dr Peacock is such a fastidious guardian of the truth, why does he wilfully mislead students of Hudson by reviewing Brian Bailey's biography under a bogus name? By pretending to be J. P. Johnson, when he is in fact Dr Alf Peacock, he has ensured that some crucial late-twentieth-century source material for Hudson is now invalid and, sad to say, totally useless. Ironically, had some pro-Hudsonian journalist or historian done the same thing in the nineteenth century, they would have been damned, like Richard S. Lambert, by Peacock's vitriol-drenched pen. Ultimately, Alf Peacock's sly attempt to score points off a fellow biographer has completely destroyed his credibility as an historian.

Brian Bailey himself was unaware that Dr Peacock had used a pseudonym in his review (indeed this was my little secret, until the publication of this book). But he is none too impressed with the good doctor anyway, taking him to task on a number of counts. He criticises Dr Peacock for 'throwing little new light on Hudson the man', which is a damning verdict on Dr Peacock's 150,000-plus words and copious footnotes, and he picks up on a number of errors of fact – just as Dr Peacock did with Lambert. How George Hudson himself, who dealt in grand visions rather than minutiae, would have been amused by these petty, vicious and, on occasions, deceitful arguments in his name.

There are, however, a couple of important misconceptions about George Hudson that do need to be cleared up. For example, he is often quoted as saying, in his Yorkshire dialect, 'Mak all t'railways cum t'York'. He never made this comment. Indeed he was obsessed with preventing Edmund Beckett Denison's Great Northern Railway Company from building a direct London-to-York route. But that did not mean, as Dr Peacock ingeniously tries to argue, that Hudson did not have the interests of York at heart. Nor does it mean that Hudson did not wish York to be a major railway centre. He did.

It was also widely believed that George Hudson's wax effigy at Madame Tussaud's, which was first unveiled in 1848, was hurriedly removed when he fell from grace. This misconception stemmed from a cartoon in *Punch*. In fact Hudson's wax effigy survived him and was not removed until 1877 – six years after his death. No doubt the knowledge that this effigy was standing proudly in a popular London tourist attraction, while he was rotting away in poverty-stricken exile in France, would have brought a wry smile to the old man's face.

Meanwhile, *The Yorkshireman*, which published some scurrilous items about Hudson in its time, alleged that Hudson had been awarded a doctorate in philosophy by a German university. There is no evidence for this and it is likely that *The Yorkshireman* used this false story, allegedly based on a report in a Liverpool paper, to make fun of Hudson's lack of formal education. If so, the paper stooped disgracefully low – especially since it was meant to be both radical and enlightened. Unfortunately, this rumour was then repeated by Richard S. Lambert and could so easily have passed from folklore into fact.

Finally, and most importantly, it is wrong to portray George Hudson as a cynical crook. He was never criminally prosecuted for his alleged offences, which is interesting, given the wave of anti-Hudson sentiment which swept the country between 1849 and 1852. He never openly broke the law, he simply took advantage of its deficiencies. That enabled him to defend himself plausibly and cogently, especially since he himself did not believe that he was a criminal. And why should he? Nobody complained about his 'sharp accounting practices' when dividends were high, and they had ample opportunity to do so. It was only when dividends fell that the Railway King was left exposed and friendless. The hypocrisy and self-interest of some of Hudson's shareholders still beggars belief today.

Yet Dr Peacock, armed with thousands upon thousands of words, still moves in for the kill – by denouncing George Hudson as a criminal and suggesting, in a chapter devoted entirely to Lambert, that Hudson's sympathetic biographer was a highly dubious character. Time and time again Dr Peacock takes the side of George Leeman, a self-seeking opportunist if ever there was one, against George Hudson. In his essay 'Leeman and York Politics' (1981), Dr Peacock accepts that Leeman had complete control over York City Council once Hudson had fallen, but denies that he was a 'greedy tyrant' like his predecessor. He fails to support this with any substantial evidence. In any case, I would suggest that it is preferable to be a 'greedy tyrant' than a man like Leeman who was deeply implicated in the kidnapping and subsequent imprisonment of the ailing and elderly George Hudson in Whitby in 1865. Dr Peacock thinks it is unfair that today George Hudson is more famous than George Leeman. In fact it would be a travesty if it were the other way round.

Overall, posterity (Dr Peacock excluded) has treated George Hudson rather more kindly than his contemporaries. The scale of Hudson's achievement, the breadth of his vision, his enormous energy, his capacity for hard work and, last but not least, his humility and integrity in the face of poverty and exile, are now beginning to be appreciated. There is one city, however, where the attitude towards the Railway King remains ambivalent and confused. How ironic that this city should be York, the place that Hudson loved, and benefited, the most.

CHAPTER NINETEEN

York, the City that dare not Speak his Name

The sleepy old archiepiscopal city of York would, indeed, willingly have us forget that short but vivid chapter of her history when she allowed herself to be seduced away from her traditional repose and dignity, and be committed to take part (even a central part) in the national scramble for filthy lucre and commercial pre-eminence. Railway business was the occasion of the seduction; and George Hudson, the linen draper of College Street, was the seducer

Richard S. Lambert

There stands, some 150 yards from York's magnificent station, a marble statue. The subject of the statue, a forbidding-looking man in a Victorian frock coat, is grasping a roll of papers in his right hand and is gazing determinedly ahead of him. Clearly he is a man of some importance to merit such a prestigious position in the city which is steeped in tradition and overflowing with historical jewels. Many visitors and, indeed, some residents believe that this formidable man is George Hudson, the great Railway King, who presided over one of the proudest periods of York's modern history. They are wrong. The man is George Leeman, Hudson's greatest enemy, who ultimately destroyed him. The irony is immense, the symbolism telling. The erection of a memorial to Leeman was the ultimate rejection of Hudson and all that he stood for. York, in Pontius Pilate-like fashion, had washed its hands of one of its greatest sons.

It is doubly ironic that the citizens of York had subscribed £20,000 to the cost of a statue to mark the city's pre-eminent role in the growth of the railways in the nineteenth century. Originally the money was going to have been spent on a statue of George Hudson, but Hudson's fall from grace in 1848, followed by lurid revelations about his business dealings, turned York against him. Therefore it was decided, with a kind of twisted logic, to honour George Leeman instead. What a convenient way to soothe an over-ripe conscience. And how reassuring to have Leeman, the epitome of moral and financial rectitude, gazing out across the city, instead of Hudson, the man who had brought shame on York.

That is how the city fathers would have felt when the statue to Leeman was built. It mattered not that Leeman himself resorted to base tactics to destroy Hudson or that Leeman, without Hudson's achievements, would have been a run-of-the-mill provincial solicitor. It is often argued, notably by Leeman's great champion Dr Peacock, that Leeman was the white knight in shining armour who rode to York's rescue as it was sinking under the weight of Hudson's gross misdemeanours. That is misleading. It is more accurate to suggest that Leeman, the canniest of businessmen, helped to destroy Hudson for his own ends. It is no coincidence that, with Hudson out of the way, Leeman fulfilled his dual ambitions of becoming Lord Mayor of York (three times) and the chairman of the North Eastern Railway

Company. Worse still, he helped to put an ageing and infirm Hudson in jail in 1865 to prevent him becoming MP for Whitby. Poor Hudson was hardly a threat to Leeman then, so the so-called knight in shining armour was acting out of pure vindictiveness.

Does such a man deserve a statue? Well, the city of York certainly thought so. And not just a statue, either. Leeman Road is one of the most popular routes into the city, as it snakes through some of the city's less salubrious suburbs, before culminating at the foot of his statue on the edge of the city centre. However, it would be stooping to Leeman-like levels of vindictiveness to lobby for the removal of either Leeman's statue or his name from Leeman Road. It would be much better, surely, to redress the balance by honouring George Hudson in a similar fashion.

At one stage in York's history, Hudson's name was everywhere – in the city's streets, newspapers, churches and council chamber. Now it takes a good deal of detective work to unearth any trace of Hudson in his beloved city at all. There are a couple of perfunctory plaques, one outside the old drapers' shop in College Street and one outside 44 Monkgate (where, incidentally, his beautiful garden is now a car park), and an inscription, dated 1838, on Victoria Bar off Nunnery Lane. Then there is a George Hudson Street, but this street must rank as the ugliest, dingiest and dirtiest street in the entire city. It links Rougier Street with Micklegate, but has no other discernible purpose today at all. It is home to a boarded-up supermarket, a couple of council offices, a tarted-up pub and an Indian take-away. The fact that the pub was once called The Railway King, but is now part of a national chain, simply adds insult to injury. Is this really the best York can do to honour one of its most famous sons?

It is true that a new (and desperately ugly) office block off Tanner Row, belonging to British Rail's Eastern Region, was named

Hudson House in 1968. The decision to remember the Railway King in this way was taken by 500 railway staff and it is gratifying that Hudson was chosen ahead of George Stephenson and George Leeman. Hudson House, comprising two four-storey and two six-storey office blocks, now houses Railtrack, GNER and Arriva personnel following the privatisation of British Rail and is a nerve centre of York's business life. Hudson supporters are delighted that Hudson House towers over Leeman's statue (which is just two hundred yards away), but the sad fact remains that Leeman's statue greets many visitors to the city, while Hudson House is off the beaten track.

It is worth pointing out that York, together with the north-east of England, boasts some of the finest railway architecture in England, primarily because of George Hudson. Hudson's close relationship with George Townsend Andrews, who designed the first York Station at Toft Green, as well as the De Grey Rooms, guaranteed that the north of England has more listed railway buildings than anywhere else in the country outside London. Hudson had the money and the drive, Andrews the intellect and the aesthetic vision. Together they ensured that the railway revolution was not just about blood, sweat, tears and dividends, but about beauty as well.

Meanwhile, the York headquarters of GNER and Railtrack lie directly between Hudson House and the statue of Leeman. These headquarters house a fascinating copy of a portrait of George Hudson by John Andrews, painted in 1845. Hudson is wearing his trademark white waistcoat in this portrait, which is said now to be in the possession of the Hudson family. It is worth seeing this picture, even if it is only a copy. But beware. It is symptomatic of the perceived lack of interest in the great man that it is hidden away in a boardroom and that anyone wishing to see it has to jump through a series of infuriating bureaucratic hoops. There is another portrait in York's Mansion House, this one by Francis Grant, which is afforded a somewhat higher profile, but it is still difficult and time-consuming to get permission to infiltrate the Mansion House's inner sanctum. Ironically, the only one of these three portraits which is on show to the general public is in Sunderland, where Hudson is treated with the respect and honour that York simply cannot muster.

The Sunderland portrait, also by Sir Francis Grant, is housed in the splendid Monkwearmouth Station Museum, overlooking the River Wear. The museum, which is dedicated to George Hudson and the development of the docks in Sunderland (the two are inextricably linked), is the heart-warming tribute to the Railway King and a potent reminder of his tremendous legacy to the town. The station itself, built in 1848, is far grander than the majority of the stations which were springing up across Britain at the time. This was because Hudson wanted to mark the successful start to his career as MP for Sunderland and to make a permanent impression on his adoptive town. He achieved both aims with consummate ease and the station's classical portico and Ionic columns make it one of Sunderland's most attractive buildings today. In 1848, however, the station's beauty was secondary to its strategic and practical importance. At the time there was no railway bridge over the River Wear and passengers wishing to cross into the town centre had to walk or take a horse-drawn cab to the other side of the river.

Monkwearmouth Station decreased in importance when the North Eastern Railway Company extended the line across the Wear and built a new station called Sunderland Central in 1879. Nevertheless it remained in use for another ninety years, until it closed to passengers in 1967. The line, however, remains open — which gives the museum an air of vibrancy and authenticity as trains pass the old station every day. It is also lovingly preserved and cared for and a potent reminder of the town's glorious industrial past.

George Hudson, most appropriately, dominates Monkwearmouth Station Museum. As you walk in, Grant's imposing portrait on the left immediately grasps the attention and does not let go. Painted in 1846, at the height of Hudson's fame and fortune, it is a faithful, if slightly flattering portrayal. At the time Grant was the most renowned painter of society in the country, following his excellent portrait of Queen Victoria a couple of years earlier, and that of Hudson was exhibited at the Royal Academy in 1847. The trademark white waistcoat is very much to the fore, as is the railway bill held firmly in the right hand, but the most striking feature of the painting is Hudson's face. Is there just a hint of suspicion and wariness in those intelligent and penetrating eyes? It would not be surprising if there were, as his enemies were beginning to circle around him, like vultures, even then.

Elsewhere in the museum, which is close to a shrine to George Hudson, are two pictures celebrating the historic opening of the South Docks in Sunderland on 20 June 1850. One is by Mark Thompson and the other by John Wilson Carmichael. In Carmichael's depiction of a day of hearty celebrations, the eye is drawn to a cheery, slightly corpulent, figure who is waving his bowler hat merrily in the air. It is George Hudson, King of the Docks for a day. A nearby audio-visual display tells the story of the Sunderland Docks and makes the point that Hudson's decision to buy the Durham and Sunderland railway, together with the Wearmouth Dock Company, in 1846, paved the way for the opening of the South Docks. Had he not done so, there is no way that Sunderland would have had a thriving dockland enterprise in the mid-nineteenth century. But because he did, the quantity of coal exported from the Wear rose by fifty-six per cent between 1851 and 1858. Thanks to George Hudson, Sunderland became a thriving port, transporting coal mined from the nearby Durham pits to all parts of the country. Fittingly, within days of his death, the Wear Commissioners decided that the Sunderland Docks should be named Hudson Dock North and Hudson Dock South.

On the way out of the museum, it is impossible not to have another look at Grant's portrait of Hudson. It is easy to get lost in thought and reflection in front of this powerful picture, but an imaginative caption writer (possibly the curator of this little gem of a museum?) brings us back to reality with the words, next to the painting: 'If it were not for George Hudson, you would not be standing here.' That is a stimulating way in which to underline Hudson's importance to Sunderland and to make the viewer think very carefully about his influence and achievements. It is a crying shame that there is nothing remotely comparable to this in York.

There are a number of ways in which the city of York could rectify this unfortunate situation, if York City Council and York Civic Trust, the two primary guardians of the city's heritage, so wished. To begin with, there should be a public monument to honour George Hudson and to underline the tremendous debt that the city owes to him. While it would be both presumptuous and precipitous of me to suggest what form this monument should take and where it should go, I do believe that a gleaming modern statue within York Station itself would be extremely appropriate. In this way, all visitors coming to, and leaving, the city would catch a glimpse of one of the main architects of its prosperity.

Secondly, it would be tremendous if either of the portraits of George Hudson in York, both sheltered from the public eye, could be placed on permanent display in York City Art Gallery. There are already a number of paintings from the Richard Nicholson collection in the gallery and it would be highly appropriate if Hudson hung beside these, since without Hudson, Nicholson would never have had the money to indulge in his expensive hobby of buying fine art. Moreover, one of the main roles of a provincial art gallery is to record and celebrate local history – and a portrait of George Hudson would be a most significant addition to the gallery's excellent collection.

Thirdly, it is disappointing, and just that little bit strange, that the National Railway Museum does not draw attention to the crucial role that George Hudson played in the development of the railways, and the development of York as a railway city, in the nineteenth century. It was precisely because York had such a rich railway history that the National Railway Museum opened there in 1974. A small room, full of Hudson memorabilia, would be an appropriate addition to the Railway Museum's excellent collection. Once upon a time there was such a collection, commemorating Hudson and his empire, at the Londesborough Arms (formerly Mrs Tomlinson's Hotel) in Petergate, York, but the pub and the collection have both long since disappeared. The collection, I gather, was dumped in a skip by some bone-headed workman, never to be seen again. Meanwhile, the railway museum, perhaps in conjunction with York City Council's Leisure Services department and the Yorkshire Tourist Board, could organise a George Hudson trail, taking in York Station, Hudson House, the old York Station on Station Rise (where you can still see the old platforms), the Mansion House, the Guildhall, Holy Trinity Church in Goodramgate, the College Street shop, with its original stone-flagged floor, and 44 Monkgate, where Hudson's elegant living room remains pretty much intact and a statuette of him stands in the hall. It would be an illuminating and rewarding tour.

Fourthly, it should not be too difficult for the planners at York

City Council to find a more salubrious road than the dreadful George Hudson Street with which to mark the Railway King's achievements. Impressive and prestigious new housing, retail and industrial developments are springing up all over York, as the city embraces the technological revolution, and they all need names. It would be fitting if George Hudson, who presided over the railway revolution in York, provided one. After all, there are a number of lesser heroes who have already been honoured in this way. Extensive research has uncovered a Hudson Court deep in a development in York's hinterland, but that is as far as it goes. A superb new housing development, which borders the station on one side and Leeman Road on the other, could so easily have carried Hudson's name. Instead it is called St Peter's Quarter. No one doubts that St Peter was a worthy disciple of Jesus, but his connection with York is tenuous, to say the least.

Finally, and arguably most importantly, it would be wonderful if York acknowledged the debt the city owed to George Hudson and apologised for the way it has treated him. In 1972, after five hundred British Rail staff had voted to name their headquarters Hudson House, Dr John Shannon, the chairman of York Civic Trust, commented that it was time York said: 'Hudson, come back, all is forgiven.'

Today, thirty years later, Dr Shannon believes that the city has still not apologised sufficiently:

There is no doubt that George Hudson made a tremendous contribution to the prosperity of York by making the city a major railway centre. This contribution is all too easily forgotten because he died in poverty and disgrace. It is time that his legacy was properly recognised. If you look at his grave in the little churchyard at Scrayingham, near Malton, it is covered in moss and weeds. It is easy to forget what a great man, and what a great citizen of York, he was.

It was York Civic Trust who campaigned successfully to have Railway Street renamed George Hudson Street and to have Hudson's portrait restored to the Mansion House walls thirty years ago. Now I think the Trust would be very interested in any plan to erect a monument to George Hudson. Such a monument would be thoroughly deserved and would be an appropriate addition to York's landscape.

It was William Shakespeare who wrote in *Julius Caesar*: 'The evil that men do lives after them, the good is oft interred with their bones.' Completely the opposite is true with George Hudson. His good lives after him, and York especially has been the beneficiary.

Hugh Murray, York's premier historian, is also in no doubt that George Hudson has been harshly treated:

> OK, so Hudson paid his dividends out of capital and bent the rules a little, but there have been far worse crimes than that. Much more importantly, he laid the basis for the city of York's prosperity and enabled it to become a major railway centre. He may not have actually said that he would make all the railways come to York, but that's what he did. The city today owes him a great deal and I think it is only fair and just that he should be honoured in some way.

It does seem strange that York's two most famous criminals, Guy Fawkes and Dick Turpin, have achieved cult status in the city, whereas George Hudson – whose misdemeanours were less serious than those of either of these two rogues – remains out in the cold.

Indeed, when it was decided to rename Railway Street as George Hudson Street in 1971 to mark the centenary of Hudson's death, there was some animated correspondence in the columns of the *Yorkshire Evening Press*. It was suggested that it was immoral to honour such a shady character and the Archbishop of York, Dr Donald Coggan, was criticised for presiding over the renaming ceremony. The archbishop was unabashed, though he may well have reflected that the choice of the street to be named after George Hudson left a great deal to be desired.

It is tempting to suggest that Dr Alf Peacock, one of York's foremost historians, has added to the city's distaste for Hudson with his aggressive and negative two-volume biography. That, however, would be unfair. While Dr Peacock presents a most unflattering, and unbalanced, picture of his subject, his exhaustive research has done all Hudson scholars and fans alike a tremendous service. Dr Peacock clearly believes that Hudson was a charlatan and a fraud of Maxwellian proportions, and argues vehemently that the Railway King was interested only in promoting himself, rather than the railways or the city of York. It is perfectly possible, as well as desirable, to draw a completely different conclusion from the facts that Dr Peacock has so assiduously assembled. That is the joy of history.

However, it is reassuring, in view of York's lack of appreciation for one of its greatest benefactors, to know that the spirit of George Hudson is alive and well at Newby Park. This was Hudson's favourite house of all, and it afforded him tranquillity and refuge during his darkest days. Today it is the home of Queen Mary's, a leading Yorkshire private school for girls, and staff and pupils alike are very much aware of Hudson and his extraordinary life. This is primarily due to Darrell Buttery, the deputy headmaster, who is a keen Hudson student. Mr Buttery nearly bought 44 Monkgate when it came on the market in 1968 for £5,500 (it is now worth nearly £500,000) and he is an avid collector of Hudson memorabilia. One of his prized possessions is a splendid poster from 1846, advertising the forthcoming sale of prints of Sir Francis Grant's portrait of Hudson, which now hangs in Monkwearmouth Station Museum. These prints, part of a limited edition, were priced from two to six guineas, which is a telling reflection of his popularity at the time.

Darrell Buttery ensures that the older girls at Queen Mary's are well aware of Hudson's crucial role in the history of mid-nineteenth century Britain. They are well versed in the story of Ann Hudson and the Duke of Wellington; they know that the painter William Etty used to travel by rail to nearby Topcliffe Station (which has now disappeared off the face of the earth) before being met by Hudson in his 'carriage and four'; and they know that Newby Park, with its fine oaks, rolling lawns and peaceful River Swale, was Hudson's pride and joy, especially when the rest of the world had turned against him. The Railway King would be flattered to know that his memory arouses both interest and affection today in the very house he loved the most.

Elsewhere in George Hudson's native county, his name lives on. The sweet little country cottage where he was born, the last on the right-hand side of the main street in Howsham before the Howsham Hall School, is called Hudson's Cottage. It looks ridiculously small today, too small to house the whole Hudson clan, and it is likely the family occupied the next-door, semi-detached cottage too. There is also a George Hudson Way in Market Weighton, close to the York–Hull railway line and the Londesborough estate, which Hudson owned for just a few ill-fated years. Finally, we must not forget Hudson Street in Whitby, named in honour of the popular and prestigious West Cliff development. So, if Howsham, Market Weighton and Whitby (not to mention Queen Mary's and

Sunderland) can celebrate George Hudson's life, what is stopping York? It is high time that the city redressed the balance.

There is a deeper point to be made, too, a point which is touched upon at the end of Brian Bailey's biography. The city of York, led by the self-interested George Leeman, turned against George Hudson because he was supposedly corrupt. But who corrupted Hudson, if not York itself? When the young Hudson arrived in the city, fresh from the innocent Howsham fields, he knew precious little about business and even less about politics. He learned quickly. Having observed life closely in York from the comfort and safety of his College Street drapers' shop, he understood only too well that he had to play the game by York's rules if he wanted to succeed. The city was a jungle, and only the fittest survived and prospered. Had George Hudson displayed the virtues of a saint (as his enemies suggest he should have done and which George Leeman himself patently didn't), he would have remained in College Street for the rest of his life. York, meanwhile, would have missed out on the railway boom.

There was genuine concern in York in the 1830s that the city was falling badly behind its West Yorkshire neighbours as the effects of the industrial revolution began to become apparent. There was some serious money being generated in the West Riding, and York could only gaze across to Leeds and Bradford in envy. The city, meanwhile, was no longer the grand social centre that it had once been in the eighteenth century, and it was in danger of becoming a backwater, famous only for its fading historical treasures, its increasingly squalid houses and streets and burgeoning underclass.

It would be simplistic, of course, to attribute York's rapid rise as a railway city – with all the attendant benefits – to George Hudson alone. But the sheer force of his personality and the massive range of his vision were so instrumental in propelling York to the very forefront of the railway revolution. Moreover the foundation of the York Union Bank, Hudson's influential role in the House of Commons and his three stints as Lord Mayor gave the city a national profile in his heyday. If George Hudson was the Railway King, then the city of York was his court. Today it is time for this court, once again, to pay homage to its former king. Is that really too much to ask?

CHAPTER TWENTY

The Last Word

When a true genius appears in this world,
you may know him by this sign:
the dunces are all in confederacy against him

Jonathan Swift

One of the easiest, and most dangerous, mistakes that historians can make is to impose their own contemporary morals on their subjects. Whereas it is true that there are absolute standards of human behaviour, much of what we do occupies the grey area between right and wrong. We may, for example, do right for the wrong reasons and wrong for the right reasons. Crucially, throughout our lives, we are heavily influenced by our immediate environment. It is, therefore, both dangerous and misleading to judge the behaviour, and especially the business dealings, of George Hudson by the standards of the late twentieth and early twenty-first century. Yet that is exactly what Hudson's detractors have done. While William Gladstone, arguably the greatest statesman of the Victorian era, praised Hudson's vision, courage and entrepreneurial skills, his opponents preferred – and prefer – to call him a fraud and a villain. In the nineteenth century, these opponents were motivated by (at best) political differences and (at worst) greed, jealousy, opportunism and an inflated sense of their own worth.

So it is crucial to understand the age in which George Hudson lived and the way in which he responded to its challenges, its opportunities and its pressures. The wide-ranging and far-reaching consequences of the British industrial revolution, the most significant socio-economic phenomenon for a millennium, dominated the nineteenth century and led directly to the advent of the railways. The railways, in turn, were the most stimulating, the most revolutionary and the most dislocating of all the technological advances of the past two hundred years (with the possible exceptions of the car, the bomb and the internet). It is difficult to imagine the romance, the awe and the excitement created by the railway age, but imagine it we must if we are to understand George Hudson fully. For those who love art, J. W. M. Turner's *Rain, Steam and Speed* in the National Gallery is a wonderful starting point.

By the early 1830s the magic, and the potential, of speed had begun to infiltrate and grip Britain's psyche. These were the most exciting of times, unless, of course, you happened to be William Huskisson, the leading Conservative politician who was knocked down and killed by one of George Stephenson's trains at the opening of the Liverpool to Manchester railway in 1830. A single branch line could transform the fortunes of a community; a single viaduct could enhance a panoramic landscape; and a single station could become the jewel in a town's or city's architectural crown. Railway mania gripped almost every corner of the land and affected every class of society. It was possible to get almost anywhere by train – a situation welcomed by the lower middle and working classes whose previous contact with the world outside their front doors had been minimal. Meanwhile the network of 'iron roads', which were spreading through the heart of Britain's countryside like tentacles, provided seemingly infinite commercial possibilities for the nation's entrepreneurs – and a tremendous boost to the nation's wealth.

The young George Hudson was perfectly positioned to take advantage of the railway revolution. He was not only energetic, enterprising and clever, which are all admirable qualities, but he was also rich. Indeed, he had money to burn. The £30,000 which had been left to him by his great-uncle Matthew Bottrill in 1827 was the passport into the top echelons of York society and beyond. The circumstances of this most welcome legacy might have been shrouded in mystery, but its consequences were crystal clear. Hudson had money to invest and spend – and he was simply waiting for the right opportunity to present itself. That is why the meeting at Mrs Tomlinson's Hotel in Petergate, York, was so crucial. The city's leading lawyers, businessmen and tradesmen had gathered together there to discuss the possibility of bringing a railway line to York in order to rescue their city from the obscurity into which it was slowly sinking. George Hudson was the only member of this hastily convened committee who had the vision and the money to turn the dream into a reality. His opponents argue that he was lucky to be in the right place at the right time, but that conveniently ignores why the other committee members, rather than Hudson, did not force the pace. As Machiavelli, the ultimate political pragmatist, once pointed out, luck favours the hard-working and the brave.

The growth of Britain's railways was haphazard, chaotic and exceptionally fast. This growth was driven by a combination of unrelated circumstances, and often hinged upon the emergence of a man such as George Hudson. There was no strategic planning and little thought was given to where the railways would go, so long as they made money. William Gladstone tried as best he could to regulate the railways when he was at the Board of Trade in 1844, but even such an accomplished politician as he could not curb or direct their development. They had an impetus and a character all of their very own and it is not surprising that arguments still rage today as to the best way to finance and manage Britain's railways.

By 1848, Hudson controlled nearly 1,500 out of the 5,000 miles of railway in England. Had the country not been ravaged by a vicious recession during the mid to late 1840s, it is probable that the dividends from three of his four companies, namely the York and North Midland, the Midland and the York, Newcastle and Berwick, would have been paying dividends of between eight to ten per cent and the siren voices of a few dissatisfied shareholders would have been drowned out. King Hudson would have continued to reign.

It is now time, once and for all, to demolish the myth that George Hudson was a bloated, ignorant, drunken, boorish fraud. Had he been anything like that, he and his grand plans would have got no further than the back bar at Mrs Tomlinson's. A much fairer, and more illuminating, description of Hudson the man comes from Morier Evans's essay *Facts, Failures and Frauds*. In continuation of the personal description quoted earlier (page 55) Evans writes:

While Mr Hudson strongly appreciates material conditions, and respects, above all things, soundness in the subjects which engage his attention, he is, on the other hand, easily excited under sympathetic conditions to take an ideal view, which disposes him, whenever the opportunity appears to be afforded of realising his aspirations, whether these are well founded or not, to overleap or set aside restrictions of a conventional, personal, material, or even moral character, if any of these are in his way – obstacles that would fill, for others, the whole field of vision.

Such, indeed, is the man who has become identified with one of the most memorable periods of industrial progress, who aided materially to promote those designs which were presently seized upon and adopted in a spirit of general enthusiasm; who not only extended, but fortified, or rather consolidated, a portion of the growing power, succeeding, as far as he did succeed on grounds partly fictitious and partly real, and failing – not because his schemes were inherently impracticable, but through not observing the point at which their further prosecution was desirable. Taking a retrospective glance at the whole of his career, there are many features in it deserving credit . . . he has done the State some service and the country, both directly and indirectly, permanent benefit.

In other words, George Hudson was ideally suited to running and dominating the railways in their infancy in Britain. This was a cut-throat, greedy and unstable world, which needed a leader with vision, decisiveness and drive. The new railway companies, springing up at an alarming and uncontrolled rate, attracted the capital of the rich and famous, the landed gentry and middle-class tradesman and, on occasions, the poor and the needy. There were plenty of people who were prepared to enjoy a company dividend of ten per cent without lifting a finger to earn it, but there were precious few who were prepared to devote their whole lives to making those companies work. Hudson was one of those precious few, none of whom were beyond moral reproach. So it is worth considering his achievements in this field, especially since those achievements are so often denigrated.

In the astonishing fifteen years between that historic meeting at Mrs Tomlinson's Hotel and his downfall in 1849, George Hudson laid the foundations, almost single-handedly, of this country's modern railway network and ensured that the city of York, which he loved so dearly, would become the railway capital of the north of England.

In 1849, when the Railway King was effectively dethroned, Britain had half the railways in the world. That amazing statistic puts the scale of Hudson's achievement into context.

George Hudson's railways stretched from London to the Scottish Borders and from Great Yarmouth to Bristol, bringing amazing benefits to almost every town on almost every route. He had, as the historian G. M. Trevelyan once memorably wrote, 'scored his mark across the face of England'. And he had also begun to create some kind of order out of anarchy, beginning the process of amalgamation which would eventually lead to the nationalisation of the railways. Starting from the Midland amalgamation of 1843, Hudson worked steadily towards the unification of all lines between Rugby and Edinburgh. He would have gone further, but for the bitter opposition he faced in the form of Denison and his Great Northern line. Nevertheless, his achievement was immense.

How did he persuade so many investors to back his schemes? He did it by using the skills he had learned as a young politician on the back-biting York Corporation. He promised, he threatened, he cajoled, he dissembled and, crucially, he paid the best dividends in the country. As Richard S. Lambert points out:

> How could a group of timid tradesmen, who wanted to win
> a fortune by gambling without risk, be persuaded to agree to
> the necessary bold annexations, leases, purchases, or exten-
> sions, which alone could transform a petty local line into the
> nucleus of a national trunk system? A loud voice, a blustering
> manner, a little jugglery with figures, would indeed go a
> long way with such people. But unless they had a personality
> to lead them, they would fall into despondency at the first

check, forget all their ambitions, and allow themselves to be bought out at a loss by some unscrupulous rival.

Even George Hudson's most ardent admirers will admit that 'a little jugglery with figures' is being exceptionally kind to a man who raised creative accounting to an art form. It would be futile to deny that Hudson's financial transactions were highly dubious, and it was most irregular to pay dividends out of capital, but he argued that everything he did was in the interests of the railway companies he ran. The problem was that he had difficulty in differentiating between his own interests and those of his companies, but that is a failing common to autocratic businessmen. King Louis XIV's famous dictum '*L'état, c'est moi*' sums up Hudson's attitude to his companies perfectly. This is not an excuse for his behaviour, but it is an explanation. And that is why, when he was confronted with allegation after allegation of financial impropriety between 1849 and 1853, he did not react like a guilty man. He was quite prepared to justify what he had done.

It is essential to remember that George Hudson was simply behaving in exactly the same manner as the other managers and directors of Britain's railway companies across the country. They were making up the rules as they went along, as occasionally happens in fast-growing new industries. No one complained, of course (not even the holier-than-thou Leeman), when these companies were successful, but when the going got tough, and the dividends shrank, Hudson the hero suddenly became Hudson the villain. What a graphic and shameful example of hypocrisy and greed.

It is astonishing, when George Hudson's tremendous contribution to the industrial development of Britain is weighed on the scales of history against his financial misdemeanours, some commentators claim those misdemeanours to be more important. That kind of logic, however, comes straight from the pages of *Alice in Wonderland* and it is reassuring to note that Hudson's reputation as one of the greatest Victorian entrepreneurs is growing apace.

However, it was not just George Hudson's contribution to Britain's railway network, and York's economic prosperity, that marked him out as an exceptional man. He was also a hard-working parliamentarian, a tremendous patron of Sunderland and Whitby, a generous benefactor of a whole host of charitable causes, remarkably humble and uncomplaining in adversity, and a caring husband and loving father.

His critics suggest that George Hudson was a flawed and unsatisfactory human being, but this assessment – born of jealousy and hatred – does not bear careful scrutiny. Having found himself in trouble in his early teenage years, when he was drummed out of the comfortable surroundings of the village of Howsham for getting a local girl pregnant, he arrived in the forbidding city of York without a penny or a friend to his name. Armed only with an introduction to a local draper, he could have been forgiven for sheltering in York Minster and throwing himself upon the mercy of God. Courage and enthusiasm, however, are two excellent qualities and young George had both in abundance. He was well equipped to make his way in the city of York, where he would soon challenge the complacency and the self-interest of the city fathers.

A judicious marriage and a welcome financial windfall eased his way into the higher echelons of York's back-biting society and its viperish politics, where he was immediately at home. While young George was not inherently deceitful and devious, he soon learned the necessary political tricks to ensure that he prospered as well as survived. He was, though, confident and thick-skinned, which are invaluable characteristics in life's dark jungle. Dr Alf Peacock, in particular, attacks Hudson's conduct as he ascended the greasy pole of York politics, but Dr Peacock refuses to accept that Hudson was only playing the same game as his political opponents. It is interesting, though, that this eminent York historian, who has done more than anyone to perpetuate Hudson's reputation as an unscrupulous villain, has a bust of this villain in his front room!

If George Hudson had been a truly flawed and unpleasant human being, his deficiencies would have inevitably spilled over into his personal life and affected his family. It is true that his brother-in-law Richard Nicholson committed suicide, but this was due primarily to Nicholson's over-ripe conscience and his inflated self-esteem, rather than Hudson's influence. Richard Nicholson killed himself, not because he was overcome by remorse at what he had done, but because he was about to be exposed. His pomposity and overweening self-importance was his problem, not his brother-in-law's. It is also true that Ann Hudson's engagement to George Dundas was broken off, in the wake of her father's downfall, but it is unlikely that Ann would have been happy marrying into a family more concerned with her father's reputation than her own sweet and innocent nature. In any case, she found true love with her Count Suminski, so no permanent damage was done.

Leaving these two regrettable incidents aside, however, there is ample evidence to suggest that George Hudson was a generous and caring family man. After his initial amorous adventure in Howsham, he appears to have steered a much more conventional sexual path. There is no evidence whatsoever to suggest that he was unfaithful to his wife Elizabeth before his exile – and only unsubstantiated rumours of his infidelity in France. Since Elizabeth lacked both looks and intelligence, this was some achievement. While Hudson himself was no oil painting (although Sir Francis Grant did his best), his wealth and power in the 1840s would have made him attractive to a certain kind of woman. That he did not succumb to this temptation is certainly to his credit.

One of the most accurate barometers of the state of a marriage are the children. So it is significant that George, John, Ann and William were all well balanced, happy and successful in their different fields. George Snr ensured that his money bought the very best education available (Harrow and Christ Church, Oxford, for the boys and a top Hampstead finishing school for Ann). There were plenty of temptations for young men in Victorian England and many succumbed to drink, gambling and women. George, however, was an accomplished barrister and inspector of factories; John was a brave soldier; and William a hard-working doctor. None of the children possessed the character defects and fault-lines which all too often spring from a dysfunctional upbringing and inadequate parents. The love between George Snr and his youngest son William was underlined when George died in William's arms.

It is easy to forget that George Hudson spent almost as many years in exile as he did running his various railway enterprises. And, while he exhibited a number of unattractive characteristics during the height of his power, he was incredibly brave, loyal and philosophical as he eked out a pretty miserable existence in some of France's less salubrious boarding houses. He was brave, because he rarely complained about his straitened circumstances; he was loyal, because he never betrayed any of his friends or, for that matter, his enemies; and he was philosophical because he realised he had lived a turbulent and exciting life, and was grateful for the experience. His loyalty is arguably the most interesting characteristic of the three, because he could have ruined a number of leading politicians, financiers and businessmen. He kept quiet to his dying day.

George Hudson was also an accomplished parliamentarian between 1845 and 1849, and it was only in his later years, when drink got the better of him on occasion, that he let himself and his constituents down in the House of Commons. He played an important part in the events leading up to, and beyond, the terrible split in the Conservative Party over the Corn Laws and was a trusted confidante of Lord George Bentinck, the driving force behind the Tory Protectionists. He piloted numerous complex railway Bills through the Commons and, in 1844, the year before he was elected to represent Sunderland, he impressed William Gladstone with his enterprise and vision.

Richard S. Lambert, in one of the most perceptive passages of his biography, puts the scale of George Hudson's achievement into perspective thus:

George Hudson is perhaps the only businessman of 100 years ago whom we can easily imagine at home in the modern world. Other giants of the early stages of our industrial revolution pale into insignificance beside him in respect of personal energy and capacity for simultaneously directing many distinct and complex enterprises. The slow-moving world of 1845 was fascinated, above all, by the speed at which he worked. But Hudson had no telephones or cables, no typewriters or dictaphones, no aeroplanes or first-class hotels to ease the rapidity of his communications. By an unheard-of display of physical vigour he contrived to keep his fingers upon the threads of operations over a front that stretched from London to Newcastle and beyond. And *what* operations.

These operations can be broken down into four distinct areas: the railways, the docks and other industrial projects; banking and finance; property; and politics, both local and national. At the height of his power, he controlled a vast network of enterprises, which no other contemporary could begin to match. He laid the foundations of the modern British railway system; he built the docks at Sunderland; he generated wealth in Whitby; he founded the York Union Bank; he owned an amazing portfolio of properties in Yorkshire and London; and he was Lord Mayor of York three times, whilst representing Sunderland in the House of Commons for fourteen years. He would have represented Whitby in Parliament, too, at the ripe old age of sixty-four, had he not been cynically removed from the scene and thrown into prison. Most people would have been satisfied with just one of these successes, but the indefatigable Hudson never rested on his laurels until illness and poverty finally sapped his boundless energy.

It is impossible to quantify the scale of George Hudson's achievements, though the London *Evening Standard* tried, as we have seen, in 1846. Here, in full, is this most significant passage again:

Mr Hudson gave a dinner on Thursday to some happy hundreds in the Guildhall of York – but was that all? No, Mr Hudson was yesterday giving, and has for months and years of yesterdays been giving dinners to hundreds of thousands not less happy than the guests by whom he was surrounded in the Guildhall. He has found the labourers standing to be hired when no man hired them and he has given them employment and good wages and, we repeat it, good dinners – for the labourer who receives from 22s to 23s a week can, according to his habits, command a good dinner . . . Two hundred thousand well-paid labourers, representing, as heads of families, nearly one million men, women and children, all feasting through the bold enterprise of one man, and not feasting for one day or one week, but enjoying abundance from year's end to year's end. Let us hear what man, or class of men, ever before did so much for the population of a country?

In the light of everything he achieved, the savage, relentless attacks of Hudson's enemies seem remarkably petty and mean-spirited, especially since his name remains blackened to this day. A man is often vilified for who he is rather than what he has done, and this was certainly the case with George Hudson. He did not fit in with either the self-serving, parochial and abstemious York establishment or the more snobbish and intellectual elements of London society. In York, the priggish Meek and the hypocritical Leeman ensured that he never had the full confidence of the city he served and loved so well, whereas in London, the many *faux pas* of his wife Elizabeth made the Hudsons the laughing stocks of the chattering classes. George Hudson never complained, though. The farmer's boy from Howsham had the thickest of skins – and he certainly wasn't prepared to change his character to appeal to the sanctimonious Leeman or the refined sensibilities of Dickens or Carlyle.

It is significant, however, that Hudson ultimately triumphed over his merciless enemies. Although they forced him into prison, bankruptcy and exile, and made him forsake his family as well as a cherished parliamentary seat at Whitby, they could not, and did not, hound him to his death. The generosity of his friends enabled him to return to England and spend his twilight days in congenial and loving surroundings. How appropriate that he died, not alone and penniless in an anonymous French hostel, but in the house of his wife Elizabeth and in the arms of his son William. In the circumstances it was a happy, and victorious, death.

The victory, though, is not yet complete. As Dr John Shannon of York Civic Trust pointed out, even though the good that George Hudson achieved has lived on after him, this 'good' is not universally recognised. Since his death, Hudson has been shabbily treated both by the city of York and by some historians. This book is but a small attempt to set the record straight and to nail the lie, once and for all, that he was a common, unprincipled swindler. He was, in fact, one of the greatest entrepreneurs of the Victorian age, whose achievements remain with us today, while his misdeeds have vanished into the mists of time. It is time that the Railway King regained his crown.

Epilogue

It is now eighteen months since I trampled my way through the weeds and the nettles in the little churchyard of Scrayingham to look at George Hudson's grave for the very first time. Today the weeds look wilder and the nettles more menacing, while the grave itself is in danger of being obliterated by undergrowth, lichen and moss. It is a desperately sorry sight.

Much has happened during that time. Britain's rail network, once the proudest and most efficient in the world, has stumbled from one crisis to another. A series of tragic accidents, combined with union unrest and a chronic lack of direction following privatisation, has brought the industry to its knees. Railtrack is losing money more quickly and more spectacularly than Hudson himself ever did, while public confidence in the railways has been eroded by rising fares and falling standards. The Railway King's golden legacy is in danger of being destroyed.

The city of York, meanwhile, has been coming to terms with the shattering closure of its railway carriageworks, where some of the finest trains of the twentieth century were built. Once again, this was a direct consequence of the chaos caused by privatisation. It was feared that the closure could have a devastating effect on the city's precarious economic base, but the imaginative redevelopment of the carriageworks' Holgate Road site has breathed new life into York. It is a touch ironic, though, that one of the flagship office blocks in Holgate Park is called Leeman House! In stark contrast,

George Hudson Street is looking shabbier, sadder and dingier than ever and is now a ghastly memorial to a great man.

However, George Hudson is fondly remembered elsewhere in Yorkshire and beyond. Thanks to Darrell Buttery, the deputy headmaster of Queen Mary's School, Baldersby, and a tremendous supporter of Hudson, his pupils are extremely proud that the Railway King once owned the building in which they now live and learn. Meanwhile the accountants of the York-based firm Garbutt and Elliott enjoy working at 44 Monkgate, even if Hudson's accounting was somewhat less scrupulous than their own; and the friendly clerk at the reception desk of the French Embassy in London is well aware that one of the greatest British entrepreneurs of the Victorian age was the very first owner of Albert Gate East.

Back at Scrayingham churchyard, though, the outlook seemed gloomier. A hundred years after George Hudson's death, architectural historian Sir Nikolaus Pevsner wrote in his seminal *Buildings of England*: 'In Scrayingham churchyard, S of the W end of the church, is the humdrum grave of George Hudson + 1871, once the railway king.'

Humdrum? Once the railway king? Seldom has a short sentence contained words of such melancholy resonance. But then, echoing across the rolling acres of North Yorkshire, came the distant hoot of the York to Scarborough train, just as it had done eighteen months previously. How reassuring, and how appropriate, it was to hear that George Hudson was still having the last laugh.

Bibliography

Bailey, Brian. *George Hudson* (Sutton, 1995)

Blake, Robert. *Disraeli* (Methuen, University Paperbacks, 1969)

Burgess, Leslie. *Sounding Brass* (available at York City Library, 1951)

Carlyle, Thomas. *Latter Day Pamphlets* (Chapman and Hall, 1898)

Evans, D. Morier. *Facts, Failures and Frauds* (Groombridge, 1859)

Fawcett, Bill. *A History of North Eastern Railway Architecture, Vol. I: The Pioneers* (North Eastern Railway Association, 2001)

Feinstein, C.H., Ed. *York 1831–1981: 150 Years of Scientific Endeavour and Social Change* (Ebor Press, 1983)

Gash, Norman. *Sir Robert Peel* (Longman, 1972)

Hill, David. *In Turner's Footsteps* (John Murray, 1984)

Johnson, J. P. (aka Dr Alf Peacock). *Hudson, Goodrick and Glory* (York History, 1996)

Lambert, Richard S. *The Railway King: A Study of George Hudson and the Business Morals of His Times* (George Allen and Unwin, 1934)

Machiavelli, Niccolò. *The Prince* (Penguin Classics, 1961 edn)

Magnus, Philip. *Gladstone* (John Murray, 1954)

Peacock, Dr Alf. *George Hudson, Vols I and II* (A. J. Peacock, 1988–9)

Peacock, Dr Alf. *George Hudson and the Historians* (York History, 1974)

Peacock, Dr Alf, and Joy, David. *George Hudson of York* (Dalesman Books, 1971)

Ridley, Jasper. *Lord Palmerston* (Constable, 1970)

Tomlinson, W. W. *North Eastern Railway* (David and Charles, 1967)

Wilson, Robert. *The Life and Times of Queen Victoria* (Cassell, 1887)

Young, G. M. *Victorian England: Portrait of an Age* (Oxford University Press, 1936)

Index